The Groaning of Creation

God, Evolution,
and the Problem of Evil

Christopher Southgate

Westminster John Knox Press
LOUISVILLE • LONDON

Scripture quotations from the New Revised Standard Version of the Bible are copyright © 1989 by the Division of Christian Education of the National Council of the Churches of Christ in the U.S.A. and are used by permission.

Book design by Sharon Adams
Cover design by Lisa Buckley
Cover art: A Lion Devouring Its Prey, 1905 (oil on canvas), Rousseau, Henri J. F. (Le Douanier) (1844–1910)/Private Collection/The Bridgeman Art Library

First edition
Published by Westminster John Knox Press
Louisville, Kentucky

This book is printed on acid-free paper that meets the American National Standards Institute Z39.48 standard. ♾

PRINTED IN THE UNITED STATES OF AMERICA

08 09 10 11 12 13 14 15 16 17 — 10 9 8 7 6 5 4 3 2 1

Library of Congress Cataloging-in-Publication Data

Southgate, Christopher, 1953–
    The groaning of creation : God, evolution, and the problem of evil / Christopher Southgate.
        p. cm.
    Includes index.
    ISBN 978-0-664-23090-6 (alk. paper)
    1. Theodicy. 2. Good and evil. 3. Creationism. 4. Evolution. 5. Eschatology.
I. Title.
    BT160.S67 2008
    231'.8—dc22

                                                                    2008002524

To my best teachers:
Hal Dixon and Charles Napier
for their wisdom, kindness, and intellectual example

Contents

Preface

In the summer of 2005 I had the privilege of watching orcas from an open boat in the Juan de Fuca Straits between Vancouver Island and Washington state. To see these magnificent creatures (sometimes called killer whales) at close quarters, and to hear their communications on hydrophones, was an unforgettable experience. Power, beauty, community, mystery, all were there in the ten minutes or so of the "pod" passing. More, these creatures were utterly fluent and masterful in an environment, the ocean, to which human beings are only tentative and limited visitors. I could not help be reminded also of Holmes Rolston's description of orcas hunting down a sea lion, tossing it playfully in the air, prolonging its agony, before it was killed.[1]

Reading later about the Vancouver Island orcas, I learned that they are salmon-eaters, but that "transients" also come into the same waters, orcas who exhibit the predation on sea lions and other mammals to which Rolston referred. Apparently underwater recording equipment is now sufficiently sophisticated to distinguish the two kinds of orca, and the prey animals also can. Dolphins will swim alongside the fish-eaters, but "have been known to hurl themselves up the beach in a suicidal frenzy to escape the mammal-hunting orcas."[2]

Out in the buffeting Pacific swell I give thanks to God for power, beauty, community, and mystery in creation, and drawing a deeper breath I give thanks too for the creation that contains the murderous play, and suicidal frenzy of escape, and human beings' steadily gathering knowledge of these things through the enterprise we call science.

And there, in a parable, is the matter of this book. I seek to show that the evolving creation is an ambiguous place with an ambiguous history, and that God may be both praised and questioned when God's creation is contemplated honestly. I write as a Christian theologian, presupposing that the world was created out of nothing by a God we can describe and relate to as Trinity. What follows is in no way an effort to prove the existence of such a God; rather it is an exploration of models of the triune God in relation to creation, and of what that means for human beings. Above all it is an exploration in theodicy, posing the question, how can God be understood as good, just, and loving in a world full of suffering? But beyond that I also seek to ask, what is the human *calling* in respect of this ambiguous world, so out of the last two chapters come also proposals in environmental ethics.

This study confines itself rigorously to the suffering of nonhuman creatures. That is not to devalue the vast extent of human suffering, or to suggest that I do not care about it or regard it as one of the most intense problems for any believer in a loving and saving God. It is rather to counteract in a small way what I see as the overwhelming preoccupation of theodicists with human suffering, such that often even passages that start by addressing the wider issue of creaturely suffering revert almost at once to a consideration of humans.

The book is intended to be accessible to the nonspecialist reader, so as much as possible the denser pieces of discussion have been left in the endnotes to each chapter. No expertise either in the biological sciences or in systematic theology is presumed. Chapter 1 defines the nature and extent of the problem for theodicy involved in the pain, suffering, and extinction associated with evolution. I look at why neither physical death nor pain *of itself* is the problem, and briefly at the history of this debate. In chapter 2 I look at types of argument that stand in the way of our engaging with the debate, such as creationism; intelligent design; models of God that remove the idea of God's having created all that exists, or dispute God's goodness; and schemes in which all the disvalues in creation can be blamed on a "fall." Chapter 3 presents a scheme for understanding different types of theodicy, and uses that scheme to categorize the evolutionary theodicies that are currently proposed in the field. In chapter 4 I offer my own proposal as to a Trinitarian theology of creation and redemption. That proposal is taken forward in chapter 5 with a consideration of eschatology: is it meaningful to speak of nonhuman creatures having an existence after death that might in some way mitigate the evil of suffering in this life? In chapter 6 I turn to the human calling, to be contemplatives of creation, or co-creators with God, or perhaps stewards or priests of creation. And finally in Chapter 7 I examine two important proposals for how human freedom might work itself out in respect of the nonhuman creation—a move to vegetarianism and a project to end biological extinction.

Acknowledgments

The first major presentation of the argument of this book was to the 2000 Senior Seminar Series at the Ian Ramsey Centre in Oxford. That paper was later published as "God and Evolutionary Evil: Theodicy in the Light of Darwinism," in *Zygon* 37, no. 4 (2002): 803–24. My presentation (of ideas jointly developed with Andrew Robinson) to the 2005 CTNS/Vatican Observatory Conference on Physics, Cosmology, and Theodicy at Castelgandolfo has appeared as Christopher Southgate and Andrew Robinson, "Varieties of Theodicy: An Exploration of Responses to the Problem of Evil Based on a Typology of Good-Harm Analyses," in *Physics and Cosmology: Scientific Perspectives on the Problem of Evil in Nature*, ed. Nancey Murphy, Robert J. Russell, and William Stoeger, SJ (Vatican City and Berkeley, CA: Vatican Observatory and Center for Theology and the Natural Sciences, 2007), 69–90. My paper to the 2006 European Society for the Study of Science and Theology in Iaşi, Rumania, is published as "The Creatures' Yes and No to Their Creator: A Proposal in Evolutionary Theology, Kenotic Trinitarianism, and Environmental Ethics," in *Creation's Diversity: Voices from Theology and Science, Issues in Science and Theology 5*, ed. Willem B. Drees, Hubert Meisinger, and Taede A. Smedes (London and New York: T&T Clark/Continuum, 2008), 58–77. I also presented to the 2006–7 Exeter Theology Department's graduate seminar the core of the article "Creation as 'Very Good' and 'Groaning in Travail,'" published in *The Evolution of Evil*, ed. Gaymon Bennett, Martinez J. Hewlett, Ted Peters, and Robert J. Russell (Göttingen: Vandenhoeck and Ruprecht, 2008), 53–85. My paper to the 2008 Exeter Colloquium on "Vegetarianism as Spiritual Choice" will appear as "Protological and Eschatological Vegetarianism," in *Eating and Believing: Interdisciplinary Perspectives on Vegetarianism and Theology*, ed. R. E. Muers and D. J. Grumett (London and New York: T&T Clark/Continuum, forthcoming).

James Dickey's poem "The Heaven of Animals" is from Dickey's collection *The Whole Motion: Collected Poems 1945–1992*, © 1992 by James Dickey and reprinted by permission of Wesleyan University Press.

All quotations from the Bible are from the New Revised Standard Version unless otherwise specified.

My thanks go to my own university and department at Exeter, to David Moss and colleagues on the staff of the South West Ministry Training Course, and to students on the modules "God, Humanity and the Cosmos" and "Evolution, God and Gaia" who helped me refine my ideas. Also to all the staff at the Center for Theology and the Natural Sciences at Berkeley, where I spent a most generative few weeks as a visiting scholar in 2005, and to the Arts and Humanities Research Council for their support of the projects "The Use of the Bible in Environmental Ethics" (AH/D001188/1) and "Vegetarianism as Spiritual Choice in Historical and Contemporary Theology" (AR119101). I also thank the Council of the South West Ministry Training Course for sabbatical time and support.

Among the senior scholars generous with their time and attention I thank in particular Bob Russell, Keith Ward, Holmes Rolston III, Celia Deane-Drummond, Jack Haught, and Denis Alexander. Conversations with Exeter colleagues Jeremy Law and Mark Wynn were very important at key junctures in the project. All those at the Castelgandolfo meeting were unstinting in their support, especially Wesley Wildman, Philip Clayton, Tom Tracy, Mark Worthing, and Denis Edwards. I pay special tribute to the late Arthur Peacocke, whose encouragement over many years was such a help to me, and which included his advocacy of the importance of my 2002 article in *Zygon*.

I have greatly valued recent collaborations with the teams on the AHRC grants, and thank in particular Dave Horrell and Cherryl Hunt for permission to use their developing insights on Romans 8. I have treasured over many years the supportive friendship of Richard Burridge and Wentzel van Huyssteen. Over the years two other, very different collaborations have been particularly important to me, both in catalyzing my imagination and in insisting on a properly critical approach to its fruits. These have been with my poet colleague Richard Skinner, also a student of the science-religion debate, and my theologian and philosopher colleague Andrew Robinson. Richard valiantly read the whole first draft of the book; my debt to Andrew's thinking will be evident particularly in chapter 3, where our categorization of theodicies owes a great deal to his initiative. I am grateful too to Ruth Harvey Regan for a most attentive reading of chapter 6. The final production of the manuscript would not have been possible without the help of my diligent and ever-cheerful research assistant Katie Endacott (also a careful and critical reader of the first draft), and the dedicated and expert professionalism of Philip Law and his staff at Westminster John Knox Press.

All remaining errors, infelicities, and obscurities in the work remain the sole responsibility of the author.

For the love of my family, especially that of my wife, Sandy, no words of thanks and praise could ever be enough.

1

Introduction

1.1 THE "GOOD" AND THE "GROANING"

One of the core assumptions of Christian thought is the affirmation that God's creation is good. The beautiful rhythms of the first chapter of the Hebrew Bible culminate in the assertion that "God saw everything that he had made, and indeed, it was very good" (Gen. 1:31). However, humans have always known that the nonhuman creation contained violence and pain; the young lions, to quote the Psalmist, roar, seeking their food with God (Ps. 104:21). Tennyson wrote in *In Memoriam* that humanity

> Trusted God was love indeed
> And love Creation's final law—
> Though Nature, red in tooth and claw
> With ravine, shrieked against his creed[1]—

Charles Darwin (1802–89) famously gave evolution its first comprehensive rationale in *The Origin of Species* in 1859.[2] In the light of his proposals on natural selection (1.2), he wrote this to J. D. Hooker: "What a book a devil's chaplain might write on the clumsy, wasteful, blundering, low and horridly cruel works of nature!"[3]

Christian theologians of Darwin's time were very much aware of the tension between such judgments and a straightforward affirmation of creation as good. So J. R. Illingworth, writing in the important collection of Anglican essays *Lux Mundi* (1888), could say: "The universality of pain throughout the range of the animal world, reaching back into the distant ages of geology, and involved in the very structure of the animal organism, is without doubt among the most serious problems which the Theist has to face."[4] This is a telling quote. Though animal suffering was known before Darwin, the narrative of

1

evolution that emerged in his work stretched the extent of that suffering over millions and millions of years and millions of species, most of them now extinct. What is more, pain was "involved in the very structure of the animal organism," or at least of the evolutionary process, as I shall show below.

So in the light of this vast narrative of nature as struggle, "clumsy, wasteful, blundering, low and horridly cruel," it becomes far harder to assert the creation's goodness, and easier to side with Paul's assessment of the creation as "groaning in labor pains" (Rom. 8:22, often translated "groaning in travail"). It is the task of this book to show that God's creation can be seen as *both* good *and* groaning.

1.2 EVOLUTIONARY THEORY

Darwin saw that variations in biological forms were always arising, also that typically there are always more members of a species born than can reproduce successfully. He concluded that there will always be competition for scarce resources, and only those variations that were well adapted to their environment would give rise to descendants. Those variations would be "selected for," and the other variations would tend to disappear from the population. This is the essence of his theory of "natural selection," and of its enormous explanatory power.[5] Its implication is plain: less well adapted members of a species will tend to have a shorter life and fewer descendants. Further, the success of many species depends on their predating upon other species.[6] The competition to reproduce will drive the characters of species toward greater and greater excellence, and systems of predation will generate excellence in predator and prey alike. In Holmes Rolston's wonderfully telling phrase, "The cougar's fang has carved the limbs of the fleet-footed deer, and vice versa."[7] Species as we know them are as they are because of the pressure of natural selection and predator-prey cycles.

We can now see why pain and violence are endemic in nature. We can also see the beginnings of a possible theodicy; values arise in evolution along with the disvalues. Darwin himself wrote: "Thus, from the war of nature, from famine and death, the most exalted object which we are capable of conceiving, namely, the production of the higher animals, directly follows. There is grandeur in this view of life, with its several powers, having been originally breathed into a few forms or into one; and that, whilst this planet has gone cycling on according to the fixed law of gravity, from so simple a beginning endless forms most beautiful and most wonderful have been, and are being, evolved."[8]

As I shall discuss in detail in section 3.3, this type of argument is a key resource for evolutionary theodicists. "Grandeur" accompanies the groaning, and the groaning may be the only way by which "exalted objects" may arise.

But before we can address this, we need to characterize more carefully the problem of suffering in the nonhuman creation.

First I acknowledge that the view of Darwinian evolution given here is a highly simplified one, and needs much qualification. Competition is not the only strategy organisms use; cooperation, between individuals of a species, and between species, is also very common. And evolutionary theory is itself "evolving."[9] The ways in which variations arise and are transmitted are much more varied and complex than was imagined when "neo-Darwinism" (the combination of Darwinian evolution with genetics) first cohered in the 1940s. Nevertheless, the problem of evolutionary theodicy in its essentials rests on the core of the theory as already outlined. I have already quoted the distinguished American environmental philosopher and theologian Holmes Rolston III, whose work has been an important inspiration for my own. Rolston's verdict on an evolving creation is that it is "random, contingent, blind, disastrous, wasteful, indifferent, selfish, cruel, clumsy, ugly, full of suffering, and, ultimately, death" but also "orderly, prolific, efficient, selecting for adaptive fit, exuberant, complex, diverse, regenerating life generation after generation."[10] Both sets of qualities are accommodated within the scope of an evolutionary worldview. That is the problematic this book explores.

1.3 OBJECTIONS: PERHAPS THERE ISN'T A PROBLEM AFTER ALL

A series of objections need to be logged at this point, though none of them in my view stands up to scrutiny. An ancient recourse is that of Augustine, that though "this is the appointed order of things transitory. Of this order the beauty does not strike us, because by our mortal frailty we are so involved in a part of it, that we cannot perceive the whole, in which these fragments that offend us are harmonized with the most accurate fitness and beauty."[11] Well, we have now a far greater understanding of the nonhuman world than was possible in a prescientific age. We see keenly the extent of its beauty, indeed the "fitness" of evolved creatures, and yet the abundance of suffering sticks out all the more as a problem for theodicy.[12]

Equally, it is sometimes said that nonhuman creatures do not really feel pain, or that they do feel pain but not in the way that humans do, not accompanied by awareness of mortality, or anticipation of pain before it is near, or the loss of hope. These are responses that depend on those advanced systems of temporally aware memory, consciousness, and culture that seem to be completely unique to humans. I concede that nonhuman animals may not have, probably do not have, that narrative of their lives, that sense of a long future stretching out before them which suffering may truncate or impoverish, that characterizes (adult) human experience. Animals do not experience, as far as we know, that situation we call "the collapse of all our hopes," and there may be types of human mental illness for which there is no animal correlate. It is very important to admit that we do not know what the experience of other creatures is like. We shall never know, this side of paradise, what it is like to be a cat, or yet a bat.[13] *cf. H. G. Wells*

But to acknowledge that our awareness of these fascinating questions is limited is not to say that we have no knowledge at all. A telling case in the United Kingdom is the debate about the hunting of red deer with hounds, in which a scientific study showed physiological evidence of severe distress in the hunted animals.[14] Nonhuman creatures may not carry around with them an awareness of death as humans do, but they know the experience of acute pain, and when that pain comes with no avenue of relief, it seems to me that it constitutes not merely a useful physiological response, but actual suffering.[15] Animals may not know the experience of existential dread, but higher animals know what it is to be trapped, to lose their freedom of action; observation of zoo animals alone tells us that. In the wild this type of suffering comes as they are cornered by predators, or succumb to disease or injury.

To sum up, intense and protracted pain and/or fear among creatures, particularly when the creature senses that there is no chance of relief, may justifiably be termed suffering, and there is ample evidence that this exists, particularly in creatures that have complex brains processing information from pain-detection systems.

Another objection we can dismiss without much difficulty is that of Kenneth Miller in his *Finding Darwin's God*. For Miller, "The brutality of life is in the eye of the beholder"; it simply depends whether you view life from the point of view of predator or prey. He goes on, "We cannot call evolution cruel if all we are really doing is assigning to evolution the raw savagery of nature itself. The reality of life is that the world often lacks mercy, pity, and even common decency."[16] Suffering, pain, waste, and extinction in the nonhuman world, for Miller, are just facts of nature. They have no moral content, and we should not project on them moral categories, which properly belong only to the sphere of human beings. This must seem to a Christian theologian a most curious position. It is an aspect of what Robert J. Russell has called "theodicy lite."[17] If one poses the question, why is the nonhuman world of value? the normal Christian response would be: because God created it and pronounced it good, because God continues to hold it in existence from moment to moment, and to nurture it with the divine love. So the sufferings of creatures *must* be a problem for Christian theology, even when no human beings are directly involved in the "transaction."

It is worth taking up that last observation for a moment, just to point out that this problem of suffering within the nonhuman creation is a problem only for theists,[18] and indeed for those theists who want to believe in a creator God who is also good and benevolent. Quentin Smith writes:

> Not long ago I was sleeping in a cabin in the woods and was awoken . . . by the sounds of a struggle between two animals. Cries of terror and extreme agony rent the night, intermingled with the sounds of jaws snapping bones and flesh being torn from limbs. . . . A clearer case of a horrible event in nature, a natural evil, has never been presented to me. It seemed to me self-evident that the natural law that *animals must savagely kill and devour each other in order to survive* was an evil natural law and that the obtaining of this law was sufficient evidence that God did not exist.[19]

If there is no God, the problem resolves itself. Without a belief in a creator God, and indeed a loving creator God, there is a natural and easy response to suffering in the nonhuman world. "That's just the way things are"; the rhythms of predation are "just nature's way," which we should not question (let alone attempt to tamper with).[20] As Michael Lloyd notes, the problem is that much worse for the theist who also believes that God's self-giving love finds its truest expression in the example of Christ, whose life was the very reverse of self-preservation.[21] For Lloyd, as for many writers we shall encounter in these pages—Denis Edwards, John Haught, Jay McDaniel, Niels Henrik Gregersen, and Robert J. Russell, to name but a few—the suffering of nonhuman creatures is a problem because it seems to call into question the goodness of the God who made this creation. Where I would diverge from Lloyd is the point at which he concludes that some sort of fall of creation from God's original intentions must have taken place. I consider this strategy in detail in section 2.6. To anticipate that discussion for a moment, this postulate of a "cosmic fall" to account for suffering will not do for two reasons:

1. Because there is no scientific evidence that the biological world was ever free of predation and violence. Evidence of predation, and of the extinction of species, goes back as far as the fossil record can take it.[22]
2. This point is crucial: As I indicated above, the suffering of creatures is *instrumental*. It serves God's purposes, if those purposes are to realize more and more sophisticated and better adapted ways of being in the world. "Darwin's God" seems to *use* natural selection to further those ends, and that means more and more intricate ways of competing with other individuals and predating upon other species. It is the weak, always, who go to the wall in this system, the erratically swimming fish that attracts the shark, the lame antelope calf that is singled out by the hyena pack, the floundering zebra that is seized by the crocodile.

The quotation from Smith given above provides me an opportunity to clarify what type of exercise I am carrying out in this book. I am not seeking to prove the existence of God to those who do not believe, or yet to refute arguments against the existence of God. I am working within the community of belief to face the problems and tensions that come as we try to understand the God who made this world and who, Christians believe, acts to save it.

1.4 SEEING THE CREATION TRULY

What Smith writes is also a reminder of the importance of seeing the creation as it is, and not with over-romantic spectacles on. There is a great danger in this area of work either of sentimentalizing animal experience, doing what one might term "bambi theology," or of minimizing the extent of animal suffering. Much film of the natural world focuses on its beauty, and (understandably) does not engage with the suffering of animals as they struggle with chronic disease or the effects of parasites, or die lingering deaths from inefficient predator attacks or their own injuries. I ask the reader for the duration of this book to be realistic about these phenomena and not to romanticize them. In doing so I follow other writers who have emphasized the same need. There is outstandingly honest nature writing in, for example, the work of Aldo Leopold and Annie Dillard.[23] Lisa Sideris, who has written particularly eloquently about the work of Holmes Rolston, also issues a plea to avoid sentiment.[24] Michael Pollan writes:

> Without predators to cull the herd deer overrun their habitat and starve—all suffer, and not only the deer but the plants they browse and every other species that depends on those plants. In a sense the "good life" for deer, and even their creaturely character, which has been forged in the crucible of predation, depends on the existence of the wolf. . . . From the point of view of the individual prey animal predation is a horror, but from the point of view of the group—and of its gene pool—it is indispensable. So whose point of view shall we favor? That of the individual bison or Bison? The pig or Pig? Much depends on how you choose to answer that question.[25]

Again we see how disvalue, in particular to the individual animal, may be of value to the species as a whole. I take this up in more detail in sections 3.3–3.4, but for now simply reiterate that we must assess the experience of other creatures using the best array of scientific tools we can (together with that intense poetic contemplation which an observer like Dillard brings to nature) without allowing sentiment to get in our way.[26]

1.5 REFINING THE PROBLEM

To help us refine the problem I draw on the writing of another skeptic's view of the natural world, this time of the Galapagos Islands, which did so much to inform Darwin's work.[27] The biologist David Hull writes:

> What kind of God can one infer from the sort of phenomena epito-mized by the species on Darwin's Galapagos Islands? The evolution-ary process is rife with happenstance, contingency, incredible waste, death, pain and horror. . . . Whatever the God implied by evolution-ary theory and the data of natural selection may be like, he is not the Protestant God of waste not, want not. He is also not the loving God who cares about his productions. He is not even the awful God pic-tured in the Book of Job. The God of the Galapagos is careless, waste-ful, indifferent, almost diabolical. He is certainly not the sort of God to whom anyone would be inclined to pray.[28]

emotive language

It is worth distinguishing the "charges" Hull lists: "happenstance, contin-gency, incredible waste, death, pain, and horror." These fall into different cat-egories in terms of our analysis:

1. Mention of *happenstance* and *contingency* is interesting in the context of theodicy. It could be taken in two ways. It might imply that a God who allows an element of chance within creation would not know the sorts of phenomena to which such evolution might give rise. However, such a-gnosis in God is out-side the normal range of theologizing about creation. We can easily concede Hull's point that such a God might not be worthy of worship. But suppose God did indeed intend the sort of evolving biosphere science now describes. Many of those working at the interface of science and theology have emphasized that such a world seems necessarily to involve (on our current understanding of the universe) the creation unfolding according to the interplay of chance and phys-ical law. Though happenstance and contingency are ingredients in the costs to creatures of the processes of evolution by natural selection, they are not those costs themselves.[29]

2. *Horror* is part of some humans' reaction to the process, but not part of the process itself. Though certain evolutionary strategies such as parasitism and infanticide arouse a negative aesthetic response in us, I doubt whether this constitutes an extra category of concern to the theodicist beyond those of pain and death—especially given the very particular and limited nature of our aes-thetic perspectives.[30] *Pain* is experienced by individual organisms possessed of more than minimal sentience, if they are exposed to parasitism or predation (and perhaps even more so if they die of disease). Pain is a necessary concomi-tant of a richer experience of the world in higher animals.[31] There has to be

pain if there are to be higher organisms with sophisticated processing of their environment; there has to be the suffering that goes with predation if there are to be lions. Pain and suffering can, moreover, be seen as part of the way the evolutionary process optimizes the fitness of organisms, and the fitness of ecosystems. Pain cannot be excessive, because counterproductive pain would be nonadaptive and would therefore be selected against.[32] *Yes!*

However, just as some human beings never seem to have any opportunity for fullness of life, so the experience of many individual animals, such as the newborn impala torn apart alive by hyena, seems to be all pain and no richness. There are innumerable sufferers of the processes of predation and parasitism, including organisms for which life seems to contain no fullness, no expression of what it is to reach the potential inherent in being that creature. Indeed the "overproduction" typical of biological organisms virtually guarantees this. These organisms may be regarded as in some sense the victims or casualties of evolution.

3. *Death* is a thermodynamic necessity; it would be impossible to imagine biological life without it. It is also the prerequisite of "regeneration" (so Rolston) and of "biological creativity."[33] It seems to me that death need not be considered a problem, if it follows a fulfilled life.[34]

4. What of *incredible waste*? Need we consider the processes of cosmic development that result in destruction and "discarding," the "waste," as it might be said, of all sorts of entities other than life forms, from stars which go supernova to terrestrial to mountains eroded away to hummocks? Here I draw on Rolston's analysis of value in his *Environmental Ethics*.[35] He makes a convincing case for intrinsic value inhering in every *living* thing, on the grounds that every organism is an entity which experiences and processes its environment (in however primitive a way) in order to live and reproduce. This is a distinctive property of life, and a distinctive locus of value. Theologically, one may recall the phrase from the Nicene-Constantinopolitan Creed that describes the Holy Spirit as "the Lord, the giver of life."[36] Life is a very particular gift of God in creation; the experience of every life form must therefore be part of our consideration of the costs of that creation. The star that must "die" in order that heavy elements may form in its supernova has no "experience" of a parallel sort. So our consideration must be of the "waste" of living things. I touched earlier on the pain, suffering, and lack of fulfillment associated with the overproduction typical of most organisms. But there is a further important element in apparent waste: the extinction of so many millions of species, each of which was an "attempt" on the part of the evolutionary process to establish a particular niche, and many of which (like the dinosaurs) *had* to die out if mammals were to flourish. The concept of waste is not perhaps the most appropriate one, since this seems suggestive of creatures being made to be

Indeed it's not ... at all.

thrown away, rather than of a creative process with concomitant casualties. There is, moreover, a sense, as Rolston and others have emphasized, in which nothing in the biosphere is ever wholly "wasted," since the free-energy content of one organism is at least partially recycled in the content of others. But *extinction* is always a loss of value to the biosphere as a whole. A whole strategy of being alive on the planet, a whole quality of living experience is lost when any organism becomes extinct.[37]

So we can now refine the problem of evolutionary theodicy: it consists of the suffering of creatures and the extinction of species. How are we to relate this to God the creator and redeemer of the world? The problem has three different theological aspects:

1. One problem is at the level of *ontology*—the fact of God's giving existence to a world containing nonhuman suffering and extinction. This extends the theological problem posed by human suffering.

2. The problem of God's responsibility for a world containing so much creaturely suffering, death, and extinction is intensified in any scheme that imputes *long-term purposes* to this process of divine creation, in the sense of God desiring certain values to arise through the process. This may be the best possible world for the evolution of living things such as ourselves, and yet the question remains as to whether the creation of such a world is the activity of a good God. Other creatures—for example, those whose extinction made possible the rise of the mammals—begin to seem no more than means to the divine end.

The more I think through this issue, the more I see that this *teleological aspect* of evolutionary theodicy is the sharpest edge of the problem. We saw above that natural selection is driven by competition for scarce resources; it therefore promotes better and better adaptation, more and more diverse and excellent strategies for surviving to reproduction. No one who has seen at close quarters the surge of a full-grown orca through the water, the prowl of a leopard through long grass, or that quicksilver stalling turn by which a peregrine returns to the stoop—all products of the refinement of predation over millions of years—can doubt the value that arises from the process. That value, in some cases, specifically attaches to the qualities necessary for the behavior that inflicts suffering on other creatures. That same surge of power is what enables the orca to batter as huge a creature as a gray whale until its strength is gone. The leopard moves silently to within killing distance, but may then take several minutes to dispatch a full-grown antelope.[38] The peregrine's skill enables it to attempt prey which is itself flying at full speed, and may only be maimed by the stoop, leading perhaps to a lingering death in the woods (if the fox is slow to come). Suffering among the weak and less well adapted is *intrinsic* to the evolution of sophisticated creaturely attributes. So if we believe God desired the development of such values—complexity, diversity, excellence of adaptation—then, again, the sufferers are means to God's ends. What sort of God is that? Is that, in Hull's phrase, "a God worthy of worship"?

3. If some scheme of redemption of nonhuman species is used to compensate for these difficulties, there is work to do at the level of *soteriology* (the understanding of salvation), since traditional Christian redemption theory has focused on an event in the history of humanity—a particular crucifixion of a particular member of a historically contingent species, lately arrived after 3.8 billion years of evolution had already passed by. What place, it must be asked, does this view of redemption have when our focus widens to embrace the whole of evolutionary history?

1.6 RESPONSES TO THE PROBLEM
FROM DARWIN ONWARD

Philosophers had been exercised by the character of nature long before Darwin. These concerns formed part of David Hume's famous critique of the design argument.[39] But Darwin's scheme both *extended* the narrative of creaturely suffering over vast spans of geological time, and *embedded* that suffering within the process by which value arose.

We saw above that Darwin was very aware of the ambiguity of the view of creation that he was proposing, its grandeur, its apparent blundering cruelty. He wrote to his friend the American naturalist Asa Gray, "I cannot persuade myself that a beneficent and omnipotent God would have designedly created the Ichneumonidae with the express intention of their feeding within the living bodies of caterpillars."[40] Gray, in contrast, thought an evolutionary scheme posed fewer problems than special creation, because it gave a *reason* for the suffering; it was part of the process by which evolution had given rise to human beings. Moreover, "A process in which the laws were designed but the details left to chance might explain nature's more repulsive products without having to ascribe them directly to divine action."[41] Such indeed was the most characteristic type of (constructive) theological response to Darwin—a sense that God "makes things to make themselves,"[42] and that theology was thereby liberated from a model of God as the distant designer of every detail of the natural world. Aubrey Moore, another of the contributors to *Lux Mundi*, wrote as follows:

> The one absolutely impossible conception of God, in the present day, is that which represents him as an occasional visitor. Science has pushed the deist's God further and further away, and at the moment when it seemed as if he would be thrust out all together Darwinism appeared, and, under the disguise of a foe, did the work of a friend. It

has conferred upon philosophy and religion an inestimable benefit, by showing us that we must choose between two alternatives. Either God is everywhere present in nature, or he is nowhere.[43]

So among the theological responses to Darwinism was a very positive one, which saw evolution as opening up a model of God as immanent in creation, and as giving that creation freedom to generate its own forms. (We shall see that approach taken to its logical conclusion in the work of Ruth Page; see section 4.4.) Such thinking should have been the ideal springboard for a concentrated look at the problems of evolutionary theodicy as I have outlined them. In the light of that it is curious how little progress has been made along these lines since those late-nineteenth-century debates.[44]

It is hard to know exactly why this problem has been so neglected in theological work. As I indicate above, it was clear to Darwin and Asa Gray, and to the theologians of the *Lux Mundi* volume. C. C. J. Webb, writing in 1911, regarded "the problem of the suffering of the lower animals" as "the most difficult part of the problem of pain."[45] John Hick, writing in *Evil and the God of Love* (originally published in 1966) cites this view of Webb's, but still comes to the issue from an invincibly human-centered view.[46]

There may be something in the argument that the sheer horror of the extent of moral evil in the twentieth century prevented theodicists from looking elsewhere in the creation. On this view the date of Webb's book, 1911, may be significant. It preceded the suffering in the trenches of the First World War, which did so much to corrode the idea that human beings in the European nations were progressing to a new pinnacle of civilization. It may further be argued that the realization of the full significance of natural selection as the way the characteristics of organisms were refined over very long time periods, and with enormous struggle and suffering, had to await the "neo-Darwinian synthesis" by which the insights of Darwin were combined with genetics (see section 1.2 above). This synthesis is often dated to the publication of Julian Huxley's book *Evolution: The Modern Synthesis* in 1942[47]—by which time, again, the minds of theologians were being massively concentrated by humans' inhumanity to each other. C. S. Lewis did address animal pain in *The Problem of Pain* (1940), though strikingly he refers such pain both to Satan's fall (see section 2.6 for a critique) and always to humans and their salvation. "The error we must avoid is that of considering them [animals] in themselves. Man is to be understood only in his relation to God. The beasts are to be understood only in their relation to man, and through man, to God."[48]

It may be that theology needed the critique of such anthropocentrism (focus on human interests) provided by ecological writers[49] in order to be able to look beyond narrowly human concerns. It may simply be that the problem of evolutionary theodicy is so intractable, and requires such delicate theological handling—in particular of the doctrine of the Fall (see section 2.6)—that few have wanted to attempt it. Perhaps such theodicy needed the pioneering work that was done on the concerns of animals by Albert Schweitzer;[50] arguably it needed the great vision of progressive evolution so controversially offered by Pierre Teilhard de Chardin[51] (explored further in section 2.5). The problem has certainly gained focus from recent studies of the neurophysiology of animals,[52] and increased awareness of the evolved character of their patterns of behavior.

Space does not permit a full survey of the literature that might be relevant to the history of this debate. The earliest book from the contemporary era that I shall draw on is Andrew Elphinstone's *Freedom, Suffering and Love*, published in 1976. Though not primarily a book on evolutionary theodicy, it has the resolutely evolutionary approach to the Fall (and the condition of humanity) that this book needs as a basis. Other important early work can be found in Arthur Peacocke's Bampton Lectures of 1978, Richard W. Kropf's *Evil and Evolution* (1984), Holmes Rolston III's *Science and Religion: A Critical Survey* (1987), and Paul S. Fiddes's *The Creative Suffering of God* (1988). Jürgen Moltmann's creative approach to evolution and its healing (an approach which itself evolved) can be found in his Gifford Lectures *God in Creation* (1983) and in *The Way of Jesus Christ* (1990).[53]

To confine myself in this study to the suffering of nonhuman creatures is not to denigrate the vast extent of human suffering. It is rather to counterbalance in a small way the preoccupation of theodicists with human suffering.

In this book I shall repeatedly refer to examples of suffering caused by predation. I find as a human who is part of a society which has managed to insulate itself from large predators that the hazards and arbitrariness of exposure to such predators captures the imagination particularly tellingly.[54] Nonhuman suffering is also, of course, caused by disease and parasitism as well. As Rolston points out, parasitism is in a sense even more disturbing than predation, since it nourishes simplicity at the expense of complexity, and often causes protracted pain as the host's strength is drained away.[55]

1.7 A KEY MOVE IN EVOLUTIONARY THEODICY

I discuss strategies in evolutionary theodicy in much more detail in chapter 3, but here I anticipate a key argument that has been advanced in different ways by many important thinkers and especially by Rolston.[56] The general tenor of this argument is to accept that there is a problem of evolutionary suffering, but to regard it as the inevitable and necessary price of the realization of values through evolution, and the price is worth it. The world is a package deal;[57] to have the values, one must have the disvalues. This does not do complete justice to Rolston's position, as we shall see in sections 3.2–3.3, but it is an important argument, recently reformulated by Robin Attfield.[58]

I need to make clear at the beginning of this book why that answer is not enough—why it is not an adequate theodicy in and of itself.[59] In what follows I am helped by David Bentley Hart's moving theological response to the Indian Ocean tsunami of December 2004, *The Doors of the Sea*.[60] The implication of Hart's argument is that the burden of theodicy in respect of natural evil does not depend on the eighteenth-century struggle between a Leibnizian conviction that this is the best of all possible worlds and the skepticism of a Voltaire. *Rather the crux of the problem is not the overall system and its overall goodness but the Christian's struggle with the challenge to the goodness of God posed by specific cases of innocent suffering.*

It is the struggle so powerfully conveyed in Fyodor Dostoevsky's depiction of the character of Ivan in *The Brothers Karamazov*.[61] A long passage in which Ivan pours out his shattered faith at his brother Alyosha culminates in the words:

> Listen: if everyone has to suffer in order to bring about eternal harmony through that suffering, tell me, please, what have children to do with this? It's quite incomprehensible that they too should have to suffer, that they too should have to pay for harmony by their suffering. Why should they be the grist to someone else's mill, the means of ensuring someone's future harmony? . . . I absolutely reject that higher harmony. It's not worth one little tear from one single little tortured child. . . . I don't want harmony. . . . The price of harmony has been set too high, we can't afford the entrance fee. And that's why I hasten to return my entry ticket. If I ever want to call myself an honest man, I have to hand it back as soon as possible. And that's exactly what I'm doing. It's not that I don't accept God, Alyosha; I'm just, with the utmost respect, handing Him back my ticket.[62]

Hart explains:

> The secret of Ivan's argument . . . is that it is not a challenge to Christian faith advanced from the position of unbelief; more subtly, it is a challenge to the habitual optimism of pagan fatalism or empty logical determinism of many Christians advanced from the position of a deeper, more original, more revolutionary, more "Christian" vision of God and understanding of evil. For behind Ivan's anguish lies an intuition—which is purely Christian even if many Christians are insensible to it—that it is impossible for the infinite God of love directly or positively to *will* evil (physical or moral) even in a provisional or transitory way.[63]

The issue for Dostoevsky is not the plausibility of the existence of God, but the goodness of God in the face of specific, individual instances of innocent suffering. Ivan's own example is the torture of an individual child. While I do not in any way equate the suffering of an animal being torn apart by other animals with the deliberate, freely chosen torture of a human by other humans,[64] the problem in terms of the goodness of God is of the same kind. This is evolutionary theodicy at its sharpest—not consideration of the overall developmental system that evolution has made possible, but of the individual creature and its predicament.[65] Faced with myriad examples of such acute, individual, blameless suffering, one might indeed seek to return one's theological ticket.[66] In a sense this is the decision of Richard Dawkins when he writes, "The universe we observe has precisely the properties we should expect if there is, at bottom, no design, no purpose, no evil and no good, nothing but blind, pitiless indifference."[67]

To summarize the argument so far: there is a real problem in affirming with Genesis 1:31 that this creation is "very good," and indeed that it is the creation of a good God. The evolutionary process presents us with the fact of the suffering of myriad creatures (the "ontological problem") and, even worse, the thought that this suffering serves a purpose, in refining species and spurring them on to new and ever more complex and ingenious evolutionary strategies, including those of rationality and consciousness. The victims of evolution, therefore, seem to be merely means to the divine end (the "teleological problem"). Even if the system as a whole is full of value, even if it may be the only way such value could be realized in creation, the suffering of individual creatures might lead one to return one's theological ticket, either to conclude with Dawkins that evolution is just the way things are, blind, pitiless, and indifferent, or worse, that it is the product of a cosmic sadist rather than a loving Father.

Another element in the problem of evolutionary theodicy, again with both ontological and teleological aspects, is the problem of extinction. With every extinction a whole way of being alive is lost to the biosphere. A whole set of strategies for responding to the environment and to other creatures, and hence a whole set of values, is irreplaceably gone. Again it could be argued that other biotic strategies, other values, replace what is lost, and that extinction is a necessary part of the process that drives innovation and complexification. But simply to speak of that necessary exchange of value is not to have taken in the full burden of the theodicy problem. The predicament of the last representatives of a species going extinct may be a particularly acute one, as they lose reproductive opportunities and ultimately the experience of recognizing any of their own kind. Of course, that experience will vary in intensity depending on the sophistication of the sentience of the creature. But one thought experiment, at what are likely to have been among the highest levels of sophisticated perception in an extinct creature, will reveal something of the charge of theodicy that extinction represents. In 2004 results were published on the skeletons of the so-called "hobbits" of the Indonesian island of Flores.[68] *Homo Floresiensis* was a dwarf hominid, apparently with social structures sufficiently advanced to allow the cooperative hunting of the dwarf elephants of the island. Extinction of *Floresiensis* is thought to have taken place as little as twelve thousand years ago, by an unknown mechanism. It is entirely plausible to imagine the last survivors searching the island for their fellows, and a profound experience of loss at the failure to find them. This experience would be replicated in some degree in many other extinctions of sophisticated sentient creatures. Kropf is one of the few authors who is sensitive to this issue of biological extinction. He writes, "Can the emergence of even one new species, one showing greater spontaneity and intelligence, be said to justify the disappearance of a hundred others that are less gifted?"[69] I return to the issue of extinction, and the human response to it, in my last chapter. But now I go on to outline my own approach in evolutionary theodicy.

1.8 MY OWN APPROACH:
A COMPOUND EVOLUTIONARY THEODICY

I began this chapter from the affirmation in Genesis 1 that God saw creation to be very good. However, the creation that science describes for us is one in which suffering is endemic, and intrinsic to its development, a creation moreover in which over 98 percent of all species ever to have evolved are now extinct. It is a creation that will remind the scientifically aware Christian of the apostle Paul's description "groaning in labor pains" (Romans 8:22).[70] Creation, then, is both "good" and "groaning."

I do not consider that any one argument provides a satisfactory response to the problem of evolutionary suffering and extinction. In chapters 3–6 I propose a compound theodicy that treats this problem with the utmost seriousness, and seeks to propose ways in which the believer can retain his or her theological ticket, and can continue to hold to a belief in a God who is creative, redemptive, and all-loving.

A first step is to reconsider in what respects creation may be regarded as very good. In his classic commentary on Genesis Claus Westermann notes that this is an affirmation not just of creation's beauty but of its *appropriateness*; the term is more functional than reflective of a fixed aesthetic quality.[71] I would want to hold that creation is good in its propensity to give rise to great values of beauty, diversity, complexity, and ingenuity of evolutionary strategy.[72] It is also good because it is the Lord's (Ps. 24:1). But a strong emphasis within contemporary Christian theology is on creation as a continuous process, rather than something completed at the beginning of time. For this reason I am

happy to accept John Haught's point that creation is "unfinished"[73] and to side
with Wolfhart Pannenberg's conclusion that "Only in the light of the eschatological consummation may [the verdict "very good"] be said of our world as
it is in all its confusion and pain."[74] Colin Gunton in his reappropriation of
the theology of Irenaeus of Lyons claims "good *means* precisely that which is
destined for perfection."[75] Creation then will finally be *very* good at the eschaton, when God will be all in all (1 Cor. 15:28), and God's Sabbath rest will be
with God's creation.[76]

The core of my approach to evolutionary theodicy is:

- I acknowledge the goodness of creation in giving rise to all sorts of values.
- I acknowledge the pain, suffering, death, and extinction that are intrinsic
  to a creation evolving according to Darwinian principles. Moreover, I
  hold to the (unprovable) assumption that an evolving creation was the
  only way in which God could give rise to the sort of beauty, diversity, sentience, and sophistication of creatures that the biosphere now contains. As
  shorthand I call this the "only way" argument (see section 3.3).
- I affirm God's co-suffering with every sentient being in creation—the "co-
  suffering" argument (see sections 3.5, 4.2).
- I take the Cross of Christ to be the epitome of this divine compassion, the
  moment of God's taking ultimate responsibility for the pain of creation,
  and—with the Resurrection—to inaugurate the transformation of creation (see section 4.7).
- I further stress the importance of giving some account of the eschatological fulfillment of creatures that have known no flourishing in this life. A
  God of loving relationship could never regard any creature as a mere evolutionary expedient. Drawing on a phrase of Jay McDaniel's, I nickname
  this the "pelican heaven" argument (see sections 5.3–5.6).
- If divine fellowship with creatures such as ourselves is in any sense a goal of
  evolutionary creation, then I advocate a very high doctrine of humanity,
  supposing that indeed humans are of very particular concern to God. That
  does not in any way exclude a sense that God delights in every creature that
  emerges within evolution, but it leads to the possibility that humans have a
  crucial and positive role, cooperating with their God in the healing of the
  evolutionary process—the "co-redeemer" argument (see section 6.7).[77]

To advance such a detailed scheme is not to solve the problem of evolutionary theodicy, or to deny the extent to which, in the last analysis, there is a necessary element of mystery in this area. It is merely to indicate my conviction
that a combination of approaches is required to do any sort of justice to this
neglected problem. Even as I sketch the outlines of my scheme, I acknowledge
the shortcomings of all such theological enterprises. In a sense all theodicies
that engage with real situations rather than philosophical abstractions, and
endeavor to give an account of the God of the Christian Scriptures, arise out
of protest and end in mystery. There are no completely satisfying accounts,

only recourses to explorations of God and the world that are bare logical formulations, or systems of partial explanation pointing beyond themselves. But what I attempt here is what Karl Barth called theology: "taking rational trouble over the mystery."[78]

In chapter 3 I provide a classification of different approaches in theodicy, and locate my compound approach within that classification. In chapter 4 I explore how a Trinitarian understanding of creation might come to terms with a created order full of competition, struggle, and suffering. And in chapter 5 I explore the eschatological element in my compound theodicy.

I must make clear that in appropriating the text of Romans 8:19–22 and laying it, as I have just done, alongside Genesis 1:31, I am not supposing for a moment that Paul had any evolutionary awareness. Almost certainly he was thinking mainly in terms of the "bondage to decay" resulting after the sin of the first humans, as hinted at in Genesis 3. But now that we must part company with a picture of a fall from a primordial paradise (as I shall show in section 2.6), we are still left in Romans 8 with a resonant image of creaturely suffering, and yet subjection (by God) in hope, a hope somehow tied to the destiny of human beings. Paul claims that the creation "waits with eager longing for the revealing of the children of God" (v. 19) and that it "will obtain the freedom of the glory of the children of God" (v. 21); in some way or other, the transformation of the human condition, and hence of human activity, is bound up with, and will precede, the final liberation of the nonhuman creation. I explore that destiny and that connection in chapter 6, and in my final chapter I propose some implications for how humans might imagine their calling in respect of the nonhuman creation.

Before developing my own argument further, however, I want to show why certain directions that have been taken in response to the challenge of evolutionary theodicy do not form part of my overall proposal. So I turn now to these "roads not taken."

2

Roads Not Taken

2.1 INTRODUCTION

Here I consider a whole range of ways of reframing the problem of evolutionary theodicy so as not to have to address it. I concentrate in particular on some
variants of the Christian doctrine of the Fall, proposals in which the rebellion
of some entities or other, be they humans or angels, is held to be responsible
for the disvalues we see in creation. As I made clear in the last chapter I regard
that approach as scientifically dubious; I also consider it to be theologically
unfruitful. I begin by casting my net wider, however, and mentioning briefly a
range of other possibilities, each of which would short-circuit the problem
under investigation.

2.2 CREATIONISM AND INTELLIGENT DESIGN

The first road not taken—I include this for the sake of completeness—is a
biblical-literalist approach that rejects an evolutionary scheme on the basis of
the six-day account of the special creation of creatures described in Genesis 1.
Such a creationist approach receives a careful assessment from Peters and
Hewlett.[1] It relies on preferring the (supposed) scientific content of Genesis 1
to the combined witness of the physical sciences over the last 150 years. (One
of the most impressive facets of the complex of ideas that constitutes contemporary Darwinism is the sheer range of sciences that contribute to the evolutionary narrative of the Earth.[2] That is not, of course, to claim that the theory
is without its problems,[3] but in its general outlines it is very robust.) It is the
conviction of this author, as of almost all those writing in the science-religion
debate, that creationism both fails to take science seriously, and uses a very

dubious method of interpreting Scripture. The majestic account in Genesis 1 (which in itself differs both in emphasis and in detail from the creation narrative offered in Gen. 2) provides a theological cosmology that marks out certain distinctive positions (as to the relation of God to creation, and as to the status of all human beings) relative to other ancient Near Eastern accounts. There is no reason to expect from such an account that it would meet the criteria for a scientific account of the origin of the world or of living creatures, or that it would show an awareness of, for example, the myriad extinctions to which the fossil record testifies.

The second road not taken is that of so-called "intelligent design," a movement that has grown up in the last twenty years or so, and which claims that certain elements of the cosmos could not have arisen by spontaneous processes of undirected evolution. Either it is claimed that these elements—be they biological organs such as the eye or the bacterial flagellum, or biochemical systems such as the tricarboxylic acid cycle—could not have arisen spontaneously because the probability of this would have been vanishingly small[4] or that they display "irreducible complexity."[5] In either case, intelligent design theorists claim that the biological feature concerned requires the input of a designer to insert them as a complete "module" into the systems of nature. Two key questions must be posed of the explanations offered by intelligent design. First, can an explanation based on an unknown designer ever be the best of a range of scientific explanations? It is a type of explanation that must always be vulnerable to Occam's Razor; it introduces an extra entity, a designer, into the system—an entity that is untestable and uncharacterizable, over and above the range of entities included in an evolutionary explanation. As such, an intelligent design explanation—as science, as opposed to as theology—will always tend to compare badly with an evolutionary, naturalistic explanation, in terms of the criteria of compactness, simplicity, and elegance that properly form part of scientific theory selection. For an explanation based on an intelligent designer to be the best scientific explanation, all evolutionary explanations must therefore be found wanting. Given the range of evolutionary explanations actually or potentially available for any given phenomenon, this is always going to be an unlikely event. A further consideration in theory selection is fruitfulness, and it must be questioned how scientifically fruitful a designer-based explanation can be. Like a God-of-the-gaps explanation of gravity or electromagnetism, it may appear compelling to some of those contemplating the state of the relevant science at a particular historical juncture, but because it brings scientific inquiry to a stop in an unexplained entity, it will always be vulnerable to the possibility that further development of naturalistic explanations will open up a more fruitful path.

From the point of view of the present study, it should also be noted that intelligent design poses additional theological problems within the already problematic area of creaturely suffering. A Christian scheme offers no scope for a demiurge or designer operating independently of the divine creator, so if design explanations are to be offered, they must be in terms of the activity of God. We have already seen that for a creator to fulfill divine creative purposes by means of an evolutionary scheme that necessarily involves—indeed uses— the suffering of very many creatures is theologically problematic. A major strategy in evolutionary theodicy is bound to be the conviction that this process—full of disvalue though it is—is necessary to the realization of creaturely values (see section 1.7). As we shall see in sections 3.2–3.3, this line of argument is articulately developed by Rolston, Attfield, Murphy and Ellis, and Domning and Hellwig, among others. But that strategy is brought into question by any scheme which pictures God as intervening within the scheme. In particular, postulating that the key elements in creatures were designed, rather than the result of long processes of exploration under the influence of both law and chance, seems to exacerbate the problem of theodicy created by the suffering experienced by creatures. Robert J. Russell, in proposing that God uses the pattern of mutation to shape the course of evolution, is very aware that this proposal intensifies the problem of evolutionary theodicy.[6] How much greater, then, is the theodicy problem posed by a model of a God who sets up evolutionary processes, but also intervenes to insert modules within them. The proponents of intelligent design do not think that evolutionary processes are able to give rise to complexity by themselves, so those processes are therefore not the producers of values that Darwinians would claim them to be, yet those same processes still give rise to all the disvalues of creaturely suffering. Moreover, this intervening God inserts modules of complexity into the natural order, but does not seem to intervene to mitigate suffering. As we saw in section 1.6, evolutionary schemes, problematic as they are in terms of theodicy, may not actually cause as many problems as competing models. Postulating that the key elements in creatures were designed, rather than the result of long processes of exploration under the influence of both law and chance, would seem to intensify the problem of theodicy created by the suffering experienced by creatures. The only recourse from such criticisms would be to invoke fallenness in creatures, an approach I tackle in section 2.6.[7] For further consideration of the relation of God's providence to these issues in theodicy, see section 4.6.

2.3 GOD NOT THE CREATOR, OR NOT BENEVOLENT?

A possibility which has lurked on the edge of the Christian tradition since its early centuries is that the material world is in fact evil, not the product of the creative activity of a loving God, but the work of another deity.[8] Goodness, on this view, resides in the spiritual, and it comes as no surprise that material existence is full of struggle and suffering. Such schemes in the patristic era have been reviewed by my colleague Alastair Logan;[9] their enduring appeal is shown by the phenomenon of Catharism and related creeds in medieval Europe.[10] This is always a serious theological alternative to the Christian conviction that God created the cosmos *ex nihilo* (out of absolutely nothing), pronounced it "very good," and so loved it that the Divine Son took flesh and died for its healing. I note in passing one of the weaknesses of such dualistic schemes: they provide no ethical incentive to care for the Earth or its ecology. I reiterate that this study concerns itself with the hard questions posed by a rigorously monotheistic scheme. I am, then, committed to working out the implications of God being solely responsible for the existence of the created world.

Another possibility, which again lurks on the edge of Christian reflection, is that the Creator of all things is best understood as the mysterious figure of Isaiah 45:7, the Creator of weal and woe alike, ultimately sovereign and unquestionable, but not in any simple or human-understandable way a loving God. This view is pursued with logic and considerable intellectual courage by Wesley Wildman[11]—also by B. Jill Carroll in her work on the American nature writer Annie Dillard.[12] A related strategy has recently been explored by Charlene Burns.[13] Carroll writes: "To reclaim violent models of God is simply to be honest about the universe we live in and the cosmic, natural powers that seem to 'brood and fight' within it."[14] Burns takes seriously the scientific finding I noted in chapter 1 that violent predation preceded the advent of humans by millions of years. Therefore, *pace* Walter Wink, who has done so much to help contemporary theology take the reality of evil seriously,[15] humans cannot be responsible for this facet of nature. Rather as Burns says, "Violence in nature and the suffering of innocents is a fact of existence."[16] She quotes Gordon Kaufman's view that the "serendipitous creativity" of creation "inevitably brings with it the tragedies of suffering among all levels of life and the extinction of entire species."[17] Can we then give full consideration to God as the author of "weal and woe alike" and also do justice to the Christian claim that the God of the Hebrew Bible is the same God revealed through Jesus? Burns invokes the thought of Luther about the *deus absconditus* as well as the *deus revelatus* [God hidden as well as revealed]. For Luther, "God is not to be justified in the face of evil, for God is in fact responsible, making use of it through the *opus alienum Dei* [God's alien work (of destruction)]."[18] Burns's approach therefore defaults to an appeal to mystery in God, a move which I consider in section 3.4.

Wildman's approach is rather different—not wanting to link God to a transparent good of any sort. He gives a skillful critique of "determinate-entity theism" (belief in a personal God, such as the Christian conviction that God is creator and redeemer and can be known personally through God's Son and the work of the Holy Spirit), and goes on to show the weaknesses of "process theism" (see section 2.4 below). Wildman's solution is to regard God as the ground of being, whose nature is glimpsable in the beauty but also in the violence of the cosmos. His God is not a determinate entity in all or indeed in most respects.[19] Wildman writes, "Cursed to wander in search of secrets, then, let us not waste energy on defending the universe or its divine heart." His type of theism is "an awkward partner for common human moral expectations but deeply attuned to the ways of nature and resonant with the wisdom about suffering that is encoded in many of the world's religious and philosophical traditions." Wildman presses the question that we encountered in section 1.5—"Can this be called a worship-worthy God?"—and claims that plausibility is more important than religious appeal. His God is "beautiful from a distance in the way that a rain forest is beautiful." Suffering in nature is "neither evil nor a byproduct of the good. It is part of the wellspring of divine creativity in nature, flowing up and out of the abysmal divine depths like molten rock from the yawning mouth of a volcano."[20]

The essay of Wildman's from which I have been quoting is one of the most incisive and honest pieces of theological writing I have read in a long time. Why then do I not take this road of ground-of-being theism? Ultimately out of a personal conviction that I have encountered the God of "determinate-entity theism," a God knowable—insofar as God can ever be knowable—in Jesus.[21] My experience of the Christian Scriptures is that they are a way to meet with God, and that they point to Jesus' resurrection from the dead and the dynamic power of the Holy Spirit of God in the early Christian churches. Out of the tradition that has held to such a conviction—a conviction that in my case is held with all the existential doubt and struggle that any honest believer must expect—emerges the framework of Christian systematic theology to which this book seeks to make a tiny contribution. That includes the conviction that the God who raised Jesus from the dead—and so made the ultimate personal statement of the vindication of self-sacrificial love—is both the origin of all things and the universe's ultimate hope. As soon as one embraces that framework, full of questions as it is, the problem of evolutionary theodicy is inescapable and must be addressed, in all humility. *as I said: Hermeneutics*

2.4 THE GOD OF PROCESS THEOLOGY

Process philosophy arose out of A. N. Whitehead's effort to generate a radically new metaphysics that would unify the way we understand the world. In his 1927 Gifford Lectures, published as *Process and Reality*,[22] Whitehead

(1861–1947) abandoned the notion, strong in Western philosophy since Parmenides and Plato in the fifth century BCE, that what is most unchanging is most real. Instead he conceived the structure of reality in dynamic terms (an approach that goes back to Heraclitus). Whitehead set out a radical metaphysics based not on entities but on events—on an infinite series of "actual occasions." All entities are "momentary constituents of the processes of reality"; unchangingness is a property of what is "dead, past, abstract or purely formal."[23] The emphasis is on becoming, on development in time, rather than on static being.

Space does not permit a detailed analysis of this way of thinking, except to say that for process thought the central metaphor for understanding the world is that of organism, rather than that of machine. The formation of each event is a function of

- The nature of the entities involved (as in, for instance, a physicalist scheme).
- Their context and interdependence on a number of levels (in a way more characteristic of biological organisms than of inanimate objects).
- Their "experience" and their effort to "fulfill their possibilities to the full" in the given event (language deriving not merely from biology but from the analogy of human mentality).

As Ian Barbour describes, "Each entity is a center of spontaneity and self-creation, contributing distinctively to the world."[24] This assignment of quasi-mental subjective experience to all entities is known as panpsychism, or sometimes panexperientialism.[25] Note that the process scheme is neither consistent nor inconsistent with experimental observations. Nothing in science attributes any sort of subjectivity to an entity like an electron. Whitehead's scheme is true "meta"-physics.

In the last chapter of *Process and Reality* Whitehead turns his attention to God and develops his concept of a dipolar deity. According to this concept, God, who in strict process thought is one entity among others—not ontologically distinct from the rest of the cosmos—is

- Affected by the experience of all other entities (God's "consequent" nature) *and*
- Constant in character as the ground both of order and of novelty (God's "primordial" nature).

This formulation of the character of God in terms of two types of attribute in tension—responsiveness and constancy—is known as "dipolarity" (sometimes "bipolarity"). This is a very helpful way of overcoming some of the intrinsic paradoxes of theism.[26] Dipolarity, then, allows God to be responsive to the world and yet remain God. The emphasis in process models of God is on a God who experiences the world's pain and struggle, and persuades it toward paths of creativity and fulfillment. In Whitehead's famous phrase, God is "the great companion—fellow sufferer who understands."[27]

The fellow-suffering God, who does not coerce but merely seeks to persuade other beings in the direction of love, seems at first sight profoundly attractive to the theodicist. Where process schemes are at their strongest is in offering a single account of human-inflicted evil and so-called natural evil (such as earthquakes); in both cases "evil" arises from conflicts between the desire of different entities for self-actualization. God lovingly suffers with all entities and retains their experiences in God's eternal memory, but the process God does not "fix" these conflicts for the benefit of one entity rather than another. Instead God tries to lure all elements toward the optimal blend of harmony and intensity of experience.

Criticisms of process theology include concern about the loss of the classical Christian doctrine of *creatio ex nihilo*;[28] reservations about the according of experience to every entity, however primitive; and doubt as to whether ongoing divine lure, and the retention of experiences in the divine memory, are enough to do justice to the Christian hope of the resurrection and the ultimate triumph of good over evil. It is not clear to what extent process schemes can be combined with a Trinitarian understanding. Joseph Bracken has made a valiant effort to integrate process thought with classical patterns of Christian thought such as Trinity, *creatio ex nihilo*, resurrection, and final consummation.[29] His account therefore comes near to my own at a number of points, including his emphasis on human life being held within the relations of the triune persons, on the importance of self-giving, and on true freedom consisting in response to the divine will. The scheme I propose in chapter 4 is influenced by the concept of divine lure, and by a strong belief in divine co-suffering with the suffering of creatures.

Bracken seems to have an account of "natural process" on top of which the pansubjectivity of entities can operate, leading sometimes to "misguided choices" and "pointless suffering."[30] This makes me wonder what function the process scheme really serves for Bracken in his understanding of the nonhuman world. It is more straightforward theology, and more evidently in tune with the scientific evidence, to suppose that suffering comes from the *normal* operation of natural processes (even though, as I have discussed, this suffering often serves no purpose, nor leads to any apparent redemption, for the suffering creature itself).

I have a similar thought about Pailin's fine book *God and the Processes of Reality*. Pailin is prepared to abandon panexperientialism and to readmit into his theology the doctrine of *creatio ex nihilo*. His eventual approach comes out curiously similar to that of Arthur Peacocke (of whom more in section 3.5), which makes me wonder to what extent Pailin remains a true process theologian. *So*

So my feeling in the end is that if what makes a process theologian is the emphasis on the dynamic character of the cosmos, and on divine responsiveness and co-suffering, within an understanding of God as ultimately good and ultimately sovereign, then I can subscribe; but if it involves taking on the Whiteheadian metaphysic, and the primacy of creativity and openness of process over even the will of God, then I must rule this another road not to be taken.

An extreme version of the move process theodicy makes is found in Hans Jonas, a Jewish philosopher whose own mother died in a concentration camp. Jonas is particularly sensitive to the stricture that if we say anything at all about God today, we should not say anything we would not also be willing to repeat in the presence of the children of Auschwitz. Although this point has already been well taken—perhaps particularly well by Kenneth Surin[31]—it bears restating and restating. But the model of God to which Jonas is driven is an extreme one; his God empties Godself of mind and power in giving the creation its existence, and then allows the interplay of chance and natural law to take its course. God's only further involvement is that God holds a memory of the experience of the creation; he receives his being back "transfigured or possibly disfigured by the chance harvest of unforeseeable temporal experience."[32] However authentically held, this position is a form of "sub-deism" (to borrow a phrase of Clare Palmer's), not a basis for a Christian theology of creation and involvement with the cosmos. As John Haught notes, Jonas needed in his model of God a stronger sense of promise, ultimate hope, lying behind nature's struggles and yearnings.[33] As it stands, Jonas's God is to my mind not the sort of God to whom anyone would be inclined to pray.

2.5 TEILHARD DE CHARDIN

Pierre Teilhard de Chardin (1881–1955), the French theologian and anthropologist, remains the most famous (or notorious) embracer of evolution as a working out of God's purposes in the world (see especially his *The Phenomenon of Man*).[34] Teilhard regarded the progress of evolution as leading by a near-inevitable sequence from the "hylosphere," a world containing only inanimate matter, to the "zöosphere," the world of living organisms. (Thus far Teilhard seems to foreshadow in a remarkable way recent thinking on the self-organizing properties of matter.) He thought this process of "intensification" and "centration" had then led to the "nöosphere," the realm of consciousness and cultural information, which would spread throughout the world and become more and more dominant until mind became the central reality, and all creation would converge on the "Omega Point," which he identified with the consummation of the cosmos in Christ (as in Col. 1:20). Again, one might say that a part of Teilhard's vision has been fulfilled in the development of the Internet, a very rapidly growing web of information which is starting to cover the surface of the planet.

However, Teilhard has had very many critics, not merely in the Roman Catholic hierarchy that for many years proscribed his work. In a famously scathing review, the eminent biologist Peter Medawar rejected the scientific validity of any equation of evolution with inevitable progress.[35] R. J. Berry has recently renewed the assault.[36] Arguably, Teilhard's model is not about evolution at all, but about the redemptive process by which God gradually draws the world to its consummation.

There are great flashes of insight in Teilhard. His work foreshadows the emphasis (in Peacocke and others) on propensity to complexification in evolutionary systems (see sections 4.4, 4.6), Rolston's talk of creation "suffering through to something higher,"[37] and Polkinghorne's language of the "noetic world."[38] Yet there is in his work an overweening preoccupation with the human project that sits ill with contemporary ecological sensibilities. Teilhard's focus is always on the development of consciousness, and its ever-increasing integration over the whole planet. This is the *telos*[39] toward which the evolutionary system is attracted. Now, the scheme I propose in chapter 6 involves a key role, by God's grace, for humans as the priests and servants of the nonhuman creation, and it would be hard to imagine a Christian scheme in which God's relationship with humans did not have a special place of some sort. Freely chosen human communion with God is a special element within the creation. It was the element, moreover, by which God committed Godself to the creation in a new and saving way in the Incarnation. But to regard "hominization" of the world as *the* telos of the cosmos is to limit the scope of other creaturely value in a way that is ethically problematic, and intensifies the problem of theodicy that occupies us in this study (see section 1.5 on the teleological aspect of the problem).

Teilhard's work strongly informs Richard Kropf's *Evil and Evolution* (1984), which I discuss in section 3.2. Kropf's is one of the few examples of a book-length engagement with evolutionary theodicy, and he draws much from Teilhard. Yet it is still possible to question whether Teilhard ever really had an evolutionary theodicy. The most I can glean is from a telling but enigmatic appendix he wrote in 1948 to *The Phenomenon of Man*, in which he talks of

> A particular type of cosmos in which evil appears necessarily and as abundantly as you like in the course of evolution—not by accident (which would not much matter) but through the very structure of the system. A universe which is involuted and interiorised, but at the same time and by the same token a universe which labours, which sins, and

which suffers. Arrangement and centration: a doubly conjugated operation which, like the scaling of a mountain or the conquest of the air, can only be effected objectively if it is rigorously paid for—for reasons and at charges which, if we only knew them, would enable us to penetrate the secret of the world around us. Suffering and failure, tears and blood: so many by-products (often precious, moreover, and re-utilisable) begotten by the noosphere on its way. This, in final analysis, is what the spectacle of the world in movement reveals to our observation and reflection at the first stage. But is that really all? Is there nothing else to see? In other words, is it really sure that, for an eye trained and sensitised by light other than that of pure science, the quantity and the malice of evil *hic et nunc* [here and now], spread through the world, does not betray a certain *excess*, inexplicable to our reason, if to *the normal effect of evolution* is not added the *extraordinary effect* of some catastrophe or primordial deviation?[40]

This is a strange mixture of the "only way" argument we encountered earlier in section 1.7: evil occurs "not by accident . . . but through the very structure of the system" that gives rise to achievements "like the scaling of a mountain or the conquest of the air" but which must be "rigorously paid for"—with, in the last paragraph, a very surprising reversion to a traditional Christian approach to the Fall. It is nowhere clear how the goodness of God is maintained, given that the paying of the price seems to be done by the myriad creatures discarded by the process that leads to "arrangement and centration."[41]

All in all, it is hard to know what to make of Teilhard.[42] His work is generally regarded to be much more understandable in his native French, but as can be seen he includes some strange terminology that makes it hard to locate him within the scientific and theological enterprises of his time. As I noted above, he has been famously denounced from within evolutionary science, yet recently the distinguished biologist Simon Conway Morris lectured at the annual meeting of the British Teilhard Association (2007). Teilhard's views have often been rejected by mainstream scholars seeking to relate evolution and theology,[43] yet he has been an influence on many recent thinkers, John Haught and Celia Deane-Drummond to name but two.[44]

For recent study of Teilhard see in particular my colleague David Grumett's monograph.[45] I acknowledge that Teilhard's enigmatic work may continue to be a treasure trove of insights into sacramentality and a mystical approach to biology. I also affirm the strong conviction in Teilhard that God's project of evolutionary creation will ultimately converge on an eschaton in which God will be "all in all." But as against Teilhard, I insist that that convergence comes about not through the process of evolutionary centration, for which God lets creatures pay the price, but through the mighty redeeming act of God inaugurated in the Cross of Christ (see chapters 4 and 5).

2.6 DOING WITHOUT A FALL FROM PARADISE

I now arrive at my main concern in this chapter: the idea that the creaturely world was created free from struggle and violence, but that it has since been corrupted by the rebellious action of free moral agents. I begin with proposals based on this rebellion being by human beings. Clearly such a scheme has much resonance with the first three chapters of Genesis. (This is particularly the case if the account is read straight through, ignoring the likely difference in authorship between 1–2:4a and 2:4b–3:24. On such a reading the original dispensation implied in Genesis 1:29, by which humans were given for food "every plant yielding seed," is set aside as a result of human disobedience at 3:6. A different state of the creation arises: "cursed is the ground because of you" [3:17].)

The biblical writer(s) of Genesis offer us, not just in chapter 3 but in the remainder of the primordial history up to and including chapter 11, a profoundly important insight into the implications of human sin. Once humans seek to discover the full possibilities of their selfhood through disobedient self-assertion rather than through drawing closer to the will of the God who made them, their relationship with each other and with their surroundings is at once distorted. Mutual trust is replaced by blame, envy, and violence; what has been received as gift has to be worked for, struggled for. The analysis that follows in no way dilutes my conviction as to the centrality of this insight into human being.[46]

However, the scientific record of the Earth's long history before the advent of human beings calls into profound question any account that regards human sin as the cause of struggle and suffering in the nonhuman creation in general. Predation, violence, parasitism, suffering, and extinction were integral parts of the natural order long before *Homo sapiens*. As every T-Rex-loving six-year-old knows, there is evidence of these natural dynamics from the age of dinosaurs, which came to an end some 65 million years ago. Even the longest estimate of the time for which creatures that might be recognized as human have existed is no more than a million years at the very outside. However, despite its complete lack of congruity with the scientific narrative of the unfolding of the biosphere, a sense that human sin is responsible for factors in the natural world quite beyond our power to influence remains strong.[47] This despite its clear rejection by Britain's two leading scientist-theologians of the last thirty years. Both make clear that human responsibility for predation and parasitism in nature is untenable.[48] John Polkinghorne writes as follows: "[Physical evil] must contain impermanence as the ground of change, death as the prerequisite of new life. Its blind alleys and malfunctions will produce what humans perceive as the physical evil of disease and disaster. In that sense the universe is everywhere 'fallen' and it has always been so."[49] Arthur Peacocke is also quite clear: "Biological death can no longer be regarded as in any way the *consequence* of anything human beings might have been supposed to have done in the past, for evolutionary history shows it to be the very *means* whereby they appear, and so, for the theist, are created by God. The traditional interpretation of the third chapter of *Genesis* that there was a historical 'Fall,' an action by our human progenitors that is the explanation of biological death, has to be rejected. . . . There was no golden age, no perfect past, no individuals, 'Adam' or 'Eve' from whom all human beings have descended and declined and who were perfect in their relationships and behaviour."[50]

Patricia A. Williams objects to fall narratives on another ground as well. From her perspective they are a misreading of Genesis 2–3, which was misread long ago by Paul in order to provide the "catastrophe" from which the Christ-event is our "rescue." She notes what many commentators on the Hebrew Bible have noted, that there is no "fall" tradition elsewhere in Old Testament texts that builds on Genesis 3.[51] Disputes as to biblical interpretation are notoriously fraught, but other arguments make clear that neither the human condition nor that of the nonhuman creation can be understood as the corruption, in historical time, of a primordial paradise. The first stems from the observation noted above; there is no evidence that such a paradise ever existed. The second argument is even more important. As I noted in section 1.5, it is that the very processes by which the created world gives rise to the values of greater complexity, beauty, and diversity also give rise to the disvalues of predation, suffering, and violent and selfish behavior.

So, far from the universe being fallen through human action from a perfection initially given it by God, *I hold that the sort of universe we have, in which complexity emerges in a process governed by thermodynamic necessity and Darwinian natural selection, and therefore by death, pain, predation, and self-assertion, is the only sort of universe that could give rise to the range, beauty, complexity, and diversity of creatures the Earth has produced.* This is the first major plank in my own theodicy, what I called in section 1.8 the "only way" argument.[52] Note that I do not couch this solely in terms of the evolution of freely choosing self-conscious creatures like ourselves, creatures whom we believe to have a distinctive ability to respond to God and each other in self-giving love. I consider that the evolution of such creatures was one goal of creation, but not by any means the only one.

Two essays by Michael Lloyd are symptomatic of much Christian thinking in the Western tradition in its anxiety to defend a chronological fall of an initially perfectly good creation. It is highly significant that one of these was published in Andrew Linzey and Dorothy Yamamoto's edited *Animals on the Agenda*, and the other in a collection of essays briefing the 1998 Lambeth Conference on the essentials of the faith. A belief in an original dispensation lacking predation or violence is very influential on those advocating vegetarianism. Such thinkers tend to suggest that much of humans' cruel and exploitative treatment of animals stems from the altered state of relationships after the Fall. Also there is among many Christians a fear that questioning a doctrine as central as that of the Fall would destabilize the faith and render it liable to further depredations by secularly minded scientists.

Lloyd points out that the suffering of nonhuman creatures is a characteristically theistic problem (see section 1.3), made worse for the theist who also believes that God's self-giving love finds its truest example in Christ.[53]

He goes on to examine several possibilities for understanding creaturely suffering:

First, that it is bad but necessary and worthwhile—either because the bad contributes to the good, or because creatures need a world containing disvalues to educate them to maturity. I analyze these ways of balancing goods and harms in the next chapter. Both options engender challenges in terms of what I called in section 1.5 the teleological aspect to the problem of evolutionary theodicy—predation and animal suffering having purposes that further the flourishing of creation. That is worrying to Lloyd, because in that case these disvalues "obviously have a more direct place in the divine will than if they are seen as a strange and unwanted aberration."[54] The distinction between God allowing evil and creating evil is blurred in such instrumental approaches, and creation and redemption then seem to point in different directions.

Lloyd sees that this contradiction between God's creative intent and God's saving will would disappear if it could be established that this was the only way to produce creatures capable of freedom and love. This is the "only way" argument that I introduced in sections 1.7–1.8 and identify as a key move in evolutionary theodicy (see section 3.3). But for Lloyd it is too great a limitation on the power of God. In reply I fully accept that we could never be sure that this was God's only way to give rise to creatures such as stem from the 3.8-billion-year-long evolution of the Earth's biosphere. We can only say that given what we know about creatures, especially what we know about the role of evolution in refining their characteristics, and the sheer length of time the process has required to give rise to sophisticated sentience, it is eminently plausible and coherent to suppose that this was the only way open to God.

But if one is to avoid both the suggestion that God used for divine purposes of good an evolutionary process to which violence, suffering, and extinction were intrinsic, and the subsidiary suggestion that we can understand this apparent divine ruthlessness in terms of its being the only way to bring out God's long-term goals of beauty, value, and freedom in the created world, then the easiest way is indeed to posit that creaturely suffering is bad and not the work or will of God. That is why for Lloyd an actual, cosmic fall of all creation is absolutely necessary to a Christian theology.[55] Without it, he claims that there can be no convincing doctrine of salvation (since creation is as God intended). Indeed, as often has been remarked, it is difficult to keep a high doctrine of creation—as very good and solely the work of God—in register with a doctrine of the need for the salvation of the whole creation.[56]

But suppose the only way to arrive at certain good features of creation, including freely choosing self-conscious creatures, was via a route involving creaturely suffering. Then it is possible to postulate that the creation has unfolded as God intended it to unfold, and yet is still in need of final healing and consummation. That is my own position, which I develop in chapters 4–6. Lloyd will not allow that step. If there was no fall, he claims, then nature is as God intended and there can be no redemption. Lloyd also notes the pastoral difficulty of having to admit to those who suffer that God might have intended a world in which there is suffering. God's response to suffering, he claims, is always sorrow and protest. But again Lloyd does not take account of the possibility that there was no other way for creation to be, and that God might have suffered with and sorrowed with a creation necessarily subjected to travails in order that goods might arise.

Lloyd's third objection is an ethical one: if nature is as God intended, then that makes it difficult, for example, for us to mount a case for animal rights, since the world has been so created that animals (and by extension ourselves) kill other animals for food. This is a particularly revealing move. It is the argument of someone who has decided what ethics should say, and then works up a theology to match, instead of allowing a coherently argued theology, drawing on Scripture, tradition, reason, and experience, to inform his ethics. Lloyd fears it would also be difficult to argue against those defenders of homosexuality who regard that orientation as natural, given, hence God-given.[57] Again one senses an ethical position tugging a theology out of shape, forcing the author to defend a position that is hard to defend, and certainly hard to reconcile with what contemporary science suggests about the world.[58]

Lloyd is aware, however, of the difficulty of making human sin the reason for the properties of a wide diversity of nonhuman creatures. He acknowledges that "Since Darwin, it has not been possible to characterize all the divisions of creation as the effects of the human Fall."[59] Lloyd therefore concludes that matter must have been created good, but must have been corrupted by angelic action, and that it is here that the cosmic Fall must be located.[60]

Lloyd has to admit, however, that there is no strong evidence for the existence of these "revolting" angels, and that this element of his argument has to be "carried" by the rest. In passing here I would note the ingeniousness of Lloyd's arguments. He notes, for instance, that Eden already contained the serpent, that this garden was not the whole world, and that humankind was given a mandate to subdue the creation—all signs in Lloyd's view that the creation was not paradisal but already fallen into depravity.[61] But as he gives no details of his revolting angels, his approach to the fall effectively elides into a fourth position, namely that matter, created good, was corrupted to generate suffering by what I can only call "mysterious fallenness."

T. F. Torrance offers us a highly sophisticated version of the mysterious fallenness strategy. Creation necessarily *appears* ambiguous to us "precisely because of the double face of contingence, towards God and away from God."[62] But that is an appearance that it would be bound to have, *as* creation: it is not a defect. However, there does seem to be a radical disorder to creation, a "gaping chasm in being and order which we cannot rationally span."[63] The physicality of the crucifixion and resurrection, for Torrance, is an index that "far from evil having to do only with human hearts and minds, it has become entrenched in the ontological depths of created existence."[64] However, God does not give up the claim that creation is good but insists on upholding that claim through the Incarnation.

Torrance is willing to accept decay, decomposition, and death as manifestations of thermodynamic change, but he thinks there are problems here not easily shrugged off, not least the predator-prey relationship at the heart of the evolutionary process, and the endless waste of life at all levels of sentient and organic life. These to him are signs that evil has "infiltrated these functions and features of nature, thereby giving them a malignant twist which makes them 'disorderly' in an irrational way."[65] Torrance is clearly very well aware of the extent of evolutionary suffering and the problem it could pose for theodicy. He holds, however, that in the nonhuman creation, God "makes any obstruction or evil misdirection in nature to serve a fuller and richer end than might have been otherwise possible."[66] This is a very interesting move. It fits his general method of viewing all events through the lens of Cross and Resurrection. The creation is fallen, but God is constantly the one who brings good even out of the paths into which its fallenness leads it. Humanity, come into its true self, has a priestly task "to save the natural order through remedial and integrative activity."[67]

There is much in Torrance's scheme with which I would want to agree, not least the emphasis on the priestly and co-redeemerly activity of humans to which I have pointed in my own work. But his insistence that some elements of the creation can be separated off and regarded as twisted or distorted by the "impossible possibility" (the phrase is Barth's) of evil (the origin of which Torrance admits to be mysterious) seems dangerously like saving the theistic hypothesis by wheeling on a dualist worldview whenever the going gets rough.[68] Torrance claims that the Cross of Christ tells us "that all physical evil, not only pain, suffering, disease, corruption, death and of course cruelty and venom in animal as well as human behaviour, but also 'natural' calamities, dev-astations and monstrosities, are an outrage against the love of God and a con-tradiction of good order in his creation."[69] That is a great deal to read off from the Cross of Christ, and, as I have indicated, such a theology splits the creation awkwardly into "distorted" bits and others. Clark Pinnock writes, "Some nat-ural evils are an inherent part of the natural order and are required for life."[70] Some of them "may arise from the randomness that underlies creativity and be a by-product of the orderly natural processes that sustain life." But Pinnock goes on, falling into a similar trap to the one noted above:

> Other natural evils . . . may be due to the free will of spiritual beings who unlike ourselves possess a degree of control over nature. After all, Scripture speaks of the demonic and spiritual warfare. Are there not times when one detects a diabolical dimension to natural evil? We see nature red in tooth and claw—tornados, typhoid and plagues that sav-agely kill the innocent—and conclude that this did not come from the hand of God. . . . Jesus did not attribute things like deformity, blind-ness, leprosy and fever to the providence of God. He regarded them as evidence of the reign of darkness.[71]

I would be the last to deny the reality of spiritual evil. Logically, too, if spir-itual evil and its "powers," however conceived, are able to cause mental dis-tress, and in some way or other to "possess" persons or places, which has been the experience of the church throughout its history, then those powers must have some purchase on the physical world. And I can give no more convinc-ing account of the origin and character of these powers than Michael Lloyd, when he postulates their rebellion as the reason that the natural world is as it is (see above).[72]

What requires a careful and scientifically informed theological judgment is what balance we are to postulate between the creative providence of God and the action of powers in resistance to God. It seems to me that a Christian the-ology of creation must take with the greatest seriousness the implication of the Genesis 1 narrative that everything that came to be did so through the *fiat* of God, and that divine power has shaped all the matter and mechanisms of the cosmos.[73] Whatever processes science is able to understand as contributing to the evolution of complexity, life, richness of ability and diversity in life, and the growth of self-consciousness and freedom of choice, must be presumed to be the gift of God in creation. That includes among other things the explo-sions of supernovae, the plate tectonic activity that gives rise to earthquakes and volcanoes, competition in living systems, predation, and, at higher levels of consciousness, the capacity for selfishness, exploitation, and manipulation. So it is not appropriate to postulate that hostile powers "opened the doors of the sea" such that the power of God could not keep them closed. The tectonic movement that caused the Indian Ocean tsunami is an example of those processes that have made the Earth the lovely place that it is, and should not be regarded as in any way demonic.

R. J. Berry in his 2003 Gifford Lectures specifically takes to task those Christians who "interpret any facts which they find morally difficult as 'results of the fall' (such as 'nature red in tooth and claw,' or the enormous number of human foetuses which spontaneously miscarry)."[74] But Berry's own position is a most curious one. He simply refuses to venture into evolutionary theodicy. It is not for us to question the ways of a perfect God. Creation may not seem to us very good, but very good it always has been. "We are almost completely ignorant about the moral state of affairs before the fall [which for Berry was a specific event at the end of the Pleistocene[75]] (although we know that there were landslides and extensive floods on earth before there is any evidence of human life, and that many dinosaurs suffered from arthritis)."[76] There seems to be in the writing of this eminent scientist a puzzling blind spot as to any exploration of the ambiguity of the nonhuman creation. The crucial point is the one I made above: it was the same type of tectonic movement in the Indian Ocean that did so much to make the Earth's surface what it is, with its extraordinary diversity and richness of biosphere,[77] that caused the tragic and devastating tsunami of December 2004. It was the same competition for reproductive opportunities that refined the abilities of the cheetah, the impala, the hummingbird, and indeed the HIV virus, which also ensured that so many sentient animals would die without ever knowing what it is to flourish. Is it not more honest and coherent monotheism to accept that both types of effects—enrichment and catastrophe—are functions of the same creative process, and that the tsunami should be seen therefore not as an outrage against the love of God but a tragedy of this fecund and beautiful world, a tragedy of course made worse by human improvidence? Once this step is taken, the enterprise of theodicy, begun in all humility and with great caution, in deference to the profound reality and particularity of creaturely suffering, can begin. While investigation of evolutionary theodicy is hobbled by an insistence on relying on fall language, consideration of the really hard ambiguities of creation can never develop.

So it is with relief that one turns to an approach such as that of Keith Ward in his early book *Rational Theology and the Creativity of God* (1982). Ward clearly sees that the fall of the world through Adam "must seem a very unrealistic view to anyone who accepts some form of evolutionary theory and accepts that much evil is an inevitable consequence of such a world."[78] Likewise in the thought of Paul S. Fiddes there is a willingness to question the traditional Western account of the shape of the Christian story as a "U-shaped curve": "Paradise, Paradise Lost and Paradise regained."[79] But Fiddes's analysis in terms of "a line of tension" between "freedom and limit" distinguishes too sharply between the human situation and that of other animals. Rather I would say that there is a thread of ambiguity running through the whole of evolutionary creation, which in a creature with the consciousness and freedom of action of the human resolves itself into the tension that Fiddes describes. I return to the conviction of Williams, noted above, that "the sources of evil lie in attributes so valuable that we would not even consider eliminating them in order to eradicate evil."[80] Daryl P. Domning, seeking to expound the Catholic doctrine of original sin within an evolutionary framework, comes to the same conclusion: our evolutionary inheritance makes it utterly unsurprising that we are creatures prone to violent and greedy self-assertion, yet it is what has made us the animals we are with all the possibilities for goodness that entails.[81]

The problem of evolutionary theodicy at its most acute is not the one that eighteenth-century theodicy had wrestled with, as to whether the existence of evil might lead others to doubt the existence of God. Nor is it that there is an "excess" of suffering that causes the problem of theodicy, but which can be blamed at a pinch on some agency other than God. The problem is a more chilling one than that. It is the thought that the God who gave rise to this natural world (and whose responsibility for that world should not, as we have seen, be diluted by invoking human or angelic blame or mighty demonic powers) might not be a God worthy of worship. As we heard in section 1.7, Ivan Karamazov "respectfully returns his ticket" when he contemplates the suffering of children (specifically of a single child torn to pieces by a general's pack of hounds). What I am addressing in the first half of this book is how we might think of God in ways that do not evade God's responsibility for creation, but are compatible with the conviction that indeed God is wholly good, altogether worthy of worship, and to be glorified forever. The Christian conviction is that God may never be fully known, but is always to be worshiped. In this book I am not defending or justifying God; I am trying to see how the two propositions (a) God is creator of this ambiguous world, which is "good" but also "groaning in labor pains," and (b) God is "worthy of worship" can be held together within the community of faith.

2.7 FREEDOM, SUFFERING, AND LOVE

As I indicated at the end of the last chapter, one of the books that has greatly influenced this study is Andrew Elphinstone's *Freedom, Suffering and Love*.[82] This is a book full of care and intelligence, and one can only lament that Elphinstone's early death prevented him developing his thought further. Because his book seems little considered in this debate,[83] I spend some time here evaluating his ideas and their helpfulness for my project.

Elphinstone's manifesto is that "the present primacy of pain and unrest in the world is part of the raw material of the ultimate primacy of love."[84] Crucially, however, he realizes that this is not a reflection of a primitive perfection destroyed by human sin. He perceives the Fall as one of the largest problems in Christianity, "if not the largest of all."[85] *No need for redemption if there is no Fall*

Elphinstone sees that Christianity (at least in many of its expressions) "has been unable to give an assessment of the turbulences and unrests of the world that bear a sense of purpose, meaning or constructiveness. It has been easier to take a line of least resistance and to place the blame for all imperfections on the wickedness of man,"[86] which leads, as he goes on to say, to an exaggerated sense of the depravity of humans, and a fruitless looking backward. It also carries with it the implication that the Creator miscalculated and had to send the Incarnate Son as an emergency measure, rather than his coming being the timeless intention of God, that he might be "the Lamb that was slaughtered from the foundation of the world" (Rev. 13:8). That humans were not created in ready-made perfection but through a process of "evolutionary hazard and competition over vast aeons of time . . . has not been assimilated into the lifeblood of Christianity."[87] This is the key point I want to make in this whole discussion of fallenness. A sense of humans gradually coming to the possibility of God-consciousness can be traced back in Western theology as far as F. D. E. Schleiermacher in the early nineteenth century (who in turn draws on the motif of "theosis" dating back to Irenaeus of Lyons[88]), but the myth of lost perfection is deep in the Christian psyche and continues, as I have shown, to find all sorts of expressions for all sorts of reasons.

Farther than him

That is not to say, however, that Elphinstone adopts a wholly evolutionary model of humans' development toward God. He does not depict our "Christification" in the sort of evolutionary terms we find in Teilhard de Chardin (see section 2.5, above). Indeed he accepts the criticism that Teilhard confused salvation with future evolutionary advance. And he points out that the evolutionary end of all creatures, as far as we can see, appears to be extinction, whereas the resurrection of Christ gives us a strong hint that this is not the end of humanity. Elphinstone realizes that if he is to preserve his sense of the unique importance of the particular Incarnation of the Christ as universally relevant for all time, that must imply that evolution is effectively no longer relevant to humans' spiritual state. To put it another way, we never evolve in any meaningful way beyond the humanity that was in Jesus, so the Christ's playing a part in human affairs must mark the end of evolution's capacity to effect meaningful change in humans. To say this is not to claim that evolutionary change does not continue at a physical, biochemical, indeed neural level; rather, all the possibilities of being fully human before God have already been explored in Jesus and we can hope for nothing beyond those. It is moreover to claim with

Elphinstone that of ourselves humans cannot dominate the powers of evil to which we are prey; only through the victory and example of Christ can we truly be born into "the freedom of the glory of the children of God" (Rom. 8:21). The narrative offered here is not one of human enlightenment prevailing over human evolutionary inheritance. It is a narrative of *redemption*, leading to a freedom of an enlarged and God-breathed kind. This is for Elphinstone the freedom that leads to abundance, to Spirit-enlarged powers of mind, and to a larger perspective that dissolves much anxiety. Through the divine gift of love, "Person by person, attitude by attitude, response by response, instinct by instinct, the motive power of evolution was to be quelled and transformed, restrained and converted into the motive power of spirit."[89]

His great theme is the "divine alchemy"[90] of a love that meets pain, and the evil that often lies behind it, not with avoidance or reprisal, but with passionate (in the literal sense) engagement, facing the pain and meeting the evil with forgiveness—a familiar enough Christian theme. But Elphinstone is refreshingly clear that the material that is to be transmuted by this alchemy (made possible through the Incarnation of Christ) is the human not as fallen sinner but as evolved animal, possessed of "a tough competitive, aggressive and defensive mentality."[91] The particular human travail is not so much a sin inherited from Adam as a gradually evolved aspiration to reach higher than human capacities can appropriately go, higher indeed than the angels. (This indeed is how I would read the story of Adam and Eve's disobedience in the garden, as a description of humans as a species that never knows its place.[92])

Where I differ from Elphinstone really reflects the different focus of this study from his. His concern is very much with humankind, and human pain and its significance. This approach leads him both into a deeper exploration of the significance of the work of Christ for humanity than this study can accommodate, and to an over-emphasis on human development as the purpose of evolutionary creation. Elphinstone writes, "It is hard to find an intelligent purpose in what we know of the universe if it is not centred on the drama of the human enterprise."[93] He goes on, "The whole evolutionary process will receive its final significance as the long process of scaffolding which produced man will at some point be finally and honourably dismantled."[94]

I argue later that humans do have a fundamental role, albeit a small one, in the healing of creation, but God's purposes with creation are not wholly bound up with humanity. Far too much theology has been done on this basis, neglecting the vastness, beauty, and diversity of the rest of creation, and the abundant evidence from Scripture of God's concern for and delight in the nonhuman creation. I do not suppose therefore that the whole of God's long loving creative engagement with the universe was solely aimed at humans.[95] In chapter 5 I argue that these values inherent in living organisms, once realized, are never wholly lost, but they persist through the grace and wonder of God in some way that we find very difficult to imagine. A universe governed by the second law of thermodynamics, in which net disorder is always increasing, was the necessary "scaffolding" to give rise to these values, but they will persist long after the scaffolding has dropped away, and this universe has ceased to be a possible matrix for life.[96]

One element in Elphinstone with which some would cavil is his insistence on the primacy of pain in human experience. Even what we would think of as desire has its force through the prospect of the pain of the desire not being fulfilled. That prospect, and the actuality of the pain, drives humans to compulsive appetite and to self-assertion at others' expense. This is a compelling analysis. Elphinstone ties it up with his extensive investigation of the demonic, and of the way "the prince of this world," as the Fourth Gospel calls the devil, has used pain to control human motivations and steer them away from paths of creativity, love, and forgiveness. Again, not everyone would want to write so explicitly about the character of evil, but few would deny that there is a property in humans by which they can excuse their own evil acts,[97] fall prey to compulsively self-destructive behaviors, and become habituated to getting their own way by means of extraordinary cruelty, including the dehumanizing of other humans and the exploitation of other creatures as mere toys or commodities. All that can be framed in terms of the Pauline analysis of sin, and the Gospels' language of humans as prey to the demonic. Elphinstone, however, draws back from the move we have seen earlier in this chapter of regarding whatever is disapproved of, or thought awkward, in creation as stemming from the fall of angels. He regards the demonic as something arising out of the necessities of creative process,[98] rather than a preexistent being or beings, or a freely willed creation in and of itself. He confines his analysis of the demonic to the interaction of a factor interacting with the human will, who has "no point of leverage in the world save through the medium of man's vulnerability of flesh and mind . . . Only in mankind with his developed self-consciousness and his possession of mind and will, does there exist the effective agency through which evil intention can be crystallised into evil hard fact."[99] Occasionally one can see Elphinstone flirting with the notion that natural evil and disaster can stem from demonic activity,[100] but fortunately (in the view of the present author) he holds the line and never explicitly makes that attribution.

It will be apparent from what I have said already how important it is to be clear on this point: the forces that gave rise to earthquakes and other natural disasters are the very forces that made this biosphere possible. Those disasters should not be regarded as intrusions or corruptions stemming from angelic action against God, nor should God be regarded as unable to close the doors of the sea. God rather is to be seen as the Lord of creation, but one who is intent on acting consistently, respecting the forces by which so much of value has come into being. How then do evil powers have such a hold on the human will? Because of the consistency with which God upholds and treasures the evolved freedom of that will. The same processes that gave rise to that freedom are the ones that endowed humans with their capacities for its misuse.

Arguably, however, there is more to be said about the character of desire, and its relation to self-sacrifice, than Elphinstone's analysis conceded. I return to the theme of human desire and human self-emptying in chapter 6. My next step, however, having listed a series of roads not taken, is to see what strategies in theodicy might be helpful in respect of the nonhuman creation, to categorize those approaches, and to locate my own understanding within that scheme.

3

Strategies in Evolutionary Theodicy

3.1 INTRODUCTION

In Chapter 1 I considered the precise nature of the problem of evolutionary theodicy. I showed there that the crucial issue is not *pain*—a necessary concomitant of a richer experience of the world in higher animals—or *death*—a thermodynamic necessity, and, I would argue, no source of evil if death follows a fulfilled life. Nor is the issue *the loss of nonliving entities*. The heart of the problem is that the experience of many individual living creatures seems to be all suffering and no richness. These unfulfilled organisms may be regarded as in some sense the victims or casualties of evolution.[1] I also indicated in section 1.5 that each of the massive number of species that has gone extinct is a loss of value within the biosphere and itself contributes to the problem of evolutionary theodicy.

In section 2.6 I made clear that the classical theological view of the problem of violence and suffering in nature—to see it as a product of the human fall into sin—is not tenable. Attempts to think beyond this sin-preoccupied approach can already be seen in the work of Thomas Aquinas. Taxed by the problem of nonhuman suffering Aquinas writes: "Since God, then, provides universally for all being, it belongs to His providence to permit certain defects in particular effects, that the perfect good of the universe may not be hindered, for if all evil were prevented, much good would be absent from the universe. A lion would cease to live, if there were no slaying of animals; and there would be no patience of martyrs if there were no tyrannical persecutions."[2] For Thomas, then, the goodness of the world is axiomatic, and necessary evils must be seen in that larger context.

3.2 GOOD-HARM ANALYSES

What we see in the quotation from Aquinas is a balancing of goods and harms, and a theodicy based on the conclusion that the goods balance the harms in a way appropriate to the model of God being defended.[3] With my colleague Andrew Robinson I have identified three ways in which such a good-harm analysis (GHA) may be formulated:[4]

1. Property-consequence GHAs: a consequence of the *existence* of a good is the *possibility* of it causing harms. The classic instance of this is the free-will defense in respect of moral evil.
2. Developmental GHAs: the good is a goal that can only *develop* through a *process* which includes the possibility (or necessity) of harm. The most familiar version of this is John Hick's "Irenaean" theodicy of the world as a "vale of soul-making" in which virtue is learned through a process that involves suffering.[5] This we term a "developmental instrumental" defense. Another type of developmental argument would be one in which harms are unavoidable by-products of a process that also gives rise to goods. This we term a "developmental by-product" defense.
3. Constitutive GHAs: the existence of a good is *inherently* and *constitutively inseparable* from the experience of harm or suffering.

Each of these "categories" of good-harm analysis may have three types of reference: human (the relevant goods and harms are restricted to humans), anthropocentric (the good accrues to humans, but the harm to a range of creatures), or biotic (both the goods and the harms may be experienced throughout the biosphere).[6] My concern here is evolutionary evil: harms to nonhuman creatures which have no human cause.[7] As I indicated in chapter 1, far too much writing in this area slips into focusing only on human concerns.

The most commonly used defense in relation to human-caused evil is a property-consequence argument based on the property of free will. Freely choosing agency may be judged such a good that all the harm which comes from its exercise is justified. I note below a major shortcoming of the free-will defense, but for now I would simply note that it is hard to extrapolate this to animals, since they do not, as far as we know, possess freedom of choice as humans do. C. S. Lewis put it starkly: "The problem of animal suffering is appalling; not because the animals are so numerous . . . but because the Christian explanation of human pain cannot be extended to animal pain. So far as we know beasts are incapable either of sin or virtue: therefore they can neither deserve pain or be improved by it."[8]

One example of an evolutionary theodicy based on a property-consequence good-harm analysis is found in Thomas F. Tracy's fine essay published in 1998.[9] He concedes that "the suffering of sentient animals is part of the problem of natural evil." But he offers two types of "property" that might provide "the general outline of a theodicy."[10] First he says: "To *be* is to be in relation to God, and in this lies the good of every creature of every kind."[11] He also notes that nonhuman creatures have all sorts of experiences humans do not have, and lack, for instance, "our capacity for despair and self-hatred." "Perhaps," then, "there is a balance between the opportunity to experience various goods and the cost in suffering of making those goods available."[12] A related argument is that of Patricia Williams: she asks, is it better to have a self or not to have a self? "The central answer to the problem of suffering . . . is that having a self compensates for almost any suffering we might endure, whether it is eventually turned to good or not."[13] Sentience, or selfhood, are the properties for which the consequence of evolutionary harms is to be accepted. These properties play the same role as freedom in the classic free-will defense to moral (human-caused) evil. However, even in the case of human beings the free-will defense does not succeed of itself. The weight of innocent human suffering, the abundance of situations in which humans are deprived of their free will, these corrode the straightforward defense. It is not sustainable except in combination with a theory of secondary goods, an eschatological perspective which, while not devaluing the present, emphasizes that the sufferings of this world are indeed as nothing compared with "the glory about to be revealed to us" (Rom. 8:18). Likewise, because intrinsic to evolutionary creation are casualties for which there is only pain, no expression of their experience, this type of defense to evolutionary evil fails unless there is some ultimate good that will actually *redeem* the individuals and extinct species concerned, not just other individuals and species that benefit from their suffering and extinction.

Evolution is a *process*, which over very long periods gives rise, as we have seen, to values combined with disvalues. I showed in chapter 1 why it is reasonable to suppose that this combination is in some sense a necessary one. So it is natural that the good-harm analyses most commonly found in evolutionary theodicies are *developmental* GHAs. Nancey Murphy and George Ellis see the disvalues in the nonhuman world as a *by-product* of the evolution of values.[14] In a sense this is a variant of the "free-process" defense expounded by John Polkinghorne.[15]

Richard Kropf's *Evil and Evolution*[16] was one of the first contemporary works to inform the debate on evolutionary evil. Kropf does not always stay to his task of teasing out the implications of evolution for the creation as a whole, and it is hard to settle for his conviction that for the believer faith in a good God supplies its own answer.[17]

But Kropf does begin to construct an evolutionary theodicy of nonhuman suffering around a grand developmental defense of a strongly teleological kind. This pattern reflects the strong influence of Teilhard de Chardin on his work (see section 2.5). The successes of evolution, Kropf judges, like the Creator in the book of Genesis, to be "very good" (Gen. 1:31). But the whole course of evolution is chance-laden, and evolution takes place only at the expense of very many other forms. Kropf therefore sees suffering as "the price being exacted from all creation in its struggle towards consciousness and freedom."[18] But then he shifts, like so many theodicists, back into an anthropocentric perspective. True freedom is only won through suffering, as in this assertion: "Human freedom is indeed the reason evil exists."[19]

Fascinatingly, however, Kropf then reverts to consideration of the nonhuman creation, and of Romans 8:20. "God has 'subjected' the whole world of nature and chance, but not for its own sake. Rather it is for the sake of infinitely higher stakes. God has taken a chance on chance, or it seems, that not only ourselves, but even all of nature, might 'enjoy the same freedom and glory as the children of God.'"[20] Ivan Karamazov's question burns on (see section 1.7)—What about the suffering of the individual creature? May not the price be too high?—but for Kropf the purpose of the universe is an unfinished symphony, parts of which, even the conclusion, remain unwritten. And yet the rehearsal will turn out to be the final performance.[21]

Kropf then returns to a focus on the costs of evolution, and of extinction in particular. He asks: "Can the emergence of even one new species, one showing greater spontaneity and intelligence, be said to justify the disappearance of a hundred others that are less gifted?"[22] There seem to be innocent victims at the species level as well as in human life. There is "a solidarity in suffering which makes it one with life and death, sin and freedom."[23] The human epic, as Teilhard de Chardin said, "resembles nothing so much as a way of the Cross."[24]

Kropf is seeing human suffering as instrumental to the final birthing of the new creation, just as evolutionary suffering was instrumental in developing the first creation. Suffering (in the Christian understanding of the human sphere) loses the element of alienation and isolation, for the whole Body suffers for one hurt part (1 Cor. 12:26). Even suffering that appears to be useless is "somehow caught up in the great movement in which, despite its seeming futility, all pain is transformed in the victory of Christ."[25] Suffering "remains the basic law of *all* existence that seeks greater being."[26] Suffering here is not seen as a "trial" or as an unavoidable by-product in the evolutionary process, but as "the catalyst of the process itself, and at all levels." Kropf infers from this that all levels are in some ways destined for and ordered toward a higher, transfigured, or even "resurrected" existence.[27] All creation has been groaning in travail in order that all creatures might share in some way the freedom of the children of God.

It is intriguing to read this evocation of Romans 8 within an evolutionary scheme, though I remain unconvinced that Kropf's strong Teilhardian sense of the ordering of evolution toward higher transfigured existence (see section 2.5) quite does justice to evolutionary science as we know it, or yet to the problem of the suffering of individual creatures and the discarding of so many species. I take up this question further in discussing John Haught's work in section 3.5 and my own proposal in section 4.4.

I have quoted extensively from Kropf because his work is not much known, but foreshadows in important ways that of a far more famous ecological theologian in Holmes Rolston III.[28] Rolston too, as we shall see, is convinced of the intrinsic place of "significant suffering through to something higher"[29] in nature, and of the need to evoke the Cross to do justice to nature's travail. I quoted in section 1.2 his resonant saying that the cougar's fang has carved the limbs of the fleet-footed deer; processes intrinsic to evolution give rise to harms, but are also *instrumental* in enhancing values. Rolston has also convincingly argued that without forms of predation, which are a principal source of suffering among the most complex of creatures, many of the characteristic values of such creatures would be absent. He writes: "The animal skills demanded [in a nonpredatory world] would only be a fraction of those that have resulted in actual zoology—no horns, no fleet-footed predators or prey, no fine-tuned eyesight and hearing, no quick neural capacity, no advanced brains."[30] This is a very important quotation, a reminder to theologians that we should not take the evolution of complex attributes for granted. Every evolved character in an organism has costs (for instance, the large and intricately wired human brain is a very fragile and energy-intensive organ, slow to develop, and requires not only extensive sustenance and systems of protection but also a long defenseless period of infancy). Every character survives because, and only because, its benefits, in terms of natural selection, have outweighed its costs. Rolston stresses that selection pressures promoted the survival of many of the attributes we most admire. This then is a developmental instrumental good-harm analysis, in which the harms are instrumental to the development of values. Rolston has articulated this in a number of very important chapters and articles, and in support of these he has adduced a number of helpful examples of behavior in natural systems.[31]

In section 1.7 above I noted the limited nature of schemes that merely consider evolutionary systems as a whole. I explained that such systemic accounts fail to take adequate account of the suffering of the individual creature, and Rolston's scheme has certainly been criticized along these lines.[32] Where, he has been asked, is the *redemption* in his theodicy?

To this question he gives a twofold answer, which takes our exploration yet deeper into the problem. First, Rolston has stressed that he sees redemption in the regeneration of other creatures—"renewed life comes by blasting the old,"[33] and in "the unrelenting conservation of biological identity." In this sense, "We will not say that nature does not need to be redeemed, nor that it has never been redeemed; on the contrary, it is ever redeemed."[34] In a recent article which acts as a passionate apology for Rolston's position, Lisa Sideris has criticized ecotheologians for wanting to dismantle the hierarchies and oppressions of which evolution consists, for in doing so we would put an end to the process itself. Instead of mistransferring the ethic of Jesus from the human sphere to the nonhuman, we would be better advised to discern God's will in the natural ordering and processes of the world we actually inhabit.[35]

My contention, however (contrary to Rolston's view), is that the regeneration of life out of the suffering of other life does not of itself "redeem" the suffering experienced by individuals, be they dying impala calves or lame cheetahs succumbing slowly to hunger. Regeneration does not comprehend all that is connoted by the word "redemption,"[36] and the suffering of individual organisms, even it promotes the flourishing of others, must still remain a challenge for theodicy. Moreover, I would argue that *extinction* must be conceded always to be a loss of value to the biosphere as a whole. A whole strategy of being alive on the planet, a whole quality of living experience is lost when any organism becomes extinct. So although what Rolston asserts in supporting a developmental instrumental approach to evolutionary theodicy is important, it is incomplete, and I would say the same for what he asserts about redemption.

That brings me to Rolston's other extension of his theodicy, again a very significant contribution to the debate. He does as Sideris advocates and seeks to discern the divine in the natural order we inhabit, and he concludes that it is "cruciform."[37] It is full of suffering, suffering that reminds us of the Passion of Christ, and which leads Rolston to the conclusion that God suffers with the suffering of creatures.[38] I now turn to some of Rolston's own examples to examine strategies for theodicy in more detail.

As I noted in the preface, Rolston describes the behavior of certain kinds of orca which, in killing sea lions, will toss their victims playfully in the air, prolonging their agony.[39] This type of orca is so feared by its prey animals that dolphins will drag themselves onto land and suffocate rather than face their predators.[40] As we consider this behavior, our focus may be on the orcas themselves. The freedom of behavior involved in their lifestyle as predators can lead to what seems to human observers like the gratuitous infliction of suffering, but it does not necessarily do so. Other types of orca do not show this behavior, and often predators (unless teaching their young to hunt) kill their prey with the minimum of energy and fuss. Focus on this behavior in orcas, then, would lead to a property-consequence approach to the analysis of goods and harms. Certain properties in created entities can lead—but need not necessarily lead—to suffering in the biotic world.

We could choose to focus instead on the orca's prey, the sea lion. We could conclude, with this focus, that the fact of predation progressively develops the abilities of sea lions as a species and leads to greater abilities and greater flourishing. Though individuals suffer, the species as a whole becomes better adapted—a developmental approach to goods and harms, one in which suffering is instrumental to the development of creatures.

We could broaden our focus still further and consider the whole ecosystem of this part of the ocean. It is a system in which eating and being eaten is of the essence. An elaborate chain of interdependent relationships builds up around this dynamic (with the pain that is necessarily caused to various creatures within the process). Focus on this chain of relationships might lead to a constitutive type of understanding of goods and harms. This is where Rolston's language of cruciform creation comes in. "The secret of life," he says, "is that it is a *passion play*."[41] By this he presumably means that, as at the Passion of Christ, the good does not have its meaning without the suffering intrinsic to it.

Another of Rolston's examples offers more insight into the dynamic between types of argument. He notes the way in which the white pelican, like a number of other predatory birds, hatches a second chick as an "insurance." The insurance chick is normally driven to the edge of the nest by its sibling, and once displaced is ignored by its parents. Its "purpose" is merely to ensure that one viable chick survives. It has only a 10 percent chance of fledging.[42]

Again, if the focus is on the pelican species as a whole, this strategy, "careless" and "wasteful" of individuals as it might seem, has "worked" for the white pelican, which as Rolston points out has lived successfully on Earth for 30 million years. The process of natural selection has developed in pelicans a strategy that is successful, although in many cases it leads to suffering. A defense based on this analysis would regard the harm as a by-product of a good process, and would therefore be a developmental by-product defense.

But if we shift our focus to the individual that suffers, the insurance chick itself, the language of tragedy returns. Rolston talks of "the slaughter of the innocents."[43] The process "sacrifices" the second chick to the good of the whole; it is intrinsic to the system that new life is regenerated out of the chick's death. The victims of the evolutionary process "share the labor of the divinity. In their lives, beautiful, tragic, and perpetually incomplete, they speak for God, they prophesy as they participate in the divine pathos."[44] "Long before humans arrived, the way of nature was already a *via dolorosa*."[45]

There is a tension here. Rolston's understanding of goods and harms remains a developmental one, but the rhetoric by which he elaborates his evolutionary theodicy (here and in the preceding case) implies a constitutive approach. So specific foci within the system can lead to the formulation of property-consequence or developmental arguments, but concentration either on the ills of the individual sufferer, or on the beauty and value of the system as a whole, will take the analysis back in the direction of a constitutive theodicy.

If we take phrases about "cruciform creation" and evolution as a "passion play" with full seriousness, the implication would seem to be that God is in these events, with the sufferers, in a way that somehow makes the suffering more and other than itself. That at least is how that language operates when it is used of Jesus' cruciform ministry and passion. And if evolutionary victims "share the labor of the divinity," and "prophesy" in their suffering, then again their experience must be more than might first appear. God must be bound up in it in a way that affects the creatures at some level or other of their experience. To say this is at once to say something more than a straightforward developmental defense would say.

3.3 THE CENTRALITY OF A DEVELOPMENTAL APPROACH TO THE GOODS AND HARMS OF EVOLUTION

I showed above that Rolston's dominant approach to evolutionary theodicy is a developmental one; certain values can only arise in the biosphere through an evolutionary process, and that process necessarily involves the disvalues of suffering and extinction generated by competition for scarce resources, and with it the development of strategies such as predation and parasitism. There is a necessary correlation between the values to which the evolutionary process gives rise and the disvalues of suffering and extinction.

Such a developmental good-harm analysis must be the starting point for any evolutionary theodicy that does not allow itself to be lured down the blind alleys—such as a spurious appeal to fallenness—that I explored in chapter 2. It is all the more important as a strategy in theodicy as soon as the question is asked, why did God not create a world free from all this suffering and struggle? Though we cannot know the answer to this question, a starting presumption must be that the formation of the sorts of life forms represented in the biosphere *required* an evolutionary process.[46]

Such an approach lies behind Murphy and Ellis's account, discussed above, and Robert J. Russell's account of "cosmic theodicy," his sense that a system obeying the second law of thermodynamics will necessarily use the same processes to engender both complexification and decay (see below). I agree with the recent analysis of Robin Attfield to the effect that there might not be any "better" created world that could be formulated for the realization of creaturely value, and that that argument in itself constitutes a theodicy, even without recourse to other components such as an appeal to eschatology.[47] Indeed the "only way" argument receives support from a surprising quarter, from Richard Dawkins, arch-antagonist of theologians of evolution. We saw in section 1.7 Dawkins's assessment of the way the natural world looks—exactly as it would look if there is "at bottom, no design, no purpose, no evil and no good, nothing but blind, pitiless indifference."[48] But Michael Ruse points out that Dawkins has also written: "If there is no other generalization that can be made about life all around the Universe, I am betting that it will always be recognizable as Darwinian life." "In short," Ruse continues, "if God was to create through law, then it had to be through Darwinian law. There was no other choice."[49]

Robert J. Russell has pushed the question back further by invoking the issue of "cosmic theodicy." He questions the assumption, implicit behind many formulations of the "only way" argument (including that of Ruse), that the laws of nature are a given. That in turn begs the question, "Why did God choose to create *this* universe with *these* laws and constants, knowing they would then make neo-Darwinian evolution unavoidable and with it the sweep of natural evil?"[50] Since we cannot know if other universes might have contained less evil than this, Russell says that "we must accept an 'agnostic cosmic theodicy.'" He calls therefore for "more complex responses to natural evil."[51] My own view is that we must still presume a version of the "only way" argument, or, perhaps clearer, the "best way" argument. We must just reformulate it in terms of a presumption that a good and loving God would have created the best of all possible universes, in terms of the balance between its potential for realizing creaturely values and the concomitant pain. But I agree completely with Russell that this move by itself is not enough, since it does not answer in any way the fact of suffering at the level of the individual creature.

All evolutionary theodicy, then, should start from a version of the "only way" argument, based on a developmental good-harm analysis. This was the only, or at least the best, process by which creaturely values of beauty, diversity, and sophistication could arise. Yet we saw above that even Rolston's resolutely developmental scheme contains hints of a richer approach, one that emerges as soon as the individual sufferer becomes the focus, as well as species and systems.

3.4 A FOCUS ON THE SUFFERING OF THE INDIVIDUAL CREATURE

In section 1.7 I showed that an evolutionary theodicy that merely concentrates on the developmental value of the process does not address the problem of individual suffering. To restate my inference from David Bentley Hart's reading of Dostoevsky: the crux of the problem is not the overall system and its overall goodness. It is the Christian's struggle with the challenge to the goodness of God posed by specific cases of innocent suffering. This problem is intensified in "instrumental" accounts in which this suffering serves the longer-term purposes of God in creation. In section 1.5 I termed this the teleological aspect of the problem of evolutionary theodicy. Ruth Page is one of the few modern theologians fully to apprehend this problem.[52] Her approach deserves much more attention than it has received, and I return to it in section 4.4. Suffice it to say for now that although Page manages to avoid a sense of God using the world for God's ends, she never avoids the ontological aspect of the problem: God still bears responsibility for all that to which God has given rise, including apparently pointless suffering.

A second strategy in the face of the problem of evolutionary theodicy would be the response implied by Job 38–41, that the ways of the creator of the cosmos are simply too awesome for us to apprehend. In a sense this *is* the most tempting rebuttal of Ivan Karamazov; our tickets are punched and nonreturnable, because we are only creatures. God is God, and can make and use anything for whatever ends God chooses. In the words attributed to God in Isaiah 55:8, "My thoughts are not your thoughts, nor are your ways my ways, says the LORD." We saw in section 2.6 that R. J. Berry is drawn to a similar approach in respect of evolutionary theodicy: it is not for us to question the ways of the Creator God. There is a fine saying by the Scottish thinker Thomas Chalmers (1780–1847) that God in God's sovereignty will not "falter from the imposition of any severity, which might serve the objects of a high administration."[53] Such a high and mysterious doctrine of God might take one in the direction of the Islamic understanding of the unquestionable will of the Creator, or indeed toward Wildman's ground-of-being theism (see section 2.3). Sideris too is attracted to the God of these chapters of Job.[54] Denis Edwards also cites these same passages, but what Edwards offers us is a resolutely Christian version of the answer to Job, in that he says the proof of God's fidelity to creation is ultimately the Cross of Christ.[55] A similarly deep-lying Christian confession lies behind Rolston's language of the passion play of creation.

It is significant therefore to note Edwards's own critique of Rolston's concept of cruciform creation. He points out that the Cross of Christ

> is not to be seen as some kind of necessary outcome of creation, or as a principle behind creation. The Cross is an unpredictable and contingent event. Christian theology needs to insist on the contingency of the cross for two reasons. First, the whole Christ-Event is to be seen as a totally gratuitous act of God. And second, the brutal act of crucifying Jesus ought not to be seen as simply the following out of a preordained divine plan, but more as God bringing life out of what was in itself a sinful and destructive act.[56]

Edwards goes on: "Talk about the creation as cruciform . . . does not yet offer a theological response. Such a response needs to talk about the redemption of creation in Christ."[57]

It is important too to see the profound differences between the Passion of Christ and the "passion play" of evolution. First, the cruciform life was *chosen* by Jesus, and from this *choice* came the saving power of his love. The plight of the "casualties" of evolution, who have suffering *imposed* on them by God for the longer-term good of others, is very different. The suffering of the myriad casualties of evolution is not freely chosen. Their share in "the labor of the divinity," to go back to Rolston's phrase, is imposed on them without, on his scheme, any reward to themselves. Moreover, Jesus himself was vindicated at his resurrection. It was not just that others profited by the benefits of his death. Rolston makes much use of the language of sacrifice, but this only sharpens the point that it is not the evolutionary victim (such as the backup pelican chick) that has *chosen* the good of others over its own. It is the *process* that has "sacrificed" the victim's interests to the interests of the larger whole.[58]

3.5 GOD'S CO-SUFFERING WITH THE CREATURE

Two further moves in theodicy may be proposed to stiffen a theodicy in respect of the suffering of the individual creature. The first is to emphasize the suffering of God with creatures, and the second is to invoke some form of eschatological redemption of the victims of evolution.

The question of whether it is appropriate to speak of God as suffering is one I consider in elaborating a Trinitarian theology of evolutionary creation in chapter 4. For now I simply note the part that the motif has played and might play in the framing of an evolutionary theodicy.

Rolston himself invokes "the divine pathos": God and creatures suffer so that evolutionary creation might suffer "through to something higher."[59] Life for Rolston is "a paradox of suffering and glory . . . the way of nature is the way of the cross"; the drama of nature is "a constructive, redemptive drama of birth, survival and maturation." God suffers within all this creaturely suffering as "diffused divine omnipresence."[60] This reflects his panentheistic view (that is, he regards the whole creation as existing within God, but God's being not being limited to the creation).

Arthur Peacocke also takes a panentheistic view, and clearly recognizes the cost of the evolutionary process in the suffering of creatures. As a biologist he is very aware of the inevitability of that cost—that there must be death to bring forth new and diverse forms of life, and that there must be pain and suffering if there are to be higher forms of sentience. But nowhere in his many compelling essays on God and the evolving world is there a wholly convincing account of how this can be reconciled with the goodness and love of the Creator God. Peacocke's God still seeks the prize of freely choosing self-conscious beings with whom to have free rational relationship, the "greater good" as Peacocke puts it, of "the kingdom of free-willing, loving persons in communion with God and each other."[61] This is in accord with Peacocke's preferred theodicy of the "vale of soul-making" (see section 3.2 above). Such a view is bound to focus on the concerns of "souls," rational beings, rather than on the more general casualties of 3.8 billion years of evolution. But Peacocke also describes a stronger link between his God and the nonhuman creation, stressing God's delight in the goodness of the world, and God's suffering "in, with and under" every element of the evolutionary process. He writes: "God suffers in and with the sufferings of created humanity and so, by a natural extension, with those of all creation, since humanity is an evolved part of it. The suffering of God, which we could glimpse only tentatively in the processes of creation, is in Jesus the Christ concentrated to a point of intensity and transparency which reveals itself to all who focus on him."[62] Fascinatingly, a slightly later essay alters this to ". . . intensity and transparency that reveals it as expressive of the perennial relation of God to the creation."[63] His thinking was clearly moving at the end of his career toward a focus on the sufferings of the nonhuman creation.[64]

In that same essay Peacocke raises explicitly the question:

> If the Creator intended the arrival in the cosmos of complex, reproducing structures that could think and be free—that is, self-conscious, free persons—was there not some other, less costly and painful way of bringing this about? Was that the only possible way? This is one of those unanswerable metaphysical questions in theodicy to which our only response has to be based on our understanding of the biological parameters . . . discerned by science to be operating in evolution. These indicate that there are inherent constraints on how even an omnipotent Creator could bring about the existence of a law-like creation that is to be a cosmos not a chaos, and thus an arena for the free action of self-conscious, reproducing complex entities and for the coming to be of the fecund variety of living organisms whose existence the Creator delights in.[65]

So we see in Peacocke a clear articulation of the "only way" argument, deployed as part of a developmental anthropocentric good-harm analysis, and bolstered by an affirmation of God's co-suffering with every creature.

Another thinker to stress divine co-suffering with evolutionary creation is John F. Haught. Haught's *God after Darwin* (2000) is one of the few recent books to take the theological implications of Darwinism really seriously and indeed to regard modern evolutionary theory as a gift to theology (see section 1.6). Haught's thinking is a fascinating fusion of process thought with Roman

Catholic thinkers, especially Teilhard de Chardin. From process thinking Haught derives his model of a God of "letting-be," of persuasive rather than coercive love.[66] All process thought is heir to Whitehead's famous description of God as "the fellow sufferer who understands" (see section 2.4). Process theology also influences Haught's conviction that "God is infinitely *responsive* to the world as well as creative and nurturing of it. . . . God . . . is influenced deeply by all that happens in the evolutionary process. Everything whatsoever that occurs in evolution—all the suffering and tragedy as well as the emergence of new life and intense beauty—is 'saved' by being taken eternally into God's own feeling of the world."[67] Haught writes eloquently of "faith's sense of the self-outpouring God who lovingly renounces any claim to domineering omnipotence."[68] At the same time Haught has a strong sense of nature's promise—that the creation groans because it is unfinished, but that God will ultimately draw it on to final fulfillment (we see here the influence of Teilhard).[69]

An assertion of divine co-suffering comes particularly easily to a process thinker such as Jay McDaniel.[70] But it also begs that question so vital in theology: So what? What does it matter to the suffering creature that God suffers with it? As Kenneth Surin crisply points out (thinking here of human suffering), if God was powerless to prevent the suffering in the first place, then "to the person in urgent need of succour, it would conceivably be just as efficacious to look to unicorns and centaurs for salvation."[71] The problem is yet more intense if, as we saw in chapter 1, the suffering of creatures in evolution may be thought of as serving the purposes of God.

As I have remarked before in this study, our purchase on understanding the suffering of nonhuman creatures is profoundly limited, and our understanding of God's experience is fragmentary to the point of incoherence. But we can still ask, what difference might divine co-suffering make, in the sort of instances we have been discussing as paradigmatic of creaturely suffering? When I consider the starving pelican chick, or the impala hobbled by a mother cheetah so that her cubs can learn to pull a prey animal down, I cannot pretend that God's presence as the "heart" of the world[72] takes the pain of the experience away; I cannot pretend that the suffering may not destroy the creature's consciousness, before death claims it. That is the power of suffering, that it can destroy selves.[73]

I can only suppose that God's suffering presence is just that, presence, of the most profoundly attentive and loving sort, a solidarity that at some deep level takes away the aloneness of the suffering creature's experience.[74] Again this is necessarily an anthropomorphic guess, but both acute and chronic suffering must isolate the creature, and may lead to what (for humans at least) is one of the most terrible of all experiences, that of dying alone, with no connection to care or fellow-feeling of any sort. God's presence to and solidarity with the suffering creature, then, is an important ingredient in an evolutionary theodicy, though not by any means a sufficient element in and of itself.

McDaniel begins his study *Of God and Pelicans* by reflecting on Rolston's remark that "If God watches the sparrows fall, God must do so from a very great distance."[75] McDaniel is convinced this must be wrong; God's care is present to every sparrow.[76] It is not enough simply to say of the back-up pelican chick that its suffering benefits the species as a whole. Redemption, McDaniel argues, must be of the particular creature concerned itself, and must involve a context in which it can respond to God's redeeming initiative. Hence his hope of "pelican heaven," and that "kindred creatures, given their propensities and needs, find fulfilment in life after death too."[77] This is a recourse not only to divine fellow-suffering (as is also found in Rolston) but, in addition, to the other way I noted above of "stiffening" an evolutionary theodicy, that of invoking eschatological compensation for the victims of evolution. McDaniel's model therefore differs from the drama of nonhuman redemption that Rolston depicts, in which redemption is understood to occur through regeneration of life in other creatures.

By focusing on the suffering creature itself, McDaniel questions whether a developmental defense based on the flourishing of other creatures, or the adaptedness of the species as a whole, can be deemed sufficient. He has his own version of the "only way" argument, in his sense that there are "necessary correlations among the capacities 1) to enjoy rich forms of sentience, 2) to suffer, 3) to inflict harm upon others, and 4) to contribute to the well-being of others."[78] He concludes: "As God lured advanced forms of life into existence, there was a risk involved, even for God. It was that creatures would evolve into manners of interaction that would be tremendously painful to one another, even as they would also enjoy opportunities for harmonious and intense experience that were tremendously rich."[79] Like Rolston I would go further and say this was not just a risk but a certainty, indeed that natural selection suggests to us that suffering is a necessary driver of progressively richer and more intense experience.

The only other taxonomy of evolutionary theodicies that I have encountered (apart from my own in "God and Evolutionary Evil" [2002]) forms part of Ted Peters and Martinez Hewlett's survey of theistic evolutionists in their *Evolution from Creation to New Creation* (2003).[80] Peters and Hewlett look at the work of B. B. Warfield, Kenneth Miller, Peacocke, Edwards, Haught, Russell, Philip Hefner, and Teilhard de Chardin.

The omission of Rolston from their list is startling, though perhaps explained by their strong rejection of thinkers who "collapse the theodicy problem into natural processes." This approach for them "represents a failure of theological nerve. It is a sell-out to naturalism and a loss to theism."[81] By this I take Peters and Hewlett to mean that redemption is an essential element in any properly Christian response to evolution, a thesis with which I thoroughly agree (see above). Their placing of thinkers is similar to the one I have developed here. Their own approach, very surprisingly, lapses back into the language of fallenness. Although they have just criticized Philip Hefner for remarking that "evil is a phenomenon that occurs after the initial articulation of the essential goodness of Creation,"[82] Peters and Hewlett themselves want to claim that they do not know theologically "why violence, suffering and death have had to play such a role in the creation up to this point . . . The struggle for survival is a mark of fallen creation."[83] So they effectively bracket out the teleological problem of evolutionary theodicy in just the way I showed was unacceptable in my discussion in section 2.6. Peters and Hewlett themselves concede, "Our answer to the theodicy problem is not a logical one. We do not invoke twists of logic to justify God for creating a world of struggle with survival of the fittest and all its accompanying waste. Rather, we point to God's promise of resurrection and renewal."[84] I warm very much to Peters and Hewlett's emphasis on the importance of a theology of the Cross, and of an emphasis on eschatological redemption, a motif I take up in chapter 5. In chapter 4 I try, without I hope too many twists of logic, to say more about theodicy and creation than they are willing to say.

4

An Adventure
in the Theology of Creation

4.1 INTRODUCTION

I regard this chapter of the book as the most speculative, the greatest "adventure." Having analyzed the various approaches to the problem of evolutionary suffering in the theological literature, I now have to try and set in place a scheme of evolutionary creation that does some sort of justice to three key Christian convictions:

1. God understood as perfectly loving and always desiring the good.
2. God understood as Trinity, which is the Christian reflection on the revelation of God in creation, in the Christ-event, in Scripture, and in the work of the Spirit in the church and the world.
3. Creation understood both *as* creation, made, loved, and interpenetrated at every moment by the energies of the triune persons of a perfectly loving God, and yet shot through with the sort of ambiguity that evolutionary understandings compel us to acknowledge—beauty compounded with suffering, beauty forged out of suffering.

I acknowledge that my account contains sundry hostages to fortune—also that whatever we seek to say of God is always lamentably partial and inadequate, at its very best only fractionally better than silence.

In Chapter 1 I outlined what I called a compound approach to evolutionary theodicy. I indicated that this would be based on the ontological claim that God gave rise to the creation (and continually sustains it as it unfolds); the teleological claim that God has goals within the creation, one—though only one—of which is the evolution of freely choosing self-conscious creatures such as ourselves; also the claim that God suffers with the suffering of every created creature. Finally at the Cross God both takes responsibility for that suffering and begins the process of transforming it toward a final consummation, in which there will be fullness of life for creatures who have never known such. I showed earlier in section 2.6 that it is inappropriate to fall back on the traditional understanding of suffering in the nonhuman creation all being the result of human sin. It is therefore necessary to find some formulation of the theology of creation that allows for a God who creates an ambiguous world, a biosphere based on an inherent coupling of values and disvalues. Many authors have believed that that means positing a God who suffers with the world even as the divine love draws it on, and I begin by investigating the validity of that claim.

I am concerned in this chapter principally with the theology of creation. At the end of the chapter I consider questions of providence, and a theology of the Cross and Resurrection as redemptive of all creation. I take up the question of a redeemed life for creatures in chapter 5.

4.2 THE SUFFERING OF GOD

A key element in my compound evolutionary theodicy (see section 1.8) is the proposal that God suffers in the suffering of every creature. The suffering of God has been a common motif in the theology of the last hundred years, especially in the light of the World Wars and more particularly the Holocaust. This motif is in tension with the classical notion of the *apatheia* of God. Platonic formulations insisted that if God truly suffered, God would not be in control of God's life, would not be self-determining.[1] Against that is, first, the biblical witness to a God who is both approachable and responsive, who grieves over the sins of the people and is stirred to wrath by their sin.[2] Second is the discomfort of many theologians at formulations that isolate the suffering of Jesus from that of the Father. Jürgen Moltmann's fine study *The Crucified God* (1973) indicated the riches of Trinitarian reflection that are released by taking leave of the classical doctrine and allowing "patripassianism," the real suffering of the Father at the passion of the Son.[3] Third, the extremes of human suffering that became known all over the world from the experience of the Holocaust made a God who did not suffer a hard God to proclaim.[4]

Sarah Coakley points out that Aquinas was familiar with the theological problems of suffering, cosmology, and human freedom, and still formulated a model of God based on attributes of omnipotence, omniscience, impassibility, and so on.[5] As Herbert McCabe shows, it is most important to understand these statements about divine attributes correctly; they are not positive statements, but negative, apophatic formulations: "perishability, decline, dependence, alteration, the impersonality that characterises material things, and so on—all these have to be excluded from God."[6] Thomas Weinandy has made a further attempt to reassert the classical doctrine of the inability of God to suffer.[7] In essence Weinandy's point is the same as McCabe's; the story of Jesus the Crucified One is "the projection of the trinitarian life of God on the rubbish dump that we have made of the world."[8] God does not suffer change, because what we see in the Incarnation is God's eternal nature.[9] This is the doctrine of divine *apatheia* brought out of its shell of Platonic idealism and into contact with the real travail of the world.

These discussions lead us back to consideration of the "poles" of the divine nature, on which I touched in discussing process thought in section 2.4. Some theologians stress the unchangingness of this nature, and that all that happens happens out of the inexhaustible eternal fund of the triune God's loving will. Therefore what happens does not, in Fiddes's term, "befall" God;[10] God does not suffer in any way corresponding to the suffering we know about as humans. There are those who say—for the range of reasons discussed above—that we must include a description of God's responsiveness to the world in its actual flow of its temporality. God lets the world happen to God and in the process both transforms the world, and also experiences new levels of empathy with creatures. God therefore attains new levels of self-realization,[11] but also of suffering.

I follow here the instincts of not only Protestant theologians, such as Moltmann, Ward, and Fiddes, but also scholars of Catholic thought, such as Catherine LaCugna,[12] that what we see in the Passion of Christ reflects the deep pathos at the heart of God in relation to created being.[13] And I take with all seriousness Fiddes's point (against Weinandy) that that means God "adapts the divine being to the actions of our world . . . God freely chooses to be open to the hurt that will befall, with its unpredictability."[14] As we saw in the previous chapter, such a conviction about the suffering of God with creation forms an important part of the evolutionary theodicy of thinkers as diverse as Rolston, Peacocke, Haught, and McDaniel.[15]

4.3 DIVINE SELF-EMPTYING

Another important if controversial strategy in contemporary theology is that of invoking divine "kenosis" (self-emptying) in creation.[16] An important way in which God has been described as giving rise to a quasi-autonomous creation, in which there is disvalue as well as value, and which may be a cause of divine suffering with suffering creatures, is through a kenotic theology of creation. This concept, which in Christian thought derives originally from the description of Christ's self-emptying in Philippians 2:7, is used both to account for God's permitting of processes that give rise to disvalue, and also to imply a way in which the divine love suffers with that disvalue. I consider here to what extent the concept of divine self-emptying can be helpful in understanding the relation of the Creator to an evolutionary creation. That relation has to be such as to give rise to biological "selves" with their own interests and behaviors. I explore how the states of those biological selves may be described both scientifically and within a theology of "deep intratrinitarian kenosis." I then try to tease out how creaturely response to the Creator may be characterized within such a theology.

It is now my contention[17] that the language of kenosis in creation tends to arise out of commitment to a questionable spatial metaphor for the God-world relation—the alleged need for God to "make space" outside Godself for the created world[18] and/or an (also questionable) commitment to incompatibilism, the notion that the free actions of creatures are incompatible with the involvement of God in every event.[19] Arthur Peacocke writes of divine kenosis as "a creative self-emptying and self-offering."[20] I have come to regard the language of divine withdrawal to allow creation to be itself as largely unnecessary to express the theological motivation underlying its use. What the proponents of kenosis-in-creation tend to describe in *self-emptying* terms can be redescribed in terms of the *self-offering* love of the Creator, through the activity of the Word and Spirit.[21]

However, I consider that kenosis *can* be extended from its original application in Philippians 2:7 in two helpful directions, which themselves mirror two important senses in which the self-emptying of Christ in Philippians can be read. "*Ekenōsen*" (he emptied himself) can be taken with the preceding clauses about Christ not seeking to snatch at equality with God. That leads naturally to an incarnational reading in which the divine Son empties himself of divine equality to take the form of a human. Or it can be taken with the following phrase, "taking the form of a servant," which leads to more of an ethical reading, attesting to the sacrificial self-giving in Jesus' life. In what follows I develop both of these understandings of kenosis. In this chapter I draw on the work of the Roman Catholic theologian Hans Urs von Balthasar in providing language for that movement of the inner life of the Trinity that enables us to understand God as the creative, suffering origin of all things. This is a theory of what might be termed "deep intratrinitarian kenosis."[22] The self-abandoning love of the Father in begetting the Son establishes an otherness that enables God's creatures to be "selves."[23] In chapters 6 and 7 I consider what ethical kenosis in humans liberated from the power of sin might lead to an appropriate response to the "groaning" of the nonhuman creation (Rom. 8:22).

First, then, kenosis within the Trinity. It is useful to distinguish von Balthasar's formulation from the "divine withdrawal" model of Moltmann. Both theologians are wrestling with the problem of how a perfectly self-sufficient Trinitarian God can give rise to a creation that is other than Godself. Both would want to see the self-sacrifice of Christ on the Cross as deeply indicative of the character of God's gracious nature from all eternity. Moltmann's kenotic model of creation uses the imagery of divine withdrawal, making a space of non-existence within which existence can be formed. One of the weaknesses of the model is the implication that there might be ontological "space" to which God is not present.[24] Von Balthasar takes kenosis "back" a stage further; it is the self-emptying love of the Father in begetting the Son that creates the possibility that other selves can be formed.[25] Divine self-giving, on this model, creates the giving of selfhood to others. That separation of Father from Son of which Molt-mann wrote with such power in his *The Crucified God* is for von Balthasar inherent, in some measure, in the very character of a God who gives existence to the other and exposes Godself to the other in vulnerable love.[26] Otherness in the Trinity is the basis for the otherness of creation.[27]

But the existence of entities other than God is only the first stage of the problem of engaging theologically with an evolutionary creation. Nonliving entities have existence, but it is a characteristic of *living* organisms that in some sense they have "agency," they have "interests" that their behavior promotes.[28] This is crucial to our exploration of the inherent ambiguity of creation, the intrinsic link between values and disvalues. The ambiguity of the creation, its apparent "groaning," relates specifically to the disvalues experienced by living creatures. As I indicated in section 1.5, there is no waste in the "death" of stars by supernova or the erosion of great mountains to hummocks,[29] no evil in the changes in the surface of Jupiter owing to the impact of the comet Shoemaker-Levy.[30] Outside living organisms there are no selves, no discrete entities with interests to which "evils" can occur.[31]

Biological selves, then, have interests that their behavior seeks to promote. At its simplest level, they derive energy from their environment and seek to avoid harmful elements in that environment. As they grow and mature, the behavior by which they exercise agency and promote their own self-interest is a function both of the species to which they belong and of their own individual identity. On the model I am elaborating, then, the relationships within the Creator God are such as make space not only for creaturely existence but for creaturely "selves" and their response to their environment. The Father whose self-abandonment begets the Son, the Son whose self-emptying gives glory to the Father, these in the power of the Spirit give rise to living selves.

Where the ambiguity of the creation becomes manifest is at the next step. *The character of created selves is typically not that of self-giving but of self-assertion, for that, in a Darwinian world, is the only way biological selves can survive and flourish.* The values in creation, then, arise out of this self-assertion.

4.4 DEVELOPING A THEOLOGY
OF EVOLUTIONARY CREATION

I now develop this theology of creation further, aware of the speculative nature of this material. I regard engagement with the ambiguous character of evolutionary creation as essential to a proper dialogue between Trinitarian theology and contemporary science. A starting premise is that in the context of such an evolutionary creation it is still meaningful to talk of creation originating by the will of God the Father and occurring through the agency of the divine Logos and the Holy Spirit, a formulation that Colin Gunton traces back to Irenaeus's phrase about the Son and the Spirit being the two "hands" of the Father in creation.[32] As Neil Messer notes, this is a "sophisticated and significant" model, ruling out the need for other mediators of creation, and emphasizing that creation stems "not just of divine power and will, but also of [the] gratuitous love" of the triune God.[33]

In what follows I am conscious that far greater minds than mine have puzzled over the doctrine of triune creation. All I claim for the present study is that it brings together an underconsidered problem—that of the real ambiguity of an evolutionary creation—and an array of resources that might not normally be combined. I explore how this "two-hands" formulation of Irenaeus might be applied to a biosphere understood as evolving by natural selection, with all the problems of theodicy—ontological, teleological, and soteriological—that that entails.

The novel combination of resources that I bring to bear includes:

- The understandings of the great Orthodox thinker Maximus the Confessor (c. 580–662) as to the "logoi" of creation.[34]
- Recent thinking about the work of the Spirit in creation by the contemporary Australian theologian Denis Edwards.[35]
- The metaphysics of the nineteenth-century Romantic poet and Jesuit Gerard Manley Hopkins (1844–89), in particular his understanding of "selving."

What follows is a consciously metaphysical scheme, which will need to be assessed according to its internal coherence, its coherence with the tradition of Trinitarian theology and with current understandings of living organisms, and its value in integrating considerations of theodicy—and environmental ethics—into closer dialogue with the theology of creation.

My first resource, then, Orthodox thought, and particularly Maximus. I approach this via a wonderful quotation given by Kallistos Ware from the thought of St. Philaret: "All creatures are balanced upon the creative word of God, as if upon a bridge of diamond; above them is the abyss of divine infinitude, below them that of their own nothingness."[36] The theology of creation begins from ontological dependence; both existence and meaning within the created order depend utterly on God.

For Maximus the Confessor, everything has meaning through its participation in the Logos.[37] The logoi, the beauty and meaning of things, are God's thoughts and intentions. The logos of a thing is therefore its nature and what God intends it to be, or as Ware puts it, "that which makes it distinctively itself and at the same time draws it toward the divine realm."[38] Note the language here of movement, even of lure, which prevents this formulation from falling into the over-static ontology that Gunton notes as a problem in the Western Platonic inheritance via Augustine.[39] Indeed over-static understandings of the nature of creatures could not accommodate the Darwinian vision of species in transition in response to naturally occurring variation and the selection pressures of their environment. So it is essential to avoid such a static view of the character of organisms. Rather, biological organisms and species are best seen as representing points and peaks within evolutionary fitness landscapes.[40] I see every such peak as a possibility imagined in the mind of God, hence possessing in Maximus's terms "logoi," divinely given patterns of being. The divine ideas to which the nature of species correspond need to be thought of not as static aesthetic ideals but dynamically and in terms of peaks in fitness landscapes, peaks that shift over time as God draws the biosphere onward. So I do not see species as static or unchanging, nor do I imagine all members of the species as clustered precisely at the top of the fitness peak. The work of the "two hands" of the Father in creation both draws onward the ever-shifting distribution of peaks in the fitness landscape, through the unfolding creative work of the Logos, and encourages organisms, through the power of the Spirit, in their exploration of that landscape, giving rise to new possibilities of being a self. This model of divine creativity has something in common with the work of the late Arthur Peacocke, in his use of metaphors such as God the improvisatory composer,[41] and also with the model of divine lure in process theology (see section 2.4). My model is distinguished from these, first, in being explicitly Trinitarian in its formulation and, second, in giving an account of how organisms are both valued by God in their nature, but also are able to resist the divine invitation to transcend that nature (see below).

This brings me to the work of the Spirit in creation. Denis Edwards has done some very helpful work both in justifying the assignment of proper roles to the persons of the Trinity in creation, and in exploring what role might be distinctively assigned to the Spirit.[42] Edwards sees the Spirit as the immanent Life-Giver, enabling creatures to be and to become. He goes on to talk of the Spirit enabling creatures to exist in their individuality and creaturely otherness.[43] In chapter 9 of *Breath of Life*, Edwards makes clear that he is pursuing a relational ontology, one moreover that shows itself aware of the ambiguous character of the relationships within an evolutionary creation. "In nature," he writes, "we find amazing and beautiful patterns of mutual dependence, cooperation and shared life. But we also find competition for survival, predation and death."[44] Edwards does not try and resolve this ambiguity, except by reference to its eventual eschatological resolution (an approach also characteristic of John Haught).[45] For Edwards, "This [relational Trinitarian] theology does not resolve the ambiguity we find in created relations. It leaves us like Job before the mystery."[46] In what follows I try very tentatively to shed some light on this mystery.

I follow Edwards in holding that "each diverse creature has its own distinct integrity. From the perspective of science, this individuality and integrity are given in all the constitutive relationships that make the entity what it is. From the perspective of theology, each individual creature has its own independent value within an interrelated universe, a value that springs from its relationship with the indwelling Creator Spirit."[47] In seeking to clarify the role of the Spirit in creation, and its relation to the work of the Logos, I propose that the work of the Spirit in creation is associated with both particularity and self-transcendence. Any individual organism is not merely an example of a type, not merely a representation of the logos that informs it; it is also its particular self, with its own particular "thisness"[48] which, like its logos, is a gift from God in creation. In my scheme this gift of particularity is seen as conferred by the Spirit, interacting with the work of the Logos. The Logos is being understood to confer pattern and common significance to the organism as a member of a species.

Insofar as it is through variation among individuals that a species "explores" new possibilities within a fitness landscape, the work of the Spirit in conferring particularity is also a work of making possible self-transcendence—both in an organism's growing to maturity in the form of its species, and in the sense of its possible exploration of new behaviors, going beyond what was previously the character of that species.[49] (It must be acknowledged that very many of these individual explorations will not lead to greater fitness or fulfillment.) The role of the Spirit may also be seen as the creation of the possibility of community, insofar as community depends on both the mutual interaction of what is particular and distinct, and the transcendence of isolated self-interest for the sake of that interaction.

Existence, pattern, and particularity are properties of all entities, so there is no violation here of the principle that the actions of the Trinity must be capable of being viewed as a single action. However we can at this point make a useful distinction between living and nonliving entities. The theology of creation outlined above has been illustrated by reference to living organisms, but it applies also to the nonliving, with the differences that (a) the logoi of mountains, deserts, and oceans, their beauty and meaning, shift on much more gradual timescales, and (b) the degree of particularity attached to nonliving enti-ties is very much less, and there is no possibility of self-transcendence (unless we take the biblical miracles as very exceptional examples). The work of the Holy Spirit in conferring particularity and the possibility of community is especially notable in the "giving of life."[50]

My third major resource is the metaphysics of Hopkins. The poet writes in what is arguably his finest sonnet, "As Kingfishers Catch Fire":

> As kingfishers catch fire, dragonflies draw flame;
> As tumbled over rim in roundy wells
> Stones ring; like each tucked string tells, each hung bell's
> Bow swung finds tongue to fling out broad its name;
> Each mortal thing does one thing and the same;
> Deals out that being indoors each one dwells;
> Selves—goes itself; *myself* it speaks and spells,
> Crying *What I do is me: for that I came.*[51]

What I want to argue, in linking the creation of biological selves to the the-ology of Trinitarian creation, is that when a living creature "selves" in the sense of Hopkins's kingfishers, behaving in its most characteristic way, and flourish-ing in so doing, it is conforming to the pattern offered by the divine Logos, the pattern of that type of selfhood imagined by the divine Word, and begotten in the Spirit out of the perfect self-abandoning love of the Father. Selving, then, takes place within what I have called "deep intratrinitarian kenosis." It is from the love of the Father for the world, and for the glory of the Son, that other selves gain their existence, beauty, and meaning, that which prevents them from reverting to nothingness. It is from the self-sacrificial love of the Son for the Father and all his works that each created entity gains the distinctive pattern of its existence, that which prevents the creation from collapsing back into an undifferentiated unity. It is from the power of the Spirit, predictable only in its continual creativity and love, which is the same self-transcending and self-renewing love as is between the Father and the Son, that each creature receives its particularity. Within each pattern or logos of created entities is a diversity of individual being, a "thisness" that is the distinctive gift of the Spirit. In its moment of "catching fire" the kingfisher is in that moment the pattern of "king-fisher." Hopkins sees this as a kind of profound creaturely yes: "what I do is me: for that I came." It is a yes of identity, but also of particularity.[52]

We can imagine these moments of creaturely yes, of the creature perfectly expressing its identity, the pattern and particularity of its existence to their full potential, most easily in higher animals, in the moments in which the creature seems perfectly to fulfill what it is to be that animal, that bird, whether it be the moment of eating the best food, accomplishing the perfect hunt, the moment of pure play. More generally, any creature's yes comes when it is perfectly itself, both in terms of the species to which it belongs and in its own individuality. The creature perfectly sounding the "hung bell" of its existence perfectly "selves." We can associate this language of perfect selving with the concept of creaturely praise of God, a concept that has been strong in various parts of the Christian tradition,[53] and which finds support in the Psalms, in particular 19:1–4; 145:10–14; 148.

What is vital to a treatment of evolutionary theodicy is to acknowledge that the character of the creation is such that many individual creatures never "selve" in any fulfilled way. I gave earlier in section 3.2 Holmes Rolston's classic example of the insurance chick that birds such as white pelicans hatch.[54] Typically this younger chick is edged out of the nest by its elder, and then ignored by the parents. It has only a 10 percent chance of fledging. The insurance pelican chick rarely has the chance to manifest the pattern "pelicanness"; instead its life, typically, is one of starvation, pain, and abandonment to early death.

To gain some theological purchase on the problematic character of evolved creation, shot through as it is with ambiguity and implicit question as to the goodness of God, we can analyze the possible states of living creatures as follows:

- "Fulfilled"—a state in which the creature is utterly being itself, in an environment in which it flourishes (including an appropriate network of relationships with other organisms), with access to the appropriate energy sources and reproductive opportunities.[55]
- "Growing toward fulfillment"—not yet mature, but still with the possibility of attaining the "fulfilled" state.
- "Frustrated"—held back in some way from fulfillment, whether by adverse mutation or environmental change, or through old age, or being predated upon or parasitized, or being unable to find a mate through competition or species scarcity.
- "Transcending itself"—through some new pattern of behavior, whether as a result of a favorable mutation, or a chance exploration of a new possibility of relating to its own or another species.

The first state is the state of true "selving," the state Hopkins talks about in his poem, and it is the "sound" of "praise" from creature to Creator: "what I do is me: for that I came." Scientifically, it is made possible by the flux of energy through the biosphere, both from the sun and from the hot interior of the Earth, and by the recycling of energy from other life forms.

Theologically, we might say that this fulfillment in the creature is the gift of existence from the Father, form and pattern from the Son, particularity from the Holy Spirit, and that the creature's praise, in being itself, is offered by the

Son to the Father, in the delight of the Spirit.[56] As I indicated in chapter 1, I hold that these states of fulfillment consummate a creaturely life, such that the death that inevitably follows them may be considered a natural end rather than itself being evil.[57]

The second state is scientifically describable in terms of the interaction of the genome with intraorganismic and environmental factors, again made possible by the flux of energy through a dissipative system. It will include pain, in many organisms, because of the need to learn an aversion to negative stimuli. As I noted in chapter 1, pain is a necessary, rather than a negative, aspect of the growth of sentient life. The Godhead that is so committed to the creation as ultimately to experience birth and infancy as a human may be imagined to take an especial delight in the growth of young organisms.

The third state, frustration, is one that Darwin's model of natural selection brings very much to the fore. Darwin recognized that biotic systems will be limit-sum games, that evolutionary strategies almost always involve the overproduction of offspring, and necessarily imply the existence of "frustrated" organisms is a precondition of other organisms "growing toward fulfillment" and "fulfilled." In the current creation, "frustration," including the actual pain caused to organisms by disease, competition, and being the victim of predators, is a necessary cost of selving. Indeed it is a characteristic of nature that the full flourishing of some individuals is at the expense of that of other individuals, either of the same species or of others. Predation is the most obvious example; competition for reproductive success is another.

Theologically we may posit that the frustration of the creature, be it of the insurance pelican chick, or the sheep parasitized by the worm *Redia*,[58] or the aging lion beaten for the first time in a fight with a younger male, is received by the Son through the brooding immanence of the Spirit, and uttered in that Spirit as a song of lament to the Father. All that the frustrated creature suffers, and all it might have been but for frustration, is retained in the memory of the Trinity.[59] Given that the same processes lead to full selving and to frustration, we must imagine this ambiguity held deep in the loving relationships within God.

I indicated above that we might (tentatively) identify perfect selving with creaturely praise, drawing on Hopkins's line, "What I do is me: for that I came." But I regard the position as more complex than that, and develop here a fuller picture of creaturely response to the Creator, which will incorporate the fourth of the possibilities given above, that of creaturely self-transcendence. I indicated above that I saw the invitation to self-transcendence in the exploration of new possibilities of being as the especial gift of the Holy Spirit in creation. The Spirit longs for creatures to transcend themselves, to find new ways of relating. Evolutionary self-transcendence is dramatically illustrated in such cruxes as the symbioses that gave rise to the first eukaryotic cells, or the Middle to Upper Palaeolithic "Transition" in *H. Sapiens*, by which the human being emerged from being an animal of relatively modest technological skills[60] to a being not just capable of great linguistic, social, economic, and artistic sophistication,[61] but also of worship and of genuine self-sacrifice. Indeed, a form of self-transcendence occurs whenever cooperation between organisms, either within a species or across species, produces new types of "selves." The various forms of "altruism" that have been described for nonhuman species are expressions of that transcendence of mere self-interest.[62] But clearly such cooperations are limited, and take place within a larger context of competition among the extended selves for scarce resources.

I have long been fascinated by a passage in Paul Fiddes's book *The Creative Suffering of God*. He writes of God's relation to the creation, "Some overall vision of the 'responsiveness' and 'resistance' of creation to the Spirit of God is needed for a doctrine of creative evolution, [and] for a proper theodicy."[63] Fiddes is arguing that we must speak of some sort of "free will in creation," of resistance and responsiveness, if we are to speak of God suffering in creation. This taps into Fiddes's conclusion that suffering must be something that befalls God, not a mere logical outworking of the divine plan.

Fiddes's language of freely chosen resistance, and of suffering that befalls God outside the divine plan, needs further exploration, particularly in the case where it is being applied outside the sphere of human choices. The sort of creation that this is presumably *is* very much part of God's plan. Indeed it is a creation, according to Paul in Romans 8:19–22, subjected to futility by God in hope that eventually it may achieve the glorious liberty of the children of God. (For further analysis of this text see section 6.1.) To realize this goal God must encounter the contingency and struggle of creatures being creatures and not-being-God. Just as the Cross, in Christian tradition, is at one and the same a shocking and blasphemous contingency, and also in some sense falls within God's plan,[64] as being the only way to bring all creation to its ultimate fulfillment, so it is part of God's plan that God encounter and bear the self-seeking and communion-denying elements in what it is to be a Darwinian creature. Immanent in all things, God must be exposed to what it is for living organisms to selve in this way.

I articulated above a suggestion of how we might understand creaturely responsiveness, the creature's yes to God—in the moment of eating the best food, accomplishing the perfect hunt, the moment of pure play. More generally the creature's yes comes when it is perfectly itself, both in terms of the species to which it belongs and in its own individuality. The creature perfectly sounding the "hung bell" of its existence perfectly "selves." How then might we understand a creaturely "no," a "resistance" to the divine will?

Von Balthasar places the tension between createdness and self-interest within a Trinitarian frame. He writes: "The creature's No, its wanting to be autonomous without acknowledging its origin, must be located within the Son's all-embracing Yes to the Father, in the Spirit."[65] What, though, *is* the creaturely no? It is, after all, not easy to associate von Balthasar's description of the creature "wanting to be autonomous without acknowledging its origin," with scientifically characterized behavior in birds, or yet bacteria. What follows is an attempt to venture onto this very difficult territory.

I am helped by an article by Patricia Williams who points out that four central characteristics of the behavior of living organisms—from the simplest upward, and including humans—are: struggle for *resources*; *reproductive* behavior; association with, and positive behavior toward, genetic *relatives*; and *reciprocal* behavior.[66] Clearly as organisms become more complex, reproduce sexually, and form communities, the latter three become more and more important. But all biological "selves" pursue some or all of these behaviors selfishly and preferentially. Resources are secured at the expense of other organisms of the same species and others. Reproduction is effected, typically, with the strongest available partner, not with the weak. The good of genetic relatives is preferred to the good of "neighbors." Biological relationships abound with cooperation, but very rarely exhibit anything going beyond our understanding of kin and reciprocal altruism,[67] into the realm of what might be called sacrifice.

Contained within the behavior of Darwinian creatures—which is understood in Christian thought to be created by God, and is the means by which there arise the extraordinary beauty of the cheetah and the gazelle, by which the orca and the porpoise, the peregrine, the hummingbird, and the honeybee, all come to be the creatures that they are—is a limitation of creaturely response. The creation is "very good," but each element of it is necessarily limited. Self-transcendence is, as was noted above, limited within the nonhuman realm. There is within the nonhuman world little sign of costly self-giving to the other, or identification with difference in community. There are some very touching examples of animal behavior, particularly in social animals. Orcas will push an ailing pod member to the surface to breathe; elephants will surround and support a sick member of the family group. But very rarely is there care for the genuinely other. In this respect the heart-rending observations of a lioness who exhibited motherly behavior toward a series of young oryxes—normally an animal preyed on by lions[68]—stands out as an example of possibilities virtually never seen (and indeed, in Darwinian terms, maladaptive).[69]

Of themselves, then, organisms other than the human show limited signs of self-transcendence. Nonhuman creatures, it might be said, then, offer a kind of "no" to the example of the triune creator's self-giving love, to the love poured out without the cost being counted. The work of the Holy Spirit in offering possibilities of community succeeds in giving rise to ecosystemic complexity, but "fails," in most of the nonhuman world, in creating any community characterized by authentic altruism, true self-giving love. Only hints of this behavior emerge, in the care given to infants in many species, in the mutual protectiveness in social groups. Complex social interactions, containing hints of genuinely altruistic behavior, are seen at their most pronounced in primate groups; Frans de Waal has argued that such species may indeed be "good-natured."[70] But these possible examples of self-transcendence are exceptions. Typically the nonhuman creature returns to God its "selving" "yes," but also a "no" to self-transcendence, to growing into the image of the Trinity of self-giving love.[71] It is in Fiddes's terms a "no of self-preservation, or the hoarding of space."[72] It is not in nonhuman creatures the "calculating, cautious self-preservation" Fiddes sees in human creatures,[73] but it is still a no to possibilities beyond the creature's present nature.[74]

God bears this creaturely "no" in God's being; it is always new and always particular, because particularity is part of the gifting of God to the creation through the Holy Spirit. God suffers not only the suffering of myriad creatures, each one precious to the Creator, and the extinction of myriad species, each a way of being imagined within the creative Word, but also the continual refusal—beyond the creation's praise—of God's offer of self-transcendence, the continual refusal, beyond all creation's flourishing, to live by the acceptance of the divine offer that would draw the creature deeper into the life of the Trinity itself. It will be apparent anew how paradoxical the theology of evolutionary creation must be, given the Christian affirmation that a good God has given rise to a good creation, and yet as we have seen the creation is shot through with ambiguity.[75] The purposes of God are, and are not, realized in the life of any given creature. God delights in creatures in and for themselves, and yet longs for the response of the creature that can become more than itself, whose life can be broken and poured out in love and joy after the divine image. Divine purposes are, seemingly, realized, after many setbacks, at the level of the biosphere as a whole, in the evolution of a rich variety of ecosystems, and eventually in the arising of a freely choosing self-conscious creature, the human being, capable of sophisticated reflection on the planet, and hence potentially a partner for God in the care of living things. But at the level of the individual creature, the divine desire for creaturely flourishing is frequently unrealized, and where it is realized, it is only so at the expense of other possibilities, and often at the expense of the flourishing of other organisms. The pattern of the creation's flourishing, then, is an *ambiguous* pattern—"yes" to God always accompanied by no—full of beauty, full even of praise, but also of selving that takes place at the expense of the flourishing of other selves.[76]

In reflecting on this model of creation's response to God, it is hard to resist the analogy of music, on which Arthur Peacocke drew when he wrote of creation as improvised fugue and to which he returned in one of his last books.[77] The melodies of selving creatures, which the immature are still learning and trying out, are won at the expense of the dissonant chorus of frustrated creatures, and over this ambiguous chorus (this state of travail and birthing) rises the improvisation of new themes being tried. God on this model is both playing the ground bass, the divine, intratrinitarian music that surrounds and blesses the whole, and also encouraging creativity, perhaps periodically stepping in, but only to avert disaster, to prevent the floor of the concert hall collapsing.[78] Within the movements of love of the triune persons, space is made for selving, and for the holding of the pain of frustration. But these processes involve not only responsiveness to the divine love, but also resistance, self-assertion at the expense of care and cooperation.

It is this nexus of considerations that offers the real challenge and excitement of evolutionary theology, a challenge too often muted by creationist and other naïve readings of the narratives both of Scripture and of science. Few theologians have really engaged with this. One who has done so, reframing the problem so as to draw the sting of evolutionary suffering for a doctrine of God, is Ruth Page.[79] Page writes: "I cannot imagine a God responsible for natural evil any more than one responsible for moral evil. . . . To those who wish to affirm full-blooded . . . [divine] making and doing, [my] version will appear anaemic. But the consequences of belief in a more virile God, who has to be responsible for the removal of around 98% of all species ever, but who fails to do anything in millions of cases of acute suffering in nature and humanity, are scarcely to be borne."[80]

Page then stresses the problems of theodicy associated with any long-term teleological scheme. She emphasizes that God "lets the world be"—drawing here on the Heideggerian term *Gelassenheit*. God creates possibilities and lets them unfold. Thus far this is a clear picture, and one to which no metaphysically aware scientist could object. But *Gelassenheit* of itself does not do justice to the Christian vision of the God involved in the world. Page is well aware of this, and she therefore also invokes a category of divine involvement she calls *Mitsein*, God's companioning of the world at every stage and locus. I do not believe this view is entirely consistent in Page. Sometimes she speaks of *Mitsein* as a nonjudging maintenance of relationship, and sometimes she uses a more familiar terminology very akin to process thought, as in her talk of "a God always present everywhere, offering both reproach and encouragement, and above all saving, forgiving, companionship."[81] Divine reproach and encouragement sound very like the steering of the cosmos to me.[82] However, Page's central point is that her divine companioning is "teleology now";

it is all for the benefit of the entity concerned, and does not use that entity as a means to an end.

It may be doubted whether this altogether relieves the theodicist's burden. After all, as I pointed out in section 3.4, God is still responsible for the onto-logical aspect of the problem—for the existence of the world in which the suf-fering takes place. Moreover, all life, from its most primitive, is characterized by differential selection of self-replicators, and only very primitive ecosystems, lacking all sentience, involve no significant cost to organisms in terms of pain and suffering. But Page might argue that life itself, life lived in companionship with God, is worth the sufferings intrinsic to its development (cf. also Tracy's approach mentioned in section 3.2). Page's scheme does go a great way to address the teleological problem of evolutionary theodicy—God using pain, suffering, death, and extinction to realize other ends.

There are many points of contact between Page's thought and the view pre-sented here—a strong awareness of the problem of suffering and extinction in evolution, a sense of God creating by creating possibilities, or even "possibil-ities of possibilities."[83] There is a consonance between this picture and my own sense of God imagining the peaks on fitness landscapes that creatures explore, and also encouraging the creature to explore new ways of being within those (ever-shifting) landscapes. I am also sympathetic to Page's appropriation of Austin Farrer's work; she writes of God thinking creatures into being but mak-ing them "follow their own bent and work out the world by themselves."[84] For Page and for Farrer, as for me, God uses creative pressure of which creatures are not aware for the satisfaction of individual life and for the evolutionary process to continue.

I consider, however, that Page has not wholly apprehended the ambiguity in creation, that blend of value with disvalue which this study explores. When she writes of "earthquakes, hurricanes, and volcanoes," and "what horror a change of climate [of which there have been many[85]] may wreak over vast areas of the world," she comments, "These are instances when the world does not fit together, and the wonder they inspire is not likely to lead to immediate thought on the goodness of God."[86] But it is precisely those great geochemical events that have shaped the wonderful biosphere of the present Earth. They *are* the way the Earth "fits together" so as to generate new long-term possibilities. And Page surely underrates God's engagement with long-term possibilities, extending beyond the immediate creatures present at any given phase of the planet's history. Consider the truly ancient predators of the world: the shark and the crocodile. Both groups of species arrived on remarkably stable peaks in fitness landscapes hundreds of millions of years ago. Both in their own way have their own beauty and fittingness (witness the extraordinary delicacy with which a crocodile, possessed of a bite power approaching that of *Tyrannosaurus*

Rex, holds its infants between its teeth). But it would be hard to imagine the Creator not desiring the further evolution of predators, just because such highly efficient strategies had already evolved,[87] any more than one could imagine God not desiring the evolution of the eukaryotic cell given the great sophistication of the bacteria that had evolved over the first billion years of the history of life. The evolutionary process, as Arthur Peacocke notes, "is characterized by propensities toward increase in complexity, information-processing and storage, consciousness, sensitivity to pain and even self-consciousness."[88] It is hard, then, to concede Page's rigid "teleology now," when to do so would be to imagine that these longer-term propensities are not also reflections of the divine desire. To deny the existence of that divine desire to relate to organisms with more and more complex consciousness is to be unable to say that a primate's life contains greater values than its most primitive evolutionary ancestors. Since, as I indicated at the beginning of this chapter, properties such as complexity and self-consciousness evolve by a process that denies full flourishing to a high proportion of the individuals and species that evolve, the long-term teleological problem in evolutionary theodicy is unavoidable.[89]

The scheme I am developing here is a strongly teleological one. It affirms the value of every creature, both as a good of itself and as a vital component of an ecosystem (it should be remembered that ecosystems typically depend obligatorily on the flourishing of microorganisms), but it also prizes self-transcendence, the exploration by organisms, either through genetic mutation or new behaviors, of new possibilities of being. It acknowledges the propensities of which Peacocke writes, and regards them as divinely imparted to the biosphere. It assigns progressively greater value to more complex organisms, and more complex interrelations of organisms. It prizes interactions of care within and across kin groups, and symbioses between species (in line with an understanding of the Holy Spirit as the former of and delighter in relationships). It claims that the Spirit longs for creatures to transcend themselves, to find new ways of relating.

4.5 THE HUMAN ANIMAL AND ITS "SELVING"

I noted above that for the kingfisher truly to "selve" was to conform to its logoi, to the pattern of kingfisher given by the Creating Word. But the human animal has access to an extent of freedom and self-transcendence that goes vastly beyond what is present in other animals. I accept, of course, all the ways in which the human sciences tell us our choices may be limited or conditioned. But I take very seriously also a theological description of the human as a freely choosing creature in the image and likeness of God. For such an animal, to "selve" is to conform (however momentarily) to the image of God the Trinity. That means to conform to the pattern of Christ, and to have accepted from the Holy Spirit the gifts both of particularity and of engagement in authentic community. That would be community characterized by the self-giving love of neighbor in which is found the true love of self, of justice, and of God.[90]

Human evolution, graced by the continual outpouring of divine love, has opened up possibilities for a "yes" to God that goes beyond mere selving:[91] a "yes" based on a sharing of resources with the weak and the non-kin, on repro-ductive processes accompanied by self-giving love and sustained companion-ship, on a recognizing of all humans as one's neighbor, and on sacrificial actions. I imagine that God responds to these possibilities with a yet more pro-found level of self-communication than is possible to nonhuman animals, and a yet more profound divine respect for the freedom of the self-conscious selves that have evolved.

That is not to say, however, that the old imperatives with regard to resources, reproduction, relatives, and reciprocity lose their hold. Indeed they develop within the self-conscious mind an addictive power. Consciousness seems to amplify the potential of humans for evil as well as good. Both our yes and our no to God take on formidable force; our no becomes ecologically the force to become a "plague species,"[92] economically to perpetuate and exacer-bate extremes of wealth and poverty, militarily and socially to ghettoize and ultimately to undertake genocide, religiously to crucify the Prince of Peace and Lord of Glory. As J. Wentzel van Huyssteen has noted, "*Homo Sapiens* is not only distinguished by its remarkable embodied brain, by a stunning men-tal cognitive fluidity expressed in imagination, creativity, linguistic abilities, and symbolic propensities. As real-life, embodied persons of flesh and blood we humans are also affected by hostility, arrogance, ruthlessness and cun-ning."[93] The combination of our cognitive and emotional resources with our biological imperatives gives us the possibility of greed, lust, rape, and exploita-tion of the weak, of the poor, of other species. With our emergent faculties comes a greater and greater need of God—a need not just to receive from God but to dwell within the life of the Trinity, to live within and from the patterns of the triune love. It is the Incarnation, finally, that opens up the being of God in a new way,[94] offering us both the most profound of examples, and a new possibility of being at home within the life of a God who has taken human experience into Godself.

The Gospels of Matthew and Luke attribute to Jesus the saying "Foxes have holes, and birds of the air have nests; but the Son of Man has nowhere to lay his head" (Matt. 8:20; Luke 9:58). To use an analogy from physics: human beings are not like particles, with a certain position and a certain mass, but like vectors, having a certain strength and a certain orientation. The Christian conviction is that Jesus gives us the example of what it is to keep one's orientation firmly and wholly on God, and to derive all one's strength from that. One's life is from moment to moment not one's own possession, but something received as a gift from God. What is said of Christ's equality with God in Philippians 2 is true of authentic human being in itself—that it is not something to be grasped at, but to be received and responded to in service of God and others. Again we see the connection between what it is to be an authentic human being and the relationships of freely given mutual love and response that are attributed to God as Trinity. Indeed Christian theology wants to go further and say not just that a human being fully alive has a quality of life that is like the quality of life that is within God, not just, in the famous saying of Irenaeus of Lyons, that the glory of God is a human being fully alive, but also that a human person living in free, loving, undistorted relationship with others has been drawn up into the life of the Trinity, and participates in that life. The human being has no true home, but only a direction of journeying, into the heart of God in Godself.

On this model the *imago Dei* is the *imago Trinitatis*, the capacity to give love, in the power of the Spirit, to the radically other, and by that same Spirit to receive love from that other, selflessly.[95] But we only grow into that image as we grow into God, as we learn to dwell within the triune love.[96] We never possess the *imago* independently of that indwelling,[97] that journeying toward God's offer of ultimate love.

Within human beings, then, grows up (such is the grace of God in creation) the possibility of a larger "yes"—of a sharing of resources with the weak and the non-kin, of reproductive processes accompanied by self-giving love and sustained companionship, of recognizing all humans as one's neighbor, and of self-sacrificial actions. I take up the question of the human calling further in chapter 6.

4.6 GOD'S PROVIDENTIAL ACTION IN THE WORLD

If we are to avoid a deist or sub-deist theodicy based only on considering why God set up this particular type of evolving biosphere and not another, we must address explicitly the question of God's continuing interaction with the creation. In section 4.7 I consider the historical moment that concentrated and symbolized God's loving and saving care for creatures: the incarnation, life, passion, and resurrection of the Christ. Here I address God's general interaction with the long history of the biosphere. Two questions need attention.

First, to what extent did God guarantee that life would arise on one or more planets, and that the evolutionary process would be fruitful? The prevailing view of the existence of life in the universe is now that it is likely to be common—that many Earth-like planets will be found. Given that life seems to have arisen so relatively quickly on Earth, within perhaps 200 million years of the end of the "cosmic bombardment," it is often presumed that life will be likely on any planet with the right composition and distance from its sun. Equally, it is often said (most famously by Stephen Jay Gould) that if "the tape of evolution" had been run again, it would have produced entirely different results.[98] In this connection it is very interesting to note the work of Simon Conway Morris, who concludes the contrary on both counts. He shows in his book *Life's Solution* that there are good arguments for supposing that Earth may be the only life-bearing planet.[99] And he has long disagreed with Gould about the directionality of evolution, pointing to the many characteristics of evolution, including the "camera eye," saber-toothed predators, and intricate social communication, which have emerged several times in different lines of descent (so-called "convergent evolution").

It is important for theologians not to produce travesties of what the biological sciences claim. Evolutionary processes do seem to contain a significant element of chance, and the history of the biosphere has been marked by great extinction events that have altered its character enormously. Nevertheless, the overall result has been one of the progressive evolution of strategies of being alive involving greater and greater consciousness and diversity, hence Arthur Peacocke's claim that God has given the process "propensities" in this direction (see section 4.4 above). To this I would add my own proposal that God both continually creates new possibilities for creatures, and may have protected the possibilities that God knew would be fruitful for the development of complex life.[100]

Robert J. Russell has suggested that God may have acted at the quantum level to influence mutation events in evolutionary history. This is part of his very carefully argued scheme of "non-interventionist objective divine action."[101] Part of the strength of Russell's scheme is his awareness of issues of freedom and theodicy. God's action to alter the course of evolution would both have to respect the freedom of complex creatures as they arose, and would also sharpen the question, why did God not prevent the many deleterious mutations that led to crippled and unfulfilled lives among creatures? God's respect for creaturely freedom might well mean that divine action at the level of mutation decreased as more and more complex creatures evolved.[102]

But our second question still tugs at us: why did the God of noninterventionist providential action not minimize creaturely suffering within evolution? As Austin Farrer put it, "Poor limping world, why does not your kind Creator pull the thorn out of your paw?"[103] Or at least, in Keith Ward's words, we can imagine that God "could act to heal and save from harm on occasion and to an extent that does not undermine the general structure of reality."[104] Wesley Wildman's telling "argument from neglect" applies here. Wildman considers that a God who will not alleviate suffering "does not pass the test of parental moral responsibility . . . We must conclude that God has a morally abysmal record of inaction or ineffective action."[105] This is one of his reasons for abandoning belief in a personal God (see section 2.3). Philip Clayton and Steven Knapp have given a thoughtful response to Wildman, in terms of the need for God to act with total consistency, in the face of the vast continuum of suffering to which God is exposed.[106]

Farrer's own answer is a clear one. He continues the passage just quoted:

> But what sort of a thorn is this? And if it were pulled out, how much of the paw would remain? How much, indeed, of the creation? What would a physical universe be like, from which all mutual interference of systems was eliminated?
>
> It would be no physical universe at all. It would not be like an animal relieved of pain by the extraction of a thorn. It would be like an animal rendered incapable of pain by the removal of its nervous system; that is to say, of its animality. So the physical universe could be delivered from the mutual interference of its constituent systems, only by being deprived of its physicality.[107]

Here we see a version of the "only way" argument I considered in sections 3.2–3.3, extended from God's setting up of the evolutionary system to God's ongoing relation to it.

The scheme I proposed in section 4.4 is based on a theology of divine companionship and co-suffering, and also of divine longing. That longing for the final transformation of creatures found its most intense expression at the Christ-event, to the significance of which I now turn.

4.7 THE SIGNIFICANCE OF THE CROSS AND RESURRECTION

Throughout the history of Christian thought, debate has taken place as to how Christ's work on the Cross affects the world. What does it mean to say that Christ died "for us" (Rom. 5:8) or "for our sins in accordance with the scriptures" (1 Cor. 15:3)? What does it mean—even more difficult to wrestle with—that the blood of Christ's cross reconciled the whole of creation to God (cf. Col. 1:20)?

Theories of atonement have often been divided into the objective—Christ's death transforms the world irrespective of any response by creatures—and the subjective—the Gospel story of the example of Christ in going innocently to his death for love of the world transforms the hearts and spirits of those "with ears to hear." In respect of the benefit to humans, a complete account must integrate the two, in the sense that objective theories also require a subjective response.

The atonement is a huge subject, full of paradox and mystery. Central as it is to my theodicy, I can only outline my approach briefly in this present study.[108] Suffice it to say that if the Cross and Resurrection inaugurate a great era of redemption of the nonhuman creation leading to the eschaton, as seems to be the implication of Colossians 1:20 and Ephesians 1:10, then the impact of the Christ-event must be an objective one. It cannot rest only on the free choice of the creatures who are the beneficiaries. This is also argued by Niels Henrik Gregersen in an important article,[109] and is the implication of Moltmann's work over a number of major books. God's ultimate self-giving in Christ makes possible a self-transcendence in humans that evolution of itself would not make possible.[110] Christ's ultimate act of kenosis, felt by his Father as the uttermost alienation,[111] begins the final phase of the creation in which the evolutionary process itself will be transformed and healed.[112] As Fiddes has shown, it is unhelpful to think of God's suffering being located only at the Cross.[113] But to return to the position of Peacocke's that I quoted in section 3.5, "The suffering of God, which we could glimpse only tentatively in the processes of creation, is in Jesus the Christ concentrated into a point of intensity and transparency which reveals itself to all who focus on him."[114] "Intensity" expresses the sheer extent of God's sacrificial love for the world in Jesus, "transparency" the way that the Cross shows to human beings what love is, at its truest, and what it can cost.

I wrote in section 3.5 of divine co-suffering with the creature as consisting of presence and solidarity. The Incarnation is the event by which God takes this presence and solidarity with creaturely existence to its utmost, and thus "takes responsibility" for all the evil in creation—both the humanly wrought evil and the harms to all creatures.[115] Karl Schmitz-Moormann put it thus: "By becoming human in the incarnation, by life, passion, and death on the cross, God paid the utmost price for the freedom of human beings to love."[116] This language of price has been problematic in the history of this debate, since it begs the question: to whom is the price paid? Hence my preference for the language of God taking responsibility.[117]

The key passage from Romans 8 that informs this study suggests that this freeing of human beings to love self-sacrificially after the model of Christ must somehow precede God's full liberation of the rest of creation. I hold to a model of atonement based on the objective freeing of humans from the compulsions of sin, subjectively appropriated by humans through faith and contemplation of the example and passion of Jesus. I extend that via the concept of "deep incarnation" that has been developed by Gregersen: the Christ-event takes *all* creaturely experience into the life of God in a new way.[118] It thereby makes possible the transformed life of creaturely selves at the eschaton. We see the first hint of the character of this transformation in the bodily resurrection of Christ.

In the next chapter I take up the question of the character of creation's final state, and show why I believe it will involve a redeemed existence for creatures that have died without knowing anything of creaturely flourishing in their first lives. In chapter 6 I consider the role of human beings, exploring in more detail Paul's conviction that the creation "waits with eager longing for the revealing of the children of God" and "will obtain the freedom" of their "glory" (Rom. 8:19, 21). Finally in chapter 7 I consider possible practical ways in which humans' role in partnership with God might be explored.

5

Heaven for Pelicans?
Eschatological Considerations

5.1 INTRODUCTION

In 1974 Keith Ward wrote, "If there is any sentient creature which suffers pain, that being—whatever it is and however it is manifested—must find that pain transfigured by a greater joy."[1] In a later book he repeated this conviction, to the effect that "Immortality, for animals as well as humans, is a necessary condition of any acceptable theodicy; that necessity together with all the other arguments for God, is one of the main reasons for believing in immortality."[2] This echoed the sentiment of a famous sermon of John Wesley's, "The General Deliverance." In this sermon Wesley, meditating on that same passage—Romans 8:19–22—which has been exercising us throughout this study, likewise posed the question as to whether there might be "a plausible objection against the justice of God, in suffering numberless creatures that had never sinned to be so severely punished . . . But," Wesley continues, "the objection vanishes away, if we consider, that something better remains after death for these creatures also; that these likewise shall one day be delivered from this bondage of corruption, and shall then receive an ample amends for all their present sufferings."[3] So for Wesley and for Ward, as also for thinkers as diverse as John of the Cross and Paul Tillich,[4] animals at least among nonhuman creatures will participate in some redeemed state. Indeed both Romans 8:19–22 and the cosmic-Christological passages in Colossians 1:15–20 and Ephesians 1:10 seem to express a clear view that "the creation" (Rom. 8) and "all things" (Colossians and Ephesians) will share the benefits of God's redeeming work in Christ.

However, when I have presented the thesis of this book in various places it is always the eschatological dimension of the argument, in particular the notion that there might be animals (and even dinosaurs) in some version of "heaven," that has attracted the most controversy. This book has endeavored to bring together science, theology, and the Christian poetic imagination. This is its shortest chapter. That future in which God "will be all in all" (cf. 1 Cor. 15:28) is the subject about which science, theology, and imagination can say least.

How little purchase cosmic redemption has on Christian theology is indicated when one consults two important books on redemption published in 2004–5. David Kelsey's otherwise admirable *Imagining Redemption* never mentions the nonhuman creation at all, and the collection *The Redemption*, edited by Stephen T. Davis and colleagues, contains only one article out of fourteen referring to this aspect of redemption. This piece, by Marguerite Shuster, reviews fifty sermons on Romans 8:18–25. Of these only eight, in Shuster's view, "have explicitly or at least generally ecological concerns."[5]

Here I seek to show that an eschatological dimension is essential in formulating an evolutionary theodicy. I explore what would appear to be the minimum contours of that dimension, and try, very cautiously, to imagine how it might be pictured. To do this I must first give a general outline of how scientifically informed work on eschatology is currently developing.

5.2 ESCHATOLOGY AND COSMOLOGY

One of the clearest conclusions of contemporary cosmology is that this universe will not persist forever; it will either collapse in on itself (the so-called "big crunch"), or expand away to infinity (so-called "heat death").[6] (Long before that, this solar system will be uninhabitable.[7]) Any continuation of the matter or information in the present universe will have to be in a different form. Ted Peters emphasizes the importance of the question when he writes: "Should the final future as forecasted by the combination of big bang cosmology and the second law of thermodynamics come to pass . . . then we would have proof that our faith has been in vain. It would turn out that there is no God, at least not the God in whom followers of Jesus have put their faith."[8]

As Peters implies, the scientific conclusion summarized above demands a theological response. John Polkinghorne and Robert J. Russell are the scientist-theologians who have done most to develop this important area of the interface of science and theology.[9] Russell has set himself to explore the "worst-case," scientifically most challenging, most "dissonant" theological account of resurrection and eschatology, and then see what purchase there might be from there on a dialogue with scientific cosmology. He is in the process of exploring the implications of a view of the resurrection of Jesus as an objective transformation of matter. He sees resurrection, then, as a mighty act of God not limited by the constraints God ordinarily imposes on Godself in relation to the creation. Russell has written of God's ordinary providential engagement with the world in terms of "non-interventionist objective divine action" (see section 4.6), action that always respects the physical laws God created.[10] But Russell sees the resurrection of Christ as the beginning of a final act that will transform the character of all creation.[11] Strikingly for the purposes of our present study, this wide-ranging eschatological vision, embracing all creation, is vital to Russell for reasons of evolutionary theodicy. It is only thus that an evolutionary creation can be vindicated. He takes the same view that I noted in Pannenberg in section 1.8, to the effect that "The long sweep of evolution may not only suggest an unfinished and continuing divine creation but even more radically a creation whose theological status as 'good' may be fully realized only in the eschatological future."[12] In the terms of the title of this present book, Russell thinks we shall see the full goodness of creation only *after* its long groaning.

Polkinghorne is working with the same set of physicist's concerns about the future of matter and how life and identity might continue in a transformed cosmos. He writes:

> It seems to me that it is the essence of humanity to be embodied and that the soul is the immensely complex "information-bearing pattern" in which the ever-changing atoms of our bodies are arranged. It is surely a coherent hope that the pattern that is me will be remembered and re-embodied by God in his eschatological act of resurrection. The "matter" of that resurrected world will be the transformed matter of this dying universe, transmuted by God in his faithful action of cosmic resurrection. It will have new properties, consistent with the end of transience, death and suffering, because it will be part of a new creation, now no longer standing apart from it(s) Creator as the "other," and so paying the necessary cost of an evolutionary world's making of itself, but fully integrated with the divine life through the universal reconciliation brought about by the Cosmic Christ.[13]

This belief in a transformed version of the present universe is, however, not the only recourse in this highly speculative area. For instance, someone committed to speaking of an eternal co-development of God and the world might take refuge in a many-universes view. The heat death of this universe would leave all that was of value persisting only in the memory of God. There it would achieve at least an "objective immortality."[14] God's ongoing relationship with physical entities would take place in other universes. Some cosmologies imagine that there may be a process by which new universes frequently (on a cosmic timescale) bud off from existing ones. What remains unclear, however, is whether structure or information could possibly survive from one universe to the next.

There is a consonance between cosmology and Christian tradition in that both suggest that this present universe in its present form will have an ending or culmination (the "eschaton"), and anything that is to do with humans and their values would have to depend on God rather than presently existing physical processes for its continuation.

Is heaven, then, a place for God and humans, or a broader redemption of all creation? What are we to make of those "cosmic-Christological" texts noted above which speak of the reconciliation of all creation taking place in Christ (e.g., Col. 1:20; Eph. 1:10)? There is an urgent need for a reexploration of these texts and their implications for our understanding of our relation to the nonhuman creation. Gunton makes an important point when he writes:

> There is in the Bible no redemption, no social and personal life, apart from the creation. It is therefore reasonable, especially in the light of Old Testament witness to the creation, to hold that the Bible as a whole is concerned with the future of creation. . . . But the fact that it is Israel and Jesus who are at the centre of God's action in and towards the world means that it is the personal that is central, the non-personal peripheral. That does not rule out an ecological concern, but it cannot be of independent interest.[15]

Human personhood, then, is taken by Gunton to be of the first importance theologically, but humanity will be redeemed, ultimately, as *part* of a new creation rather than *away* from contact with the rest of creation. Scientifically informed eschatology must try and give some sort of account of what might be continuities and discontinuities between this creation and the new one. Polkinghorne's proposal is along the following lines:

Continuities and Discontinuities at the Eschaton, according to John Polkinghorne[16]

Continuity	Discontinuity
Embodiment	No transience, pain or suffering
Temporality—since this is so fundamental to our experience	No tendency to disorder. [The idea that the eschatological state will be characterized by a suspension of the second law of thermodynamics is an idea particularly developed by Russell.[17]]
Process—God will still draw us on into the fullness of the divine life	
Personhood—the "real me" will persist, though can only do so through being held, at death, within the love of God	

Vital to this present project is my conviction that scientifically informed eschatology must also try and relate the great final transforming act of God, of which the resurrection of Christ is usually regarded as the beginning, not just to continuities and discontinuities in human life but also to our understanding of God's relation to living creatures other than human beings.

5.3 MOTIVES FOR POSTULATING THE EXISTENCE OF NONHUMAN CREATURES IN A REDEEMED CREATION

The brief survey above revealed three motives for postulating that a redeemed cosmos would be far more than merely an environment for resurrected humanity:

1. A few, profoundly enigmatic scriptural texts point in that direction. I have alluded to Paul's sudden "digression" in the argument of Romans 8 to consider the fate of the creation as a whole, and to the "cosmic Christology" of Colossians and Ephesians. In two parts of Isaiah there is mention of a transformed relationship between predator and prey animals (11:6–9; 65:25—in the former passage it is clear that this transformed relationship involves humans: "a little child shall lead them" [11:6]).

2. The second reason for believing that other creatures will have a share in the life of the eschaton is that given by Gunton in the passage quoted above, a general inference from reflection on the picture Scripture offers. Humans are always envisaged, in the Bible, in the context of the rest of creation, and it would be curious if this were not carried forward into the realm in which relationships (presumably) are to be found at their richest and truest.[18]

3. We have noted in thinkers as different as John Wesley, Keith Ward, and Robert J. Russell a conviction that a theology of creation is not enough by itself to address the problem of nonhuman suffering. A conviction as to the goodness of God also requires that we invoke the doctrine of redemption, and postulate some sort of eschatological fulfillment for creatures. I now examine this point 3 in more detail.

5.4 DOES AN EVOLUTIONARY THEODICY REQUIRE REDEMPTION OF INDIVIDUAL CREATURES?

I have stressed throughout this book the way creaturely value is bound up with disvalue. The "thorn" of creaturely suffering is also the "grace" that is "sufficient" for the drawing on of creation toward new heights of consciousness, beauty, and diversity. The evolutionary naturalism of Holmes Rolston leads him to press the question, "Does Nature Need to Be Redeemed?"[19] Rolston's sense that living things find redemption by dint of the new life that is regenerated out of the death of the old allows him to reframe his question, and to affirm that life is *continually* being redeemed. Redemption need not involve new life for the individual creature. Whereas it is the strong conviction of Jürgen Moltmann that

> a *Christus evolutor* without *Christus redemptor* is nothing other than a cruel, unfeeling *Christus selector*, a historical world-judge without compassion for the weak, and a breeder of life uninterested in the victims. . . . Not even the best of all possible stages of evolution justifies acquiescence in evolution's victims. . . . There is therefore no meaningful hope for the future of creation unless "the tears are wiped from every eye." But they can only be wiped away when the dead are raised, and when the victims of evolution experience justice through the resurrection of nature. Evolution in its ambiguity has no such redemptive efficacy and therefore no salvific significance either. If Christ is to be thought of in conjunction with evolution, he must become evolution's redeemer.[20]

It will be clear from the preceding chapters that I do not regard God's creative activity in evolution as unfeeling or lacking in compassion. As I made clear in section 1.7, I regard Rolston's position as neglecting the predicament of the individual creature, and in particular the burden of theodicy implicit in the suffering of all creatures that die without fulfillment.

But suppose for a moment that Jürgen Moltmann, Robert Russell, Denis Edwards,[21] Jay McDaniel,[22] and I were wrong that theodicy requires eschatological redemption. Suppose Rolston were right in his view that systems for the exchange of value in creation provide their own compensation, so that there is no "excess" burden of theodicy attached to creaturely suffering within those systems. My first two reasons for invoking the presence of nonhuman creatures in heaven—based on scriptural hints and general theological reasoning—would still apply. So the very difficult task of trying to imagine a new creation within which transience, death, and suffering are at an end, and containing creatures other than humans, would not be eliminated. I spell out the need for this imaginative exercise to show that it is not undertaken lightly or out of mere sentimentality, but rather because Christian teaching seems to require it.

Polkinghorne, who has tended to concentrate in his writing both on theodicy and on eschatology, on the predicament and hope of human beings, rebukes other theologians for too anthropocentric an attitude to eschatology, which "has made it difficult for many of them to appreciate fully the necessarily cosmic scope of the Creator's total concern."[23] Yet he himself limits the involvement of animals in the eschatological sphere. They will be there as types rather than as individuals, pets being an arguable exception.[24] Russell hints at the same reticence and parsimony over heaven. Having said in his 2005

Goshen Lectures that "the suffering of prehuman life must not be justified as a 'means-end' to humanity. There is no way to justify the notion of the suffering of nature, by claiming that it's somehow worth it because we got here. That's simply offensive," he goes on, "Well, each creature, *or species at least*, must have an eschatological future of its own."[25]

I concede that simple organisms may possess little distinctive individual experience or agency, and they may be represented in the eschaton as types rather than individuals. However, to assume that that is the situation of all creatures, including higher animals, runs the risk of not doing full justice either to the richness of individual animal experience, or to the theodicy problems that evolutionary creation poses. Simple organisms may be agreed to have little sentience, but in more complex creatures with sophisticated mechanisms of perception and the processing of pain, it is individual centers of experience that are subject to intense suffering, and individual animal lives that sometimes experience little or nothing of the fulfilled life that I explored in section 4.4.[26] I draw here on Polkinghorne's own logic in the chapter just quoted. He writes of human beings:

> We shall all die with our lives incomplete, with possibilities unfulfilled and with hurts unhealed. This will be true even of those fortunate enough to die peacefully in honoured old age. How much more must it be true of those who die prematurely and painfully, through disease, famine, war or neglect. If God is the Father of our Lord Jesus Christ, all the generations of oppressed and exploited people must have the prospect of a life beyond death, in which they will receive what was unjustly denied them in this life.[27]

There are interesting links between this argument and the suggestion I advanced in section 4.5 that the character of human existence is such that humans' selving is, unlike any other creature's, only found in the self-transcendence of self-giving love; it is never wholly fulfilled, because its fulfillment is ultimately found within the life of God. I claimed that, in contrast, the life of nonhuman creatures—particular lives, not just the life of the type—can experience periods of fulfillment which fully consummate that life. But clearly there are very many creatures for whom there is no such fulfillment; there is only frustration, disease, and famine, premature and painful death. And if we take seriously the hints in Colossians and Ephesians of the cosmic character of the redemption of creation in Christ, then all these creatures, we might equally argue, must have the prospect of fulfillment. This follows as soon as one rejects Polkinghorne's conclusion that animals are only representatives of their types, and considers instead their individual suffering.

It is interesting to reflect on the caution that comes over both Polkinghorne and Russell when considering the inhabitants of heaven. One of the central points of Russell's eschatology is that the second law of thermodynamics (which insists that in physical systems the overall degree of disorder must tend to increase, and that therefore decay will necessarily occur) is an element, perhaps the key element, that will be changed in the new creation.[28] But along with that must surely go the implication that there is no competition for resources, no shortage of space in heaven. We should therefore be bold in our trust of the redemptive grace of God that will populate it.

This leaves open the question of whether Moltmann is right—that "If we were to surrender hope for as much as one single creature, for us God would not be God,"[29] which would seem to imply that every creature is redeemed— or whether only those creatures that have not known creaturely flourishing gain a transformed existence. Also an open question is whether, if the new life is only a compensation for previous lack of fulfillment, such an existence need be an eternal one, or whether after a period of struggle-free flourishing a redeemed animal life might fade away? (We do not postulate that of redeemed human life, because of the promises of Scripture, and also because of a sense that human life at its truest is at home with God in a deep and eternal sense. Do we want to say any less for other creatures?) Again, if our logic tells us that the fullness of redeemed life will be lived in relationship with a whole range of other creatures, will that include creatures humans never knew, because they were extinct before we evolved? These, again, are unanswerable questions, but their difficulty does not dilute the importance of affirming redemption of evolutionary creation. All my three indicators, described in section 5.3 above, tend to compel a view that some individuals of every species may be expected to have some life with God in the eschaton. What kind of existence might that be?

5.5 EXPLORING A REDEEMED EXISTENCE FOR CREATURES AT THE ESCHATON

We saw in chapter 3 that Jay McDaniel's concern for the insurance pelican chick leads him to the conviction that "if the chick does continue in some way . . . it becomes imaginable that, in time, the pelican would experience his own fulfillment of needs and interests, his own redemption."[30] It may be asked, what is the evidence for such a "pelican heaven"? Christians have clues to the resurrected character of human existence in the resurrection appearances of Jesus, and Paul's discussion of resurrection bodies in 1 Corinthians 15, but there is very little to go on in respect of other creatures.

In particular it is very hard to make use of the eschatological visions we find in Isaiah (e.g., 11:6, the leopard lying down with the kid). They are, as Thomas

Sieger Derr puts it, "hope without details."[31] It is very hard to see how the leopardness of leopards could be fulfilled in eschatological coexistence with kids. Sideris therefore abandons all hope of making any use of these passages.[32] The poetry of Isaiah envisions animals in the new creation, but in transformed relationship that nevertheless allows them to continue to be themselves, and (perhaps most crucially in terms of the likely original sense of the passage) safeguards the relationships of animals to human beings. What these tantalizing texts do not resolve is how the eschatological fulfillment of creatures relates to their protological natures, how they were in the old creation, and the limited nature of their selving.[33]

Perhaps the easiest scheme to postulate is one based on "objective immortality,"[34] in the sense that the creatures' experience lives in the memory of God. John Haught is attracted to this view, that "the whole story of the universe and life streams into the everlasting bosom of divine compassion."[35] Such a scheme effectively dodges the difficulty in imagining a transformed relation between, for example, predator and prey animals. The experience of leopardness and antelopeness, presumably, can be held together without problem in the mind of God, since it was there that they were first imagined (see section 4.4). Thomas Hosinski puts it like this: ultimate providence is a "redemption of the suffering, fragmented, disharmonious world," in which "all creatures are not simply received into God, but are transformed, 'purged' and harmonised in the everlasting unity of God's own life."[36]

McDaniel acknowledges the power of such explanations. He reflects on the case of a gray whale systematically battered to death (being eaten alive in the process) by a pack of orcas. In such a case, he asserts, it is vital to consider redemption. He writes, "The grey whale and the orca are brought together in God's experience, as they never were in their own, and they are, in this way 'redeemed.'"[37] But McDaniel also hopes with John Wesley that subjective immortality is there for animals. "The problem is not death, it is incompleteness." The journeys of animals continue "into a still deeper form of satisfaction that represents union with the Soul itself. Once this union is realised, death can occur."[38]

Haught in his study *Deeper Than Darwin* is clearly tempted to go beyond objective immortality. He cites the passage in Tennyson's *In Memoriam* that engaged us in section 1.1, with its conviction that "not a worm is cloven in vain . . . or but subserves another's gain,"[39] and writes: "If Tennyson's hope is a realistic one, there must be some way in which the centres of striving that we call living beings would have the opportunity to attain a fulfillment proportionate to their striving."[40] But Haught is reluctant to speculate far in this direction. He continues, "What this would mean for other species of life is impossible to say."[41] Haught's instincts remain in the direction of a scheme based on objective immortality, as in this conclusion: "Somehow every event in cosmic process is salvaged and preserved eternally in God in full immediacy."[42]

I agree with McDaniel that the easiest picture of eschatological survival of creatures—an objective immortality based on survival in the memory of God—does not seem quite to do justice to the type of instance that I identified as the most problematic for theodicy. This was the case of creatures whose lives in the old creation know no flourishing, not even significant elements of the experience of what it is to be that creature, because they are killed so young, or are born with a profoundly debilitating disease. As McDaniel notes in the passage just quoted, "The problem is not death, it is incompleteness." It is tempting to press further, and explore a form of subjective immortality such as McDaniel's own proposal of "pelican heaven"[43] in which pelicanness is expressed, presumably still in relation to other creatures, without competition or frustration on the part of predator or prey. That would seem to be the closest parallel to the Christian belief in the bodily resurrection of humans, and to do most honor to Gunton's point that humans are always depicted in Scripture in the context of the rest of creation. If resurrected humans are to experience the presence of other resurrected creatures, that would seem to point to those creatures experiencing themselves, and hence to a sort of subjective immortality.

Denis Edwards provided a rich reflection on this issue in an article published in 2006.[44] He considers four possibilities: universal resurrection, which he reads as the position of Moltmann;[45] objective immortality as outlined by Whitehead and taken up more recently by Haught; a modification of the latter to include subjective existence at the eschaton, as per McDaniel; and "material inscription," a suggestion of the South African scholar Ernst Conradie.[46] Conradie regards the history of the cosmos as "inscribed in the eschaton," so that "nothing is lost," but indeed the "much richer depth dimensions" of the eschaton allow for the "transformation of the history of the cosmos."[47] "All will appear in the light of Christ's redemptive work. . . . Perhaps there may even be room for a new completion of the life stories of those who died violently and prematurely. . . . This coming alive . . . is an embodied celebration in which everyone, inscribed in the history of the cosmos, can participate in God's presence."[48]

This is a subtle idea to which Edwards is much attracted. He himself would want to insist on the role of the Holy Spirit as the one who inscribes the life of creatures in the divine life. He agrees with McDaniel that redemption for each creature will be in a form appropriate to that creature. While for some creatures that may be a subjective immortality, for others it may be that of being held in the eternal life of the Trinity and the communion of saints.[49] Lastly, he follows my own conviction that humans have a calling to participate in the healing of the world, and points to the eucharist as the classic place where that calling is enacted.[50]

Difficult questions remain. It is very hard to imagine any form of being a predator that nevertheless does not "hurt or destroy" on the "holy mountain" of God (cf. Isa. 11:9). What could the life of a predator look like in the absence of the second law of thermodynamics, and the imperative of ingesting ordered energy to ward off the ever-present slide into decay? Here I draw on a poem by James Dickey[51] that offers a fine image of the unimaginable, and which is worth quoting in full.

The Heaven of Animals

Here they are. The soft eyes open.
If they have lived in a wood
It is a wood.
If they have lived on plains
It is grass rolling
Under their feet forever.

Having no souls, they have come,
Anyway, beyond their knowing.
Their instincts wholly bloom
And they rise.
The soft eyes open.

To match them, the landscape flowers,
Outdoing, desperately
Outdoing what is required:
The richest wood,
The deepest field.

For some of these,
It could not be the place
It is, without blood.
These hunt, as they have done,
But with claws and teeth grown perfect,

More deadly than they can believe.
They stalk more silently,
And crouch on the limbs of trees,
And their descent
Upon the bright backs of their prey

May take years
In a sovereign floating of joy.
And those who are hunted

Know this as their life,
Their reward: to walk

Under such trees in full knowledge
Of what is in glory above them,
And to feel no fear,
But acceptance, compliance.
Fulfilling themselves without pain

At the cycle's center,
They tremble, they walk
Under the tree,
They fall, they are torn,
They rise, they walk again.

Dickey pictures the descent of heavenly predators on their prey as "a sovereign floating of joy" which "may take years," and the prey animals as feeling "no fear / But acceptance, compliance." The poem ends, "They fall, they are torn / They rise, they walk again."[52] This is a heaven, then, that preserves the characteristics of species, but without pain or death or destruction. Note the difference between this and the Isaianic vision of predator and prey "lying down together," and even (most difficult of all for the biochemically minded) of carnivores eating straw. Dickey's vision seems to me much truer to the scheme of continuity and discontinuity offered by Polkinghorne (see section 5.2).

Does such a heaven involve some sort of self-transcended pelicanness that is even harder for us to imagine, perhaps even involving an experience for the redeemed prey-animal that delights in the beauty and flourishing of the predator, and vice versa? This is a question theologians can never resolve, any more than we can say what would be fulfillment for the parasitic organisms that so exercised Darwin, or for the bacteria and viruses that only thrive as pathogens.[53] That we find it so difficult to picture these states of being may reduce confidence in their reality, but I return the reader to the three telling reasons for believing in some type of after-death existence for nonhuman creatures: specific scriptural texts, a general sense that human life at its richest will be set in the context of relationship with other creatures, and the need to marry a sense of the goodness of God with the evident lack of blessedness in the lives of many creatures (see section 5.3). These considerations do not depend on an ability to picture what the resurrection life of nonhuman creatures is like, any more than a belief in the findings of quantum mechanics depends on an ability to picture its often unpicturable and sometimes logically contradictory conclusions. Haught again: "It is not beyond reason to trust that [God's] eternal care could also transform local cosmic contradictions into a wider harmony of contrasts, that is, into an unfathomable depth of beauty, and that our own destiny beyond death admits of conscious enjoyment of this beauty as well."[54]

5.6 WHY DID GOD NOT JUST CREATE HEAVEN?

Intriguing as these speculations are, they must not be allowed to obscure the robust theological challenge that any scheme of eschatological compensation must face. Lurking behind all these formulations of redeemed life at the eschaton is the question: why, if an altered physics makes possible an altered and pain-free cosmos, did God not create this in the first place? For Wesley Wildman this is yet another severe problem for "determinate-entity theism"—indeed, he writes:

> I suspect that the fruit of theoretical success in articulating a coherent eschatology would only be theological disaster for determinate-entity theism. It would only reinforce skeptical questions about God's humanly recognizable moral goodness by introducing an embodiment scheme that boasts growth and change and relationality yet no suffering. In other words, *that* world and *not this* world would be the best of all possible worlds. Such a God would be flagrantly morally inconsistent.[55]

Augustine was well aware of this question of why God did not create a "better" world. His reply was that for all we know God did, but our task is to orient ourselves with love. That will not quite satisfy the modern theodicist, since we have had to face throughout this book the problem that the same process that gives rise to creaturely value also—and necessarily—involves suffering and extinction. I showed in section 3.3 that a key part of a theodicist's response would be to assert that an evolutionary scheme was the only way to give rise to such creaturely values. The response to Wildman's challenge to eschatology can only be an extension of that same argument—to reassert that this evolutionary environment, full as it is of both competition and decay, is the only type of creation that can give rise to creaturely selves. We know that, in the physics with which we are familiar, self-organization—and hence the growth of complexity, and the origin of complex selves—depends on so-called dissipative processes, in turn based on the second law of thermodynamics. This is the way creaturely selves arise. Since this was the world the God of all creativity and all compassion chose for the creation of creatures, we must presume that this was the only type of world that would do for that process. In other words, our guess must be that though heaven can eternally preserve those selves, subsisting in suffering-free relationship, it could not give rise to them in the first place.

So we are returned to our theme of creaturely selves. The best clues we can glean in respect of eschatological fulfillment will come from the case of the human being, an animal among other animals, but one with such profoundly novel emergent characteristics of selving as to engender a whole set of fresh possibilities in its relation to God. It is therefore to theological anthropology—how Christian thinkers understand human being—and to the calling of humans in respect of other creatures that I turn in the final two chapters.

6

The Call of Humanity

6.1 CREATION GROANING IN TRAVAIL

I showed in section 2.6 why I find it unhelpful to think of the "travail" of evolutionary creation as being always and everywhere the result of human sin or other rebellion against God. It is agreed by almost all commentators on Paul's description of creation's "travail" ("labor pains," NRSV) in Romans 8 that the one who subjected creation to "futility" was God, who subjected it "in hope." I begin this chapter by looking in more detail at this key text from Romans,[1] and go on from there to explore the calling of redeemed humanity. In the last chapter I examine two possible ways in which humans might exercise this calling. The passage reads in full:

> For I reckon that the sufferings of the present critical time cannot compare with the coming glory to be revealed to us. For the eager expectation of the creation awaits the revelation of the sons of God. For the creation was subjected to futility, not voluntarily but rather on account of the one who subjected it—in hope—because the creation itself will also be set free from its enslavement to corruption to obtain liberation [consisting] of the glory for the children of God. For we know that the whole creation groans together and travails together until now, and not only [the creation] but even ourselves who have the firstfruits of the Spirit, even we ourselves, groan within ourselves as we await the redemption of our body. (Rom. 8:18–23, translation by Jewett)[2]

As Hunt et al. note, "Writers on ecotheology have cited this passage ever since the field itself emerged. Many of these appeals to Romans 8 are quite brief references in general support of envisaging a positive future for the whole of creation,[3] or to encapsulate the environmental crisis (creation groaning).[4]

Others emphasise nature's value to God by using our passage to support their claims for the inclusion of nonhuman creation in God's redemptive project."

For example, "An Evangelical Declaration on the Care of Creation" (1994) declares "full good news for all creation which is still waiting 'with eager longing for the revealing of the children of God.' "[5] However, with the notable exception of R. J. Berry,[6] few of these writers offer developed engagement with biblical texts such as Romans 8. Hunt et al. conclude, "There is a general neglect of the exegetical uncertainties of the passage and its context in the letter to the Romans, and little willingness to explore in detail its ecotheological implications."

Paul's text itself is frustratingly brief and allusive. I can only agree with Neil Messer who wrote recently that "considerable reticence is in order as to the nature of this futility and the manner of this liberation."[7]

There are two key areas in this text that make it inappropriate as a mere ecotheological mantra. First is the troubling assertion that God has subjected the creation to futility.[8] This motif is elided by many ecological writers in their anxiety to profit from the notion of creation groaning in travail. To take this subjection fully into account, recognizing that we are not told what it means or how we can understand it within a contemporary picture of the dynamics of evolving ecosystems, is to realize that this is a yet more enigmatic narrative of God and world than is often appreciated.

The second major point to note is the evident anthropocentrism of the passage. As Hunt et al. note, "the redemption of the sons of God stands at the center of the story and is, indeed, the focus of the hopes of creation."

It is worth at this point drawing on a distinction proposed by Lukas Vischer between anthropomonism and anthropocentrism. Anthropomonism, in Vischer's terms, is the view that it is only human beings who are of concern in the redeeming purposes of God; human interests are exclusively important and creation exists only to serve those interests. Anthropocentrism, by contrast, he regards as accepting that human beings are of central importance in the divine economy of salvation, but not thereby implying that there is no value or eschatological purpose for the rest of creation. Vischer writes, "Anthropocentrism in the sense of anthropomonism must be rejected" but that "if anthropocentrism refers to the fact that human beings are called to fulfil a special and specific role in [the] world, it must be maintained."[9] Brendan Byrne, too, despite writing within the Earth Bible Project which sets its face against anthropocentrism,[10] acknowledges that there is a more positive view of the potential of human activity which "remains anthropocentric in the sense of according to human beings a determining role in the world (which is, after all, factually the case). But it can hardly be called anthropocentric in a negative, self-regarding, and exploitative sense."[11] Hunt et al. submit that:

a chastened and humble anthropocentrism must remain central to an ecological theology, not only because, as Richard Bauckham points out, human beings evidently do, *de facto*, have "unique power to affect most of the rest of creation on this planet,"[12] but also because it is human beings whom we address and to whom we look for responsible action in relation to creation's future. Romans 8 does indeed provide interesting resources for such an ecological anthropocentrism, since it depicts creation, humanity and the spirit as conjoined in a chorus of hopeful groaning, and links creation's hope with that of humanity, and specifically that of the "children of God."[13] The story of creation, then, is a forward-looking story in which a tragic state is being transformed, with much suffering and struggle, into one of liberation. The reason for the tragic state is not given, nor are its causes analyzed; the focus, rather, is on the co-struggles of humans and nonhuman creation that lead to freedom and glory.

Some of Paul's statements about the Christ-event stress the transformation that has already been effected in Christ (e.g., Rom. 5:18–19; 2 Cor. 5:17), but generally it is clear that this is a *process*, decisively begun yet still to be worked out through suffering and struggle (e.g., Phil. 3:12–14; Col. 1:24). Hunt et al. conclude, "Romans 8 is a particularly developed and powerful depiction of this narrative of struggle, with its insistence that it is only in conformity to the sufferings of Christ that a sharing in his glory and inheritance is attained (8:17), a narrative in which vv. 19–23 so enigmatically include the whole of creation as co-groaning."[14]

I now offer an admittedly speculative reading of key terms in Romans 8:19–22 in the light of contemporary science. I would see the "futility" to which God subjected creation as the futility of the evolutionary process. In such a process there is "a time for every matter under heaven: a time to be born, and a time to die" (to quote from the famous opening of chapter 3 of the book of Ecclesiastes, the principal source in the Greek translation of the Old Testament of the word usually translated "futility" in Rom. 8:20). There is, as I showed in chapter 1, great value generated within this "futile" cycle of birth and death.[15] But the process of evolution is profoundly ambiguous, abounding in suffering and tragedy, but also beauty and ingenuity of strategy. Occasionally a species does transcend its own nature and give rise to fresh possibilities, which in turn fall into their rhythm of birth and death. Once the process of selving and self-transcendence (see sections 4.4–4.5) had reached a certain level of complexity, God was able—through the incarnation of the divine Son within a creature—to inaugurate the process of redemption. Out of the "futility" of the evolutionary process, and the extinction of over 98 percent of the species that have ever lived, came, precariously and eventually, "hope." The rhythm of nature's birthing and dying, with all the creaturely suffering that we have seen necessarily attends it, awaited the ultimate self-transcendence of the humanity of the Christ, whose dying and rising again inaugurated a new era of possibilities. In this era human beings can find their liberty, and in doing so be transformed from one degree of glory to another (2 Cor. 3:18), and the creation itself will find liberation.

I showed in the last chapter that there were good reasons to suppose that in the "new creation" toward which the Scriptures point there will be non-human creatures living some form of resurrection life. Clearly that transformation, involving creaturely identity and experience passing through death and being reembodied in a new form of existence, must depend solely on the power and grace of God; no human initiative could bring this about, or even influence the process. So to look for signs of what the freedom of the children of God might be, and what it might make possible—in partnership with the purposes of God—we must look not at the final eschatological transformation, but into what Bonhoeffer called the "penultimate,"[16] and what a Christian vision of the ultimate might mean for human behavior in anticipation of the eschaton.

I infer from Rom. 8:21, creation's liberty awaiting that of humankind, that humans have a very special and specific role in the world. I also hold with Moltmann that the evolutionary process is in need of healing (see section 5.4). Again, I am not advancing the view that the process has been damaged by fallenness (see section 2.6) but rather that the process itself is necessarily ambiguous (chaps. 1 and 4). It therefore cannot be the last word in God's relation to creation, the state corresponding to the divine life becoming "all in all" (1 Cor. 15:28).

I propose, then, that the evolutionary struggle of creation can be read as being the "travail" to which God subjected creation in hope that the values of complex life, and ultimately freely choosing creatures such as ourselves, would emerge. It is, as Paul's language hints, a struggle that gives birth. It is a struggle in which humans and the nonhuman creation groan together, in which humans share by hard work[17] in giving birth to new possibilities of life. Norman Habel has offered a fine reading of Genesis 1 in terms of God as midwife of creation.[18] The view offered here is that, in some sense, human beings can be—if not the midwives of the new creation[19]—then at least among those that attend the birth, hold creation by the hand, and boil water as needed.

To reiterate the cautionary word I issued in section 1.8, I am not supposing for a moment that Paul of Tarsus knew anything of thermodynamics or Darwinian evolution. He may well have been dwelling, in writing of creation's "enslavement to corruption" (or "bondage to decay," as it is often translated), on the sin of Adam and God's subsequent cursing of the ground. But it is worth noting that the passage does not refer directly to the fall story of Genesis 3, also that God's action in subjecting the creation is described as being "in hope," not in punishment.[20] There is therefore a consonance between a fall-free reading of this text and contemporary scientific understandings of evolution. This consonance, as I hope to show, can be generative for our approach to understanding our calling in respect of the nonhuman creation.[21]

Such a reading of Romans 8:19–23 would suggest that the working out of the freedom of the children of God will be to do with humans having some part in the healing of the evolutionary process, and that is the suggestion I take up in chapter 7.[22]

6.2 THE FREEDOM OF THE GLORY
OF THE CHILDREN OF GOD

As I indicated in section 4.4, Orthodox thought has some intensely interesting insights to contribute to our understanding of the creation. John Zizioulas writes of the Orthodox understanding of freedom that it is "not, as with modern Western philosophy, a moral or psychological notion including the capacity of choice, but indicat[ing] the ability to affirm or deny the very existence of something involving one's own existence."[23] I take this to mean the freedom to affirm or deny the sovereignty of God as well as "to either destroy creation or affirm its existence."[24] Zizioulas goes on, "Human freedom lies in the tendency to *transcend* the limitations of nature to the point of denying nature itself or anything *given*."[25] That insight extends the analysis of self-transcendence that I gave in sections 4.4–4.5. I wrote there of the human as the creature in whom the possibility of self-transcendence had evolved to a very pronounced degree. That in itself gives rise to the freedom of which Zizioulas writes, the freedom to affirm or deny our creaturely status and our common inheritance with the nonhuman creation. In turn, that makes possible the truer freedom of the self-given self, the self freely offered to others and to God.

Another great Orthodox insight is of the cosmic significance of the eucharist,[26] and it is in eucharist that this human freedom is seen at its most characteristic. In the power of the Spirit, the self is offered, utterly, back to God whose Word made possible all selving, and in doing so the self is caught up in the life of the Trinity whose essence is self-giving. Not that the individual is caught up alone, but always in communion with others and with the creation, symbolized in the bread and the wine which are both "fruit of the earth and work of human hands." Paul saw that the true freedom of the human is made possible only by the work of Christ. Only when we are attuned to the love of Christ, rather than consumed by our own desires and fear of pain,[27] do we taste in communion the full glory of our freedom. And it is in communion that our freedom is continually renewed for the service of God and others. I return to the theme of eucharist in section 6.8 below.

6.3 HUMANS AS CONTEMPLATIVES OF CREATION

In the rest of the chapter I explore how this freedom in Christ might enable humans to work out their true role and calling in respect of the nonhuman world. I consider this first under the heading of *contemplation—seeing* the creation aright; and then under the heading of *ethics*, how to consider wisely our status and impact in relation to creation; and finally *vocation*, what is our God-given calling? In the last chapter I go on to discuss examples of *praxis*—what we might *do* as freed people in the era of God's healing of creation.

First, then, I consider the freedom truly to see the creation for itself. It will be clear from section 1.4 how important I regard it as being that the natural world is seen truly, not oversimplified or romanticized but seen for the place of suffering, struggle, and beauty that it is. Yet it is to a Romantic poet, once again to Gerard Manley Hopkins, that I turn for insight into such seeing. In section 4.4 I appropriated Hopkins's concept of "selving" to assist in the understanding of a creation both originating from the divine love and also evolving through natural selection. Another product of Hopkins's highly original poetic and metaphysical intelligence is his terminology of "inscape" and "instress."[28]

"Inscape" is a much-discussed term,[29] but for our purposes here the inscape of an entity may be considered to contain what sort of thing it is scientifically—the patterns and regularities that govern its existence—but also its particularity, its "thisness."[30] As I noted in section 4.4, every creature has both its pattern of life and membership of its species, and also its particularity as an individual creature. The scientific account of an organism is based on trends, regularities, patterns, over a range of individuals; the perception of the particularity of a specific creature, its "thisness," is more the preserve of the poet and contemplative.

Hopkins has another, related term—"instress"—which is still more difficult to pin down than "inscape." The poet seems to use "instress" for the cohesive energy that binds individual entities into the Whole, the impact the inscape of entities makes on the observer, and the observer's will to receive that impact.[31] Theologically, one might associate all three of these aspects of the relation of humans to other creatures with the work of the Holy Spirit, the "go-between God."[32] We shall see below that it is also possible for creatures to instress inappropriately, not discerning the work of God.

The value of this odd terminology is that it gives full value to descriptions of entities in scientific terms, as being examples of whatever class of entities they belong to, but also acknowledges their particularity and createdness.[33] Hopkins was keenly interested in the sort of description of the world we now call science (as witness his letters to *Nature* about sunsets[34]). But W. H. Gardner says of him that he would have parted company with the (scientific) rationalists in saying that "the human spirit must be nourished by the spurting fountains of supra-rational instress, by that 'deep poetry' which is nothing less than intuitive ontology—the knowledge of the essence and being of all things."[35] My contention is that this is a helpful way to consider what, for example, the early human cave-artists of the Cro-Magnon era (thirty thousand to twelve thousand years ago) were attempting. They strove to be deep poets of their environment as well as hunter-gatherers within it, both to see "their" animals and to "see through" them to a deeper reality.

That thought may be considered untestable, and therefore unimportant. Sadly, though paleoanthropologists may learn many things about the Cro-Magnon in the future, we shall never know much about what Hopkins would have called their "pitch," their inner sense of individuality, of being themselves, and how it caused them to view the world. Where they are of particular importance for my argument here is in terms of how humans have evolved—culturally and biologically—since then.

The biggest single cultural development has, of course, been agriculture. Though it is noteworthy the extent to which trade, and sophisticated social distinctions, seem already to have existed within prehistoric hunter-gatherer societies, agriculture gave human communities unprecedented power to alter the biodiversity of ecosystems, and to establish societies containing groups with the leisure to plan such transformations. Significantly, however, this has not been accompanied, on any large scale, by prudent conservation of the resources that allowed those communities to thrive. As I noted in section 4.5, quoting J. Wentzel van Huyssteen, "*Homo Sapiens* is not only distinguished by its remarkable embodied brain, by a stunning mental cognitive fluidity expressed in imagination, creativity, linguistic abilities, and symbolic propensities. As real-life, embodied persons of flesh and blood we humans are also affected by hostility, arrogance, ruthlessness and cunning"[36]—and, he might have added, a thoroughly short-sighted view of our own self-interest. As far as we can judge, it has always been so. Just as human hunter-gatherers were instrumental in many prey species going extinct, so there is evidence from as long ago as 1600 BCE of human over-farming leading to "the land bellowing like a bull."[37] The assumption that pre-technological human societies were always somehow in tune with, and lived sustainably in, their surroundings receives little support from the anthropological record.[38]

To go back to the terminology we have been using, humans have frequently failed to instress their environment in a way that enabled them to understand the need to preserve that environment's ability to sustain them.[39] Humans have transformed many environments, but often in ways that profoundly damaged ecological richness, and moreover which contributed ultimately to the unusability of that land for that purpose.[40]

6.4 HUMAN NATURE—SCIENTIFIC AND THEOLOGICAL UNDERSTANDINGS

I offer here first an ecological and then a theological description of the sort of creatures agricultural humans have been. Ecologically, one could claim as Reg Morrison does that with the advent of agriculture humans altered their ecological profile and by doing so became a "plague mammal."[41]

What is remarkable, particularly in the light of the accuracy and "deep poetry" with which, judging by their cave paintings, our ancestors seem to have instressed the creatures of the nonhuman world even thirty thousand years ago, is that humans still find it so hard to operate to their long-term self-interest. The current crisis over climate change can be seen as just the latest example of our inability to look to our long-term self-interest as a species. I contend that there is a profound unwillingness on the part of most contemporary human societies to understand the nonhuman world at a deep imaginative level, to instress it.[42] As a result, wherever humans interact with the nonhuman creation it tends to become impoverished, a travesty of itself.

I give a small but revealing instance from my own recent observations. On a brief visit to Japan in 2005 I went to the first capital of ancient imperial Japan, Nara. On the edge of Nara is a fine park where some of the major shrines are to be found, and within which is a herd of protected deer. On my first day I walked in the outer reaches of the park and came upon a group of these deer browsing in a meadow. They were as I have always experienced (instressed) deer, cautious herbivores to be found in elaborate social groupings, usually with the males and females separate, keeping a wary eye on the human observer. The beauty of their inscape rests not only on their grace of movement but on their social relationships and their wariness of predators, all the product of millions of years of evolution. On my second day, near the temples of Nara, deer biscuits were on sale for the tourists to buy and amuse themselves by feeding the creatures. The behavior of the deer was a revelation. They pushed and jostled one another (and humans) around the biscuit stall, males mixed up with females as they shoved and snatched. Two completely different animal behaviors, within a mile of one another. One of my abiding memories of Nara (in many other ways a fascinating and delightful place) is of a small Japanese child howling and hiding behind her parent's leg because the aggressiveness of the deer had frightened her. Perhaps that will be her impression of what deer are like for many years to come. But she had not seen, or felt, deer as they truly are, only the travesty of their behavior caused by humans using them as a source of amusement.

Clearly there are far more enlightened examples of sustainable practice, and informed and low-impact relationships with wild nature, in all sorts of places across the world. But that we are a species which routinely destroys habitats for our own purposes, and compromises evolved patterns of animal behavior, cannot be denied. Ecological descriptions, of course, offer no prescription. They do not say how things ought to be. They merely note that human beings are a particular sort of species, a plague mammal—if that term be accepted—with a long track record for transforming, and impoverishing, a range of ecosystems. Our adapted mechanisms of behavior, our evolved rationality, do not enable us to grasp the complexity of the relation between our local and our global, our short- and our long-term interest—or to the extent that we do grasp this, we are unable to form large-scale communities committed to ecologically sustainable practice.

What then of theological description? One way to formulate human unwisdom and unsustainability of practice would be by saying that humans have failed to have that mind "that was in Christ Jesus" (Phil. 2:5); they have made their advantage and glory a "snatching-matter."[43] Hopkins said of Lucifer that his sin was an exclusive "instressing his own inscape,"[44] adoring his own image rather than that of God in the servanthood of God's Christ. That constituted his fall. While not wishing to pursue the language of a historical fall, still less one from a Edenic paradisal state (see section 2.6), it is possible to regard this snatching at resources, and humans' admiring of their own image and ingenuity at the expense of truly working to understand the nonhuman world, as an index of our "fallenness." To talk of servanthood, of refusing to snatch at status or advantage, is commonplace in the discussion of right relationships between Christians, but has been sadly lacking in addressing relationships with the nonhuman world.

Humans, then, can be thought of as fallen, not only in interpersonal relationships but in relation to other creatures and our environment as a whole. A more positive way to look at our place in the world is that our true environment includes God; we can never and shall never "find our place" on this planet unless we find our home with and in the love of God, the one in whom we live and move and have our being (Acts 17:28).[45] Finding our home would mean recognizing (instressing) God's creative activity in all other species as well as our own.

All of this is not to deny the sheer extent of the challenge posed by living as a population of over 6 billion, a population within which exists huge and seemingly intractable poverty, and also huge and seemingly insatiable material aspiration. We shall need all our rationality, our poetry, and our ingenuity to engage with the challenges that now confront us. Our contemplation of and engagement with the nonhuman world must be based on a scientifically informed understanding—not merely a romanticization of wilderness, but a Darwinian appreciation of its processes.[46] But science can only take us so far. It is from theology, again, that we derive the ethical imperative to make of our lives a pattern of healing servanthood, from which the snatching that has been such a strong instinct of ours has been banished forever. The implications for human being of the theological position I developed in chapter 4 could be summarized as follows: What God fathers forth, for which he is always to be praised, is in its truest inscape the Word, which plays in return in all selving and all self-giving love to the Father. The Christ immanent in the inscapes of the world is always the suffering Christ, the Christ that bears the "no" along with creation's "yes," the Christ that bears the "no" of the human will, the Christ that-would-be-crucified. That is the Christ we discern, if our instressing of the world is true. But it is by the actual self-emptying sacrifice of Christ, the actual extremity of divine commitment to the world, the extremity that is the hinge of history, that humans are freed to make a Spirit-guided response to God and the world, a response that is not fueled by greed or addictions.

6.5 ETHICAL KENOSIS

This brings us back to the concept of kenosis, which I reviewed with some suspicion in section 4.3. I explained there it may be sounder to reserve the concept of divine self-emptying for the self-giving love within the Godhead, on the one hand, and the example of Christ's self-surrender and service on the other. For humans to respond to that example is to cultivate "ethical kenosis," putting the needs of other humans and other creatures above one's own selfish ends. I now analyze this in more detail.[47]

The first element in such ethical kenosis, after the example of Christ, is what I call kenosis of aspiration. Like Christ, the believer is called not to make of status a "snatching-matter" (see above), not to aspire to a status beyond that which is most helpful to other creatures. The essence of a kenosis of aspiration is of resisting the temptation to grasp at a role that is not God-given, not part of the calling of the individual believer or community. The consequence of such grasping is at once to fail to respect fully the status of the other creature, and to fail to receive our situation as gift from God. This is the sense in which I believe the Genesis 3 account of the Fall has a profound wisdom to it. It is an account of the tendency in human nature to grasp at more than is freely given, to seek to elevate our status beyond what is appropriate and helpful, to seek to be "as Gods." So Simone Weil writes: true love means "to empty ourselves of our false divinity, to deny ourselves, to give up being the centre of the world."[48]

And just as the Fall account in Genesis reflects a general condition rather than a historical chronology, so the status of believers as being "in Christ" is a general condition that reverses our fallenness, and makes possible the self-transcending life of which I wrote in section 4.5.

With kenosis of aspiration, however, must go a kenosis of appetite. It is possible to think of sin as "a compulsion towards attitudes and actions not always of [humans'] own willing or approving," a power that prevents humankind from recognizing its own nature.[49] This may be a compulsion to desire status over against God—the greatest and most pernicious of sins, and therefore the one on which the Genesis 3 account focuses. But it may be for power over others or for sex for sex's sake or for an excess of intake of alcohol, drugs, food, or sensation of whatever kind. All these draw us into idolatry; they make of a substance or experience a kind of substitute god. All drain away the freedom that comes from worshipful dependence on God. Particularly evidently in respect of the ecological crisis, disordered appetite harms our freedom to contemplate appropriately, and relate lovingly to, the nonhuman creation. Such appetite consumes more of the world's fullness[50] than is our share. The application of this principle of kenosis of appetite is widespread; it applies to deforestation to expand farmland for excess export crops, but also to the high-food-mile demands of the West which fuel so many unsustainable practices, to the taking of spurious long-haul flights as well as the frittering away of carbon-intensive energy in so many human dwellings.

A particular aspect of the kenosis of appetite, which links it to the kenosis of aspiration, is the kenosis of acquisitiveness. Just as we must be willing to order our ambitions and our experiences in accord with the freedom of the redeemed order, so we must order our acquisition of the material trappings of life, which again are often acquired at the expense of the well-being of others, be it through sweated labor to make trainers or printed circuit boards, or the mining that delivers exotic metals and other raw materials at great expense to human health and natural ecosystems.

I have stressed here the importance of ethical kenosis—of aspiration, appetite, and acquisitiveness being emptied out in self-giving. In section 4.5 I identified this as being the image in human life of the self-giving of the triune persons of the Godhead. Supremely, we derive this image from the example of the incarnate Christ. However, kenosis is only half of the moral imperative that I derive from an understanding of the deep intratrinitarian kenosis of the Trinity. The other half is the desire, on the part of anyone who truly loves, that the other, the beloved, should flourish in his/her/its other-ness. Within the Trinity this desire furnishes the creative impulse that allows other entities to arise within the perfect self-sufficiency of the divine life. The "other" is offered existence, form, and particularity, and beyond that the opportunity of self-transcendence, but is not coerced into being other than itself. Love between humans, in different modes depending on whether it be the love of parents for children, lovers for each other, friends for each other, or the hard, willed love for stranger or enemy, is in each case noncoercive longing for the other to flourish. All these loves depend on the primacy of love as the greatest of the theological virtues (as listed in 1 Cor. 13), made possible by the loving self-communication of God, especially in the example of Christ. So also love between humans and the nonhuman creation, which depends as I have outlined above on a real desire to know the other and respect the other for itself, and a recognition too of the other as creature belonging to and in relation with God, selving according to the pattern of itself given by the divine Word.

Such a love has to be a tough, discerning love, not mere sentiment but a real outworking of desire purified by kenosis. It is a love which recognizes that other creatures may have to be fenced away from human habitation, or controlled by pharmaceuticals or pesticides, for the human good, but still celebrates the wonder of their existence, and desires co-existence, indeed that the other might know fullness of selving and flourishing as itself, and opportunity for self-transcendence. Humans, then, are to be part, so I infer from Romans 8, of transforming the world, making it more than it currently is, starting to help to heal its ambiguity and travail. In the final chapter I explore in more detail two possible ways in which such an eschatological calling might be worked out. But first I want to refine my understanding of the human vocation in relation to the well-established debate between understandings of the human role in terms of stewardship, or more actively as co-creators with God, or more kenotically in terms of a radical equality of all creatures. (It might seem as though kenosis of aspiration would indicate that only the last-named position is tenable, but I hope in what follows to propose a richer, more nuanced understanding of the possibilities.)

6.6 A CAUTIONARY WORD[51]

Before proposing models for appropriate relationships between humans and the nonhuman creation it is important to begin by acknowledging the difficulty and peculiarity of the task. Too often this debate is characterized by one of two mistakes:

1. A neglect of the truth that humans are animals—evolved animals with a certain genetic, cultural, and social inheritance that strongly colors their behavior, animals profoundly dependent for their life on other elements in the biosphere. This neglect easily leads to a detached and manipulative attitude.

2. An over-insistence that humans are just animals, and have no distinctive capacities for moral reflection or self-conscious action. This trivializes humans' moral nature, and ignores the fact that almost every human action in the world has an impact on the rest of the biosphere in some way. Indeed, most human actions involve an implicit calculation of human needs and values in relation to those of other species.

Any attempt to characterize our relationship to the nonhuman world should recognize that we are part of the animal world through our shared genetic, metabolic, and anatomical makeup, and from moment to moment deeply and obligatorily coupled to that world, depending on it not only for the food we eat but for the oxygen we breathe. We also have the capacity to exercise choices, and, on the basis of those choices, to alter a whole range of environments in a systematic way. This capacity for systematic alteration of a whole range of environments far transcends that of any other species. It is one aspect of the distinctiveness of human beings, and it is recognized in the Christian tradition as in some way God-given, reflected in such texts as Genesis 1, Genesis 2, and Psalm 8.

Each one of the approaches explored below must be seen in the light of our kinship with and dependence on nonhuman species; we are not merely detached agents, directing the play from a safe distance of power and control; we are also actors within it. That does not mean (of course) that our role as fellow actors gives us an understanding of what it is like to experience the world as another creature. As John Habgood properly points out, appropriate consideration of the nonhuman creation must recognize its otherness.[52]

6.7 POSSIBLE CALLINGS FOR HUMAN BEINGS IN RESPECT OF THE REST OF CREATION

In a recent article I set out a spectrum of possible callings.[53] At one extreme can be seen models of human being that involve a very "high," God-given calling to be "co-creators," or even "co-redeemers" with God of the unfolding creation. Philip Hefner has proposed the term "created co-creator" as an exploratory model of humans' role,[54] and this has since been taken up in the work of Ted Peters.[55] Hefner defines the concept of the created co-creator as follows: "Human beings are God's created co-creators whose purpose is to be the agency, acting in freedom, to birth the future that is most wholesome for the nature that has birthed us."⁵⁶ *This is a strikingly future-oriented proposal*—as Peters comments, *there is a hope here for "a future that should be better than the past or present."*⁵⁷ The language of co-creation is affirmed within Roman Catholic theology by Józef Życiński. Fascinatingly, Życiński links co-creation with the working out of the Beatitudes (Matt. 5:3–11; Luke 6:17, 20–22) and their highly counterintuitive assertion that it is the poor, the meek, and the mourning who are blessed. "Happy are those who suffer for their convictions; who do not concentrate attention on themselves; who try to withdraw from every value dear to them in order to experience more deeply their enchantment with God." There is a clear link here with the motif of kenosis, which I have advanced as central to an environmental ethic. Our whole life, Życiński argues, "becomes an imitation of the style of Christ. Characteristic of that style is the connection of might and powerlessness."⁵⁸ So clearly our calling in the world is not about the exercise of might in any straightforward way.

Even more strikingly Ronald Cole-Turner proposes that humans, as co-creators, are involved in God's work of redemption as the species with the ingenuity to detect and ultimately to eliminate heritable disease.⁵⁹ At once he nuances this—in a way that is important for all those exploring this understanding of the human vocation—by adding, "Not only are we *created* co-creators; we are creatures who constantly stand in need of redemption. If we may participate in God's creative and redemptive work, it is because we ourselves are being created and redeemed."⁶⁰ I take up in the final chapter of this book a way in which we might act out a role as co-redeemers.

Co-creator and co-redeemer approaches share a conviction that human ingenuity, with the power it gives us to modify plant species and domesticate animals, to reshape environments, to make cities and parks and farms, is a God-given part of our nature. These approaches accept the great harm to which anthropocentric, or at least anthropomonist, approaches have led in the past, and nevertheless suppose that part of humanity's transformation will be the discovery of the right use of humans' gifts in respect of the non-human world.

An important understanding of humans' role in relation to the nonhuman world, still emphasizing humans' God-given specialness, is that of humans as priests of creation, the species that offers up creation's praise to God, the species that combines "the fruit of the earth and the work of human hands" in sacramental action.

This attracts a number of authors, and is usefully set in the context of the science-religion debate by Arthur Peacocke.⁶¹ Among those whose work I have already considered in this book, human priesthood of creation is espoused by thinkers as different as T. F. Torrance and Ruth Page.⁶² A related idea is beautifully expressed in this passage from Wendell Berry: "To live, we must

daily break the body and shed the blood of Creation. When we do this knowingly, lovingly, skillfully, reverently, it is a sacrament. When we do it ignorantly, greedily, clumsily, destructively, it is a desecration. In such a desecration
we condemn ourselves to spiritual and moral loneliness, and others to want."[63]

Human priesthood of creation is an idea strong in Orthodox theology, as
in this sentence from Vladimir Lossky: "In his way to union with God, man
in no way leaves creatures aside, but gathers together in his love the whole
cosmos disordered by sin, that it may at last be transfigured by grace."[64] John
Zizioulas calls for "a notion of 'priesthood' freed from its pejorative connotations and seen as carrying with it the characteristic of 'offering,' in the sense
of opening up particular beings to a transcending relatedness with the
'other.'"[65] Elizabeth Theokritoff has given a very judicious assessment of the
place of this idea in Orthodox thought, pointing out that it must be seen in
the context of the whole framework of sacramental thought and understanding of cosmic redemption.[66]

It is far easier to understand an imperative to bless and praise God for the
world than to see human priesthood as reshaping creation (though see section 7.4 for a suggestion along these lines).[67] Paulos mar Gregorios has a fine
description of this stance toward creation, calling it "reverent-receptive."[68]
In a sense, talk of priesthood does not tell us what or how much we may do,
only *how* we should do it. As Theokritoff says, "Cosmic priesthood is not a
discrete activity, something that we do in addition to living rightly in the
world. . . . It is an attitude: an awareness that all things exist for God's glory,
and a response of thankfulness."[69]

Priesthood, in other words, would seem to be compatible with a wide variety of ethical approaches (if not with the notorious thought of James Watt,
Ronald Reagan's secretary of the interior, that the impending return of Jesus
made conservation of U.S. forests an irrelevance). However, priesthood may
be criticized for failing to take adequate account of the wildness and otherness of the nonhuman world, and of that world's enormous age. Modern
humans have after all only existed for a tiny fraction of the age of the biosphere, and the Bible contains numerous references to God's relation to other
creatures without reference to a human mediating role (Ps. 104; Job 38–39;
Matt. 5:26, etc.).[70]

The notion of humans as priestly mediators between God and the nonhuman creation may also deflect attention from our evolutionary kinship with
animals,[71] and our own dependence from moment to moment on other components in the biosphere, be it the bacteria in our digestive systems or the
photosynthetic activities of plants. However, properly nuanced, human
priesthood of creation can be a most helpful overarching concept (see section
6.8 below).

At the other end of the spectrum from co-creation and co-redemption come the various radically biocentric approaches to the relation of humans to the nonhuman creation. In the thought of Arne Naess and followers of his proposal for a "deep ecology," a movement in turn much influenced by Buddhist spirituality, there is a strong emphasis on the interdependence just mentioned, on "dependent co-arising." With a sense of our dependence on other creatures goes a sense of our radical equality with other species.[72] Another source of thinking pointing in much the same direction is the writing of Aldo Leopold, in particular his "land ethic": "A thing is right where it tends to preserve the integrity, stability and beauty of a biotic community. It is wrong when it tends otherwise."[73]

In contrast to the proposal of co-creation or co-redemption described above, *this type of proposal, at most, seeks to preserve a harmonious present. More often it hankers for a return to a somewhat romantically conceived past,* when there were many fewer human beings, imposing less of a load on the carrying capacity of the planet, and more in touch with our early life as hunter-gatherers. As Thomas Sieger Derr notes, there is a fatalism in this view, which places little premium on continued human existence.[74] The past life of indigenous peoples is often celebrated without any realistic assessment of what that life might have been like.[75]

Tempting though talk of equality and plain membership is, it runs into problems in practice. As I noted above in quoting that powerful passage from Wendell Berry, human interests are constantly in tension with those of other species; can it be that there are no circumstances in which humans' survival should be preferred to the overall well-being of the biosystem within which they live? It is also questionable whether ecosystems, understood scientifically, genuinely constitute "communities." And there are powerful reservations in current scientific thinking as to whether "stability" and "harmony" are characteristics of natural systems. There is, moreover, a paradox inherent in biocentrism. Unless we lift ourselves up out of the ecosystem, experiment on it, use our distinctive rationality and ingenuity on it, and gain the perspective on it that science gives us, we cannot know what would promote the health (leaving aside talk of stability and harmony) of a system of nonhuman organisms. Derr asserts:

> The movement as a whole [biocentrism] can offer us very little real guidance about our permissible impact on the natural world. While it would allow us to feed and clothe and house ourselves, it would require of us some degree of self-limitation because of our exceptional talents, including particularly our talent for reproducing ourselves. But it is very difficult to tell what this directive might mean beyond the generalized complaint that we are too clever and thus

exceed our space too readily. We have to pretend we are less, in effect, so that other creatures may be more; but how and how much are quite unspecifiable.[76]

What then of *stewardship* as an understanding of humans' calling in respect of the nonhuman creation? This sits between the two extremes discussed above. Stewardship is less convinced of its prerogative to alter nature than co-creation or co-redemption, but it is less passively inclined and more convinced of human distinctiveness than biocentrism. Recent critics of stewardship have identified a number of problems with the concept.[77] One key difficulty is the implicit presumption that there is some state or character of the nonhuman creation, knowable by humans, that we are in a position to steward. I note also that the usual connotations of the word "stewardship" are in terms of caution about the future: *"stewardship" of "resources" seeks to provide a future no worse than the present.*

It is worth noting that stewardship may cover a wide variety of approaches. Just as it is helpful to distinguish between weak and strong approaches to sustainability,[78] it may be helpful to make a distinction in the middle of our spectrum between "weak" stewardship, which would be of a merely conserving kind; "stewardship as preservation" in Lawrence Osborn's terms, and which would incline toward the biocentric end of the spectrum described above; and "strong" stewardship, "stewardship as nurture,"[79] which would involve change as well as conservation of nonhuman environments, and would incline toward co-creation.

The discussion above reveals two important elements that complicate any effort to locate the appropriate position for Christians to adopt on the spectrum outlined above. The first element is the limited nature of our knowledge and understanding of biotic systems. Such systems are known to be very complex; it is estimated that there are millions of species not even yet described. Biological systems' sensitivity to change is also very difficult to predict, given that mathematically they will tend to manifest so-called chaotic behavior.[80]

The second element is a disagreement, not often articulated, as to what systems of nonhuman organisms *ought to be like*. I noted above the longing to find stability, beauty, and integrity within natural systems, and posed the question as to whether claims for stability and integrity can be substantiated scientifically. Lisa Sideris has criticized sharply the work of ecofeminists such as McFague and Ruether for their assumption that harmony and cooperation are fundamental characteristics of natural systems.[81] She celebrates instead the work of Holmes Rolston, whose great contributions to evolutionary theology and environmental ethics I noted in chapters 1, 3, and 5. Rolston has made an eloquent and careful analysis of instrumental, intrinsic, and systemic values in the natural world.[82] He is resolute in asserting that humans should not interfere with the workings of wild nature in wilderness areas. Even where these workings lead to great sufferings within individuals or species, humans should not intervene. This represents a strong conviction that the way that creation has evolved, under the influence of natural selection, is the way it should be. As we saw in section 3.2, creation is, for Rolston, "cruciform," a place of "tragedy,"[83] but—he might have added (paraphrasing Darwin)—there is grandeur as well as tragedy in this view of life. The nonhuman world possesses its beauty *because of* the processes that also involve the sufferings associated with predation and parasitism and which engender extinction.

But the step from scientific description to what-nature-should-be is not a strict logical step. It involves a metaphysical—indeed, for a theist like Rolston, a *theological*—judgment. The Darwinian description of the world involves no prescription as to what-nature-should-be. The impoverishment of a natural system in response to altered environmental conditions—as in the desertification of a previously forested region, the flooding of low-lying coastal systems, or come to that the onset of a new Ice Age—any of these scenarios is as compatible with the processes and descriptions of Darwinism as our present extraordinarily rich and fruitful biosphere. The changes merely lead to the selection of different populations of organisms: thorns and cacti rather than trees and ferns, saltwater fish and plankton rather than the biological communities of wetlands. Humans form judgments about which overall planetary conditions should be promoted and which striven against, judgments to which Darwinian descriptions cannot themselves give rise. The notion of a future hope for the organisms of the planet is likewise one on which Darwinism can make no comment, because Darwinism is an explanation of processes and phenomena, not an account of values or hopes.

In considering humans' relation to God and to the nonhuman creation the Christian must give an account of values and hopes. Confronted with the possibility of human-induced runaway global warming, which might ultimately render the Earth as uninhabitable as Venus, humans clearly have a duty to avoid such a huge impoverishment of the creation. (Even if we were incapable of saving our own species, we would still have that duty in respect of the Earth.) Likewise, a major exchange of nuclear weapons might not eliminate absolutely every organism on the planet, but it would be a catastrophic depletion of the biosphere.[84] Every effort must be made, surely, to prevent human activity giving rise to either eventuality.

However, our stewardly, precautionary role in seeking to ensure that the future is not radically worse than the present also applies to nonanthropogenic situations. If it were discovered that the next Ice Age was imminent (and in the *natural* macrocycles of our climate, we are heading in that direction within the next fifty thousand years) then it would surely be humans' responsibility to seek not merely to sustain human civilization (which might be done in a series of microenvironments), but to seek—if it were possible—to ward off the massive extinctions that would be associated with a major icing-over of the surface of the planet. James Lovelock has pointed out that ice ages are actually richer in overall biota than interglacials, and overall land area similar.[85] But the extinction both of many temperate-zone species and of many of the finest elements of human civilization seems a high price to pay for the flourishing of life in cold oceans. So I hold to my suggestion[86] that were a glacial to set in, humans might be right to try and manipulate the climate to reduce its impact. (Our best plan would be, presumably, to pump as much greenhouse gas into the atmosphere as possible.) So even in respect of wild nature, humans have responsibilities—arising not out of our Darwinian understanding but out of our sense of the value of God's creatures—to exert ourselves to hold the boundaries of the Earth's surface environment, the settings, as Lovelock would put it, of "Gaia"[87] within bounds which provide for a rich and fruitful biosphere. God's action to preserve God's lovely and "good" biosphere would presumably be through humans as agents. In this limit sense I consider it entirely valid to speak of human stewardship of the planet.

I also share with Bill McKibben, Rolston himself, and many deep-ecological writers[88] a sense of the importance to us, scientifically and spiritually, of the continuing existence of wilderness. Our stewardship, as conceived above in terms of seeking to protect some fruitful limits within which the Earth-system as a whole might unfold, would necessarily involve the protection of wilderness as a place consecrated to our respect for God's creation. It is in wilderness we can recognize our fellow-citizenship of the biotic community (to pick up on the language of Aldo Leopold). It is in wilderness we learn most immediately from other creatures (as out in a Dartmoor storm I learn the grain of the hill-folds from the shelter-patterns of the sheep). It is through the existence of wilderness we can reassess our sense of scale, recognizing the immensity of God and of God's work of creation, so movingly portrayed in passages such as Job 38–41 and Isaiah 40.

6.8 PRIESTHOOD OF CREATION RECONSIDERED

I noted above that the notion of human priesthood of creation does not actually offer a clear ethical prescription. Co-creatorly activity is closely connected with priesthood, and indeed is central to eucharistic practice; what we offer is both "the fruit of the earth" and the fruit of the blessing of human ingenuity, "the work of human hands." But it might also be argued that humans exercise their priesthood just as truly by being contemplatives in the sense I described above. Though we cannot hear the language of the song of all creaturely praise to which the Psalms refer (cf. Ps. 19:1–4), we can attend to it, seek to instress it to the utmost of our being; we can stand with the song in wild places, celebrate it, and offer it whole up to God.[89] R. J. Berry helpfully quotes the New Testament commentator Charles Cranfield:

> The Jungfrau and the Matterhorn and the planet Venus and all living things too, man alone excepted, do indeed glorify God in their own ways; but, since their praise is destined to be not a collection of independent offerings, but part of a magnificent whole, the united praise of the whole creation, they are prevented from being fully that which they were created to be, so long as man's part is missing.[90]

As I noted above, we cannot put human priesthood neatly on our spectrum of possible human roles at any defined point. But a lack of ethical precision does not render the idea of priesthood any less important. The tenor of the great passages on creation in the Hebrew Bible is that we have been placed in a special place by God—as created last (Gen. 1) or first (Gen. 2), as namer before God of the animals (Gen. 2:19–20), as a little lower than the angels in the song of cosmic praise (Ps. 8). This specialness is to enable us to see the created world whole,[91] and offer it up in praise. The creation of humans in the image and likeness of God (Gen. 1:26), and to praise and glorify God forever, must lie behind every description of our calling in relation to the rest of creation. Hopkins himself asserted, "The creation does praise God, does reflect honour on him, if of service to him. . . . But man can know God, *can mean to give him glory*."[92]

Insights from Orthodox thought can be profoundly helpful here. Maximus the Confessor thought of humanity as "created as the *methorios* (the boundary or frontier) between the physical and spiritual realms."[93] This is a helpful way to consider the basis for human priesthood of creation. In the article quoted in section 6.7, Theokritoff draws on the thought of Kallistos Ware in describing humans as having two roles:

1. To reshape and alter the world, giving it fresh significance and purpose."[94] (Theokritoff describes this a "kingly" role, but in the language I have been using it seems a helpful restatement of the role of a created co-creator.)
2. "To bless and praise God for the world," a "priestly" role.[95] As an individual act this is the priesthood of contemplation and understanding, which sees into the world with both realism and faith, somewhat in the way I have been describing in talking of the work of Hopkins. As a corporate act it is the priesthood of offering up the world in eucharist.[96] Our priesthood is the way this particular creature "enters the interdependence of all persons and all things in the 'cosmic liturgy.'"[97]

Ware writes of the "*logoi*" of things, their structures and patterns which "man must take the trouble to discover . . . and . . . thereafter respect."[98] We encountered this concept in section 4.4. That inner structure and pattern, along with the particularity of each created thing, is close to what I have been calling inscape. Blessing and thanksgiving are the ways we acknowledge the true nature of things—the ways, in other language, that we most truly instress them. To consecrate something is to refer it to its "original and ultimate meaning—God's conception of it."[99] This language of sacramentality, indeed of theophany, within the natural world is not, to go back to the thought of Kallistos Ware, to diminish the "isness" of each thing, but actually to enhance it.[100] There is a Godwardness to all creatures into which our priesthood fits. It is our specific gift to articulate the connection between creature and Creator. When we fulfill our mediator role, we help the world fulfill its destiny and be transformed by the light and presence of God. When we close our consciousness to what is above, we obstruct "that flow by which material things may be saturated by the Spirit."[101]

Other dimensions, though, come in from other thinkers. John Zizioulas points to the sacrificial aspect of priesthood—humans' self-sacrifice for the sake of creation as a whole, "in the image of Christ who died for all creation."[102] The Orthodox concept of the Fall tends to be one of humans' failure to grow into their potential, and we are seeing here a vision of something of the potential of humanity to be, individually and collectively, co-creators, contemplatives, and priests. Our approach to created entities should be in terms of their deep pattern, God's own conception of them. Our thanksgiving for created entities and our transformation of them should be as part of the great cosmic eucharist.[103]

Clearly there is a tension, to which Theokritoff points us, between our "activism" and our "reverent-receptive" approach (see section 6.7). We must hope that when we shape any part of creation, what we produce "will at least not contradict its beauty."[104] To put it another way, still trying to remain faithful to the Orthodox insight, part of our task as the many-faceted animal we are is not to let our struggle over the fulfilling of our own potential interfere with the ecology of praise in other entities. The given relationship of entities to God should be determinative of the way we use *our* God-given propensity to shape the environment.

We have seen in drawing on Orthodox thought the extraordinary richness of this type of approach. It will also have occurred to the reader that little in the way of a Darwinian perspective has been evident. The very positive evaluation of creation is in tension with the sense we derived in chapter 1 of the profound ambiguity of an evolving world, in which the same processes give rise to great values and profound disvalues. So, far from a sense that a created world containing this level of ambiguity might be regarded as fallen (language with which I took issue in section 2.6, but eminently understandable language all the same), the Orthodox are concerned that humans might not export their fallenness into a creation that is filled with praise, a creation of which Ware can write, "The entire cosmos is one vast burning bush, permeated by the fire of the divine power and glory."[105]

My contention is that these insights are still eminently usable even in a perspective that takes Darwinian insights and evolutionary theodicy with the utmost seriousness. The clue is, returning to our conversation with Hopkins, to have a fully rounded view of inscape (with its parallels to Maximus's concept of *logoi*). The deep pattern of all living entities does include their part in the processes of evolution by natural selection, their "selving," their "no" as well as their "yes" to God (to return to the language of section 4.4). This perspective at once helps us with what seemed awkward and unclear in the Orthodox formulations, which is what place humans might have not just in the cosmic liturgy but in the redemption of the cosmos, its transfiguration into a final altered state. To speak of the creation in the more ambiguous way at which we arrived in chapter 4 is to give space for our activism (properly understood, with all the nuances we have noted above), to impart a necessary dynamic quality to the depiction of the cosmos. The creation is no mere static hymn of praise, no mere glad repetition of eucharist, exalted thoughts though those are, but a realm in a process of becoming, accompanied by an element of "groaning." As priests we are reverent-receptive contemplatives, but also co-redeemers, caught up in a process of transformation that will lead ultimately to the new creation in which there will be no more crying (Rev. 21:4).

6.9 CONCLUSION

There are three broad contexts in which humans might have care for the creation, exerted either actively or passively. One is that of the whole surface biosphere; another is the context of what is presently wilderness; the third that in which humans live alongside the nonhuman creation and cultivate or actively manage it. I have identified a spectrum of possible roles for humans. The theme of our creation in the image of God both gives weight to a claim that humans are called to be priests of creation, and also gives us a clue as to how we might use our spectrum of roles.

We are in a sense stewards of the whole surface biosphere,[106] in that we know of certain scenarios that would eliminate all or most of that richness of life, and we have a responsibility to ward off those scenarios, to conserve at the most general level what God's loving activity over 4.5 billion years has made possible on Earth, to make sure indeed that the future is no worse than the present. And part of our status in God's image is our capacity to see that Earth as the fragile and beautiful whole that it is, and to guard it with wisdom. In this sense we are in the image of the God who looked upon the creation and found it very good, and held it safe within his rest (Gen. 1:31–2:3).

We are (within that wider perspective) fellow-citizens of wild nature. To hear other creatures' praise of their God, to recognize that they are loved for their own sake, we must quiet the thunder of our own ambitions, our own worship both of God and of idols, and we must protect places where that praise can be itself without our distorting it. We should long to hear that praise as the earliest humans heard it, and make space in our lives and our world to ensure that we do. Again, the language of stewardship may be used of this overall protecting role, but does not do justice to the role of contemplative, or praise-giver, that the wilderness can engender in us.

We are already, on a high proportion of the Earth's land surface, the ingenious innovators and managers of new ways of living in and with the nonhuman creation. Our calling is to bring this ingenuity, and the necessity of breaking the body of creation for our own needs and the needs of the future, humbly into our priesthood (cf. Wendell Berry, quoted in section 6.7). We are in the image of God the maker and innovator. We should believe, as Hefner proposes, that our future with the nonhuman creation can be better than the past or the present. But we need not see our co-creative calling solely in terms of technological innovation or biotechnological tweaking; we can create not only new strains of drought-resistant crops for use in the Sahel, but also the loving interspecies communities which are domesticated nature at its best. Our creativity can—must, if it is to be in partnership with God's—express our hope for the growth of love in the world. Our lordship and management can be expressed in service; even within the community of domesticated nature we can exert our creativity and imagination to recognize the value and dignity of the other and to serve its needs with humility and joy. This would mean radical transformation of much current agricultural practice, but only thus could our role come to be in the image of the God who in Jesus expressed lordship—domin-ion—in terms of servanthood (Mark 10:43–45).

What God alone could do, has done, once and for all, was to suffer death for the transformation of the world, to bear in the Christ the pain of the creation and of human sin. But our lives can side with that sacrifice in ways both ingenious and costly. If we were to grow into the fullness of our life under God we might be able to realize a further call—a call to participate more actively in the healing of a wild nature that may be seen both as "very good" *and* as (through the will of the same God who made it) "groaning in travail." In doing so we would be acting in the image of the God that we see, in the life of the earthly Jesus, as always moved to compassion by the need for healing.

That I see as being the most helpful *theological* analysis of what *naturalistically* can be described in Darwinian terms. A mark of humans' growing into the life of divine fellowship would be a participation in the divine transformation of the biosphere, the relief of nature's groaning. In the final chapter I turn to consider specific proposals as to how this service, this outworking of a freedom made possible in Christ, might be worked out within the biosphere.

7

Ethical Proposals and Conclusion

7.1 INTRODUCTION

The last two chapters have shown that I believe in God's eventual healing of creation (chapter 5), and that humans have a part to play in that healing (chapter 6). A constant motif of this work has been that creation is *both* "very good" (Gen 1:31) in its fruitfulness, in all the myriad possibility for "selves" and interactions that it makes possible, and in the final state toward which it is being drawn, *and* "groaning"—in that it is full of suffering, and its final liberation awaits "the freedom of the glory of the children of God" (Rom. 8:21), the growing up of humans into the loving fellowship of self-giving that is the life of the divine. A mark of humans' growing into the life of divine fellowship would be participation in the divine transformation of the biosphere, the relief of nature's groaning. But what might this mean in terms of our actual practice? What would be appropriate marks of our free engagement with co-creativity, stemming from care-ful, loving, self-emptying contemplation of the nonhuman world, of co-redemption exercised in a spirit of reverent-receptive priesthood? In this closing chapter I examine two proposals: one in relation to human diet and the keeping of animals for food, and the other in relation to the preservation of species in the wild.

7.2 ESCHATOLOGICAL VEGETARIANISM

I consider here the proposal of Andrew Linzey, director of the Oxford Centre for Animal Ethics. Linzey's conviction that the healing of creation will be a *restoration* of an original, wholly good natural order leads him to insist on an understanding of nature as fallen.[1] I explained in section 2.6 why I found that view unsatisfactory, limiting as it does our ability to appropriate the conclusions of science and the sense of ambiguity intrinsic to creation via an evolutionary process. But Linzey also appeals strongly to an eschatological argument for a new way of treating animals, based on Romans 8:19–21: creation, having been subjected to bondage, awaits the liberty of the glory of the children of God. Linzey sees this as "the decisive reference to those who ask 'What does it mean for humans to exercise a priestly ministry of redemption?' Quite simply: it concerns the releasing of creation from futility, from suffering and pain and worthlessness. . . . Such a perspective challenges at root the notion that human responsibility in the world extends only to serving and protecting our own species."[2] He goes on to say, "There can be no liberation theology without the liberation of the creation itself."[3] Problems about his commitment to a historical fall do not vitiate the power of Linzey's core proposal for an "eschatological vegetarianism"—his idea that the ending of meat eating, or more generally the killing of animals, would be a sign of human beings aligning themselves with God's eventual purposes for the creation. This warrants very serious consideration.

How, though, are to we to understand the liberation of creation, and our part in it? Much depends on which way we choose to read the sparse and poetic texts that we encountered in sections 5.3 and 5.5. As Richard Bauckham points out, the Isaianic vision in 11:6–9 talks of the reconciliation of the wild, dangerous animals with the animals that were, for seminomadic pastoralists, part of the human community.[4] On Linzey's view of predation as an unambiguous evil, and something moreover brought about by sin—be it human or cosmic—the key element here is that redeemed human behavior can be part of this reordering of the relationships of species. Sinless human leading permits reconciliation between predators and prey. But if predation is deeply embedded in the purposes of God, and is not a phenomenon either caused or exacerbated by human activity, as an evolutionary view implies, then we may question whether human activity of any sort can or should be expected to influence the predator-prey relationship. The whole tenor of chapter 5 was that only God can effect such a transformation (see also sections 6.1 and 6.9).

In an article published in 1993 Linzey sets out his central point: he believes that "it is possible and credible to believe that by the power of the Spirit new ways of living without violence can be opened up for us."[5] By refusing to eat meat, "We witness to a higher order of existence, implicit in the Logos, which is struggling to be born in us. By refusing to go the way of our 'natural nature' or our 'psychological nature,' by standing against the order of unredeemed nature, we become signs of the order of existence for which all creatures long."[6] N. T. Wright agrees that the glory of our freedom, as referred to in Romans 8, contains responsibilities.[7] Romans 8:18f. is the very text that Karl

Barth thought should be written "in letters of fire . . . across every hunting lodge, abbatoir and vivisection chamber,"[8] for Barth was very aware of the eschatological dimension of human action. He thought the killing of animals "possible only as a deeply reverential act of repentance, gratitude and praise on the part of the forgiven sinner."[9] Like Linzey he saw this passage from Romans as central. The creation waits in earnest expectation

> for what?—for the "manifestation of the children of God," and there-
> fore for the liberation of those who now keep them imprisoned and
> even despatch them from life to death. The creature has become sub-
> ject to *mataiotes* [futility], not *hekousa* [of its own will], nor according
> to its own destiny, but because of man, its subjugator. And it, too, is
> determined for liberation from the *douleia tes phthoras* [bondage to
> decay] together with the liberation of the children of God, so that for
> the moment it groans and cries with us in the birth-pangs of a new
> aeon. In this whole sphere what is good is obviously what can be jus-
> tified in face of these words, and what is bad that which cannot. A good
> hunter, honourable butcher and conscientious vivisectionist will dif-
> fer from the bad in the fact that even as they are engaged in killing ani-
> mals they hear this groaning and travailing of the creature, and
> therefore, in comparison with all others who have to do with animals,
> they are summoned to an intensified, sharpened and deepened diffi-
> dence, reserve and carefulness. In this matter they act on the extreme
> limits where respect for life and callous disregard constantly jostle and
> may easily pass into one another. On these frontiers, if anywhere, ani-
> mal protection, care and friendship are quite indispensable.[10]

Barth concludes then that "the killing of animals . . . with the permission of God . . . is a priestly act of eschatalogical [sic] character."[11] Linzey in contrast rejects all such violence as flying in the face of our possibility of acting along-side God's redemption.[12]

It is fascinating that Barth and Linzey, spurred on by the same text from Romans 8, come to such different conclusions about meat eating. Where they would both agree, however, is that the great proportion of current killing of animals is not reverent but casual, the final act in a relationship with confined animals who know no freedom to be themselves, or healthy relationship either with each other or their human owners. And "owners" is the key word here, because much of this problem stems from the reduction of animal nature to a mere commodity, which in its rearing and killing alike must be processed as cheaply as possible into products. I recall again Barth's words: "[The] good hunter, honourable butcher etc. differs from the bad in the fact that . . . they hear this groaning and travailing . . . and . . . are summoned to an intensified, sharpened and deepened diffidence, reserve and carefulness. . . . Animal pro-tection, care and friendship are quite indispensable."[13] Those words "care and friendship" seem to me to be the key. Linzey's view would be that the enhanced quality of care and friendship toward animals characteristic of the freedom of the glory of the children of God is incompatible with killing them for human purposes. Barth argues that appropriately reverent procedures for husbandry and killing can be part of a model of care and friendship.

As someone who lives on the edge of Dartmoor, Devon, which is a hill-farming area in which the landscape has been shaped for literally thousands of years by pastoralism, and where a market in locally grown organic meat is once again coming to the fore, it is hard to resist the notion that such a place should continue to be formed (while the climate permits) by community between humans and farm animals, and natural to call for that community to be characterized by care and friendship.[14] Without that community the landscape and ethos of the place would be utterly different (and, of course, the animals in question would not have any quality or unquality of life; they simply would not exist).[15]

The outbreak of foot-and-mouth disease in the United Kingdom in 2001, in which areas local to me were very badly affected, is a telling parable of the best and worst in current animal husbandry in the developed West. The outbreak was almost certainly caused, or at least greatly exacerbated, by the transport over long distances of sheep in order to gain from marginal price differentials in different parts of the country. That that was possible speaks to the cost of fuel still being lower than is suitable to the threat of climate change, and to the commodification of animals merely as units of value to be traded wherever and however human advantage might be gained from the trade. As the outbreak developed the government refused to vaccinate stock, for fear of lasting damage to the British livestock "industry" within the European Union. Instead, huge numbers of animals were slaughtered on farms and burned *in situ*. However, farmers' responses made clear that the relationship between farmers and their animals in this part of the world is more than a commercial one. The average age of farmers in the United Kingdom is currently in the late fifties. In Devon it is probably higher. But many farmers, even quite elderly ones for whom this decision could not possibly make economic sense, used their compensation money to restock their land with new herds. This points to livestock farming, at least in the context from which I write, being a vocation as well as a business, and relation with animals being a matter of care and friendship, even, in its own particular and idiosyncratic way, of love.[16]

This in its turn presses the question: can one be in I-Thou relationship,[17] indeed in servant relationship, with an animal one ultimately intends to kill? I maintain that the experience of pastoralists, stemming right back to biblical examples,[18] is that one can. As Rosemary Radford Ruether has indicated, those who do not farm can be misled here by their experience of relating to

domestic pets, a valuable cross-species relationship, but qualitatively different from other types of relations with animals.[19] Relations within farming
(and between hunters and their prey) are of course very diverse, and fall on a
spectrum on which I-Thou relation, perhaps with one's only work-dog or
dairy cow, might be at one end, and H. Paul Santmire's "I-Ens" at the other.[20]
"I-Ens" is a relationship that involves recognition of beauty and wonder, and
connotes the need for humility and gratitude. This is arguably more the relationship a free-range poultry farmer might have with a hundred chickens.
They are not known individually as Thou's, but they are recognized as having their own characters and interests, and are not simply to be used as ends.
Across the whole spectrum, I would argue, there can be a strong element of
service, and of respect, in the tending of animals.

Another theological consideration is whether there is any form of survival
after death for animals. I examined this in detail in chapter 5. This issue is
important in relation to the debate about vegetarianism because if animal existence is only in this world, then in the case of human-bred animals who suffer
some disease or other and die without any sort of fulfillment, it might be said
that it would have been better if those animals had never been bred in the first
place. No existence, it might be said, is better than flawed existence. However,
if every animal that is born is loved, cherished, and suffered with by God—and
given by God, in this life or the next, full opportunity for flourishing—then
human breeding and rearing of animals can be seen in a more definitely positive light. (However, this argument can emphatically *not* be used to justify abu-
sive treatment or cruel slaughter of animals, on the grounds that God will bind
up the wounds of the victims in a subsequent life. Cruelty and exploitation are
always injustice, and the witness of the Hebrew Bible is that the Lord always
sets his face against injustice. Nor, incidentally, could the argument be used to
justify the breeding of animals with a genetic makeup incompatible with flourishing, for that would also be an exploitative use of our ingenuity.)

Linzey's proposal is that there is now the opportunity, in many environments, to embrace vegetarianism as an eschatological sign. This could indeed
be seen as an outward and visible sign of a kenosis of aspiration, appetite, and
acquisitiveness (see section 6.5). There would be fewer "others," the good of
which might be desired, because fewer animals would be bred, but at least one
could be sure that the levels of distress (and, arguably, the dehumanization of
abbatoir workers) involved in the systematic killing of animals for meat would
be avoided. However, that would not constitute a healing of the dynamic of
predation, since that dynamic has never depended on human action. It will
only be healed by God's final action of transforming the old creation into the
new. There would moreover be a loss of interspecies community, community
which at its best can involve both humility and gratitude, and creaturely flour-

ishing on both sides—community which in itself, arguably, anticipates the interspecies relationships hinted at in Isaiah 11.

It will be clear from the above that I tend toward a position in which the breeding, rearing, and management of animals in the context of healthy methods of farming (including genuinely humane killing) can be considered a form of care and friendship between species that is an authentic part of the human vocation, part indeed that extends the possibilities of relationship between species, and is therefore not to be abandoned as part of the pursuit of an eschatological ethic. Richard Alan Young, in advocating Christian vegetarianism, concedes that "the Bible leaves diet as a spiritual choice,"[21] but he claims that "vegetarianism may be thought of as the quintessence of the kingdom, as it brings together humans and animals into a community of peace and harmony."[22] The case I make here is that certain sorts of community would be lost in a move to strict vegetarianism, which might therefore be seen as a move away from, rather than toward, the Isaianic vision.

It is fascinating to note that Luke's account of the outcome of the Council of Jerusalem in Acts 15 required of Gentile Christians only two types of restraint out of the Jewish Law: sexual morality and abstinence from food sacrificed to idols, strangled animals, and blood (Acts 15:29). These forms of abstinence are very relevant to this question. It could be held that all animals killed within a process which has no care for their well-being, but regards them only as commodities to be "manufactured" as cheaply as possible, transported wherever necessary, and killed only with concern for efficiency and not the relief of distress, have been sacrificed to the idol of human economic efficiency, whether on a capitalist or collectivist model, and are tainted thereby.[23] Not (as Paul is at pains to point out) that such food ceases to be food, capable of being eaten without the eater becoming ritually unclean, but that to eat it may be seen to be collusion (1 Cor. 8; Rom. 14:20–23). Christians might therefore feel called to abstain to avoid misleading others.[24] The constraint on strangling and on eating blood was, in effect, a requirement for humane killing and careful butchery, as well as an acknowledgment that all life belongs ultimately to the Lord. Barth, in the passage cited above, seems very aware of these constraints, and still concludes that there can be a good hunter and an honorable butcher, and, yet more controversially, a conscientious vivisectionist.

Barth recognized that vegetarianism may also be guilty at times of "inconsistencies . . . sentimentality and . . . fanaticism."[25] But he was also clear that "for all its weaknesses we must be careful not to put ourselves in the wrong in face of it by our thoughtlessness and hardness of heart."[26] It would be difficult to put this better than Wendell Berry in a passage I also quoted in section 6.7: "To live, we must daily break the body and shed the blood of Creation. When we do this knowingly, lovingly, skillfully, reverently, it is a sacrament. When we do it ignorantly, greedily, clumsily, destructively, it is a desecration. In such a desecration we condemn ourselves to spiritual and moral loneliness, and others to want."[27]

All parties are agreed that ignorance, greed, and destructiveness, manifestations in their own way of inappropriate aspiration, unsustainable appetite, and unthinking acquisitiveness are rejections of our calling to grow into God and there to discover our true freedom. Nevertheless I conclude that the keeping of animals for meat, and, in some contexts, certain forms of hunting, may be done "knowingly, lovingly, skillfully, reverently," and in a way that forms patterns of community between humans and the nonhuman creation that would be lost if meat were not eaten.[28]

7.3 GLOBAL JUSTICE, GLOBAL WARMING, AND THE GLASS ABBATOIR

I note my colleague David Grumett's point that vegetarianism has been a much stronger element in the Christian tradition than is often imagined,[29] but I also note that it has never been a general moral imperative of the tradition. That is not to say that individual Christians may not properly adopt such a lifestyle as an eschatological sign, just as other kenoses of appetite may be adopted in imitation of Christ and in anticipation of the Kingdom. We operate, as my former colleague Rachel Muers helpfully signals, in what Bonhoeffer called "the penultimate."[30] What is incumbent on Christians is in Muers's words to think about diet "in ways that focus on the better and worse choices that can be made in an imperfect world," in ways that offer us "the chance to make critical interventions in systems while recognizing one's own embeddedness in compromise."[31]

That leads me to my final point in this section. The most compelling theological argument against the large-scale keeping of animals for meat comes not out of the theology of creation, nor out of an appeal to the eschaton, but out of a sense of God's justice, and the need for human prudence.[32] Where the production of red meat in particular can be shown to be at the expense of a real possibility of feeding humans who are hungry, and where—as will be more and more the case as the twenty-first century unfolds—the keeping of animals for meat deprives humans and wild animals of supplies of fresh water, then those activities conflict with the principles of justice that are so strong in the Hebrew Bible, as indeed in many other religious and secular codes. The calculus that red meat production consumes many times the energy of the equivalent food value in cereals[33] is now augmented by calculations about the consumption of water,[34] and also about the carbon footprint of methanogens such as cattle.[35] The first two arguments are local in their ambit; some areas are suitable for arable crops and some not, some have water shortages and some not. The issue of methane production is a global concern. Climate change afflicts the poorest and most vulnerable populations in our world, raising issues of justice, and although its precise unfolding remains contentious, human prudence requires consideration of a wide range of actions to restrict its extent. Alarm over global warming is already leading to research into breeding and feeding cattle differently to restrict the damage they do to the climate. In turn this will raise religious issues for some cultures, where cattle are sacred, and possibly some concerns over animal welfare if cattle are engineered away from their "natures."

However, Michael Pollan alerts us to further complications. In much current agricultural practice, especially that which tries to minimize the use of chemical fertilizer, animals have a vital role in recycling nutrients through manure.[36] Moreover, many areas are not well suited to large-scale cereal production.[37] Abandoning the keeping of animals on such land would involve much more transport of food, again increasing the carbon footprint of feeding the world. This intricate calculation about human "oikonomics" is vital to our future. It needs to include, as I have implied, concerns about justice, sustainability, local culture, and global mitigation of the greenhouse effect.[38] At present it is done much too crudely in terms of the interests of big capital—hence, much of the pressure to commodify animals. Imperative as it is, the need for a calculation of overall "oikonomics" falls a long way away from an argument for strict vegetarianism.

Pollan's analysis of the ethics of eating animals ends with a telling exhortation. Drawing on an essay by John Berger, "Why Look at Animals?"[39] he claims that it is essential that we *see* what we are doing. Pollan writes:

> The industrialization—and brutalization—of animals in America is a relatively new, evitable and local phenomenon: No other country raises and slaughters its food animals quite as intensively or as brutally as we do. No other people in history has lived at quite so great a remove from the animals they eat. Were the walls of our meat industry to become transparent, literally or even figuratively, we would not long continue to raise, kill and eat animals the way we do. Tail docking and sow crates and beak clipping would disappear overnight, and the days of slaughtering four hundred head of cattle an hour would promptly come to an end—for who could stand the sight? Yes, meat would get more expensive. We'd probably eat a lot less of it, too, but maybe when we did eat animals we'd eat them with the consciousness, ceremony, and respect they deserve.[40]

In the end both arguments based on the original state of creation and appeals to the imperatives of the eschaton collapse into the prophetic—the argument for justice and *shalom* in the not-yet-fully-redeemed world—full of possibilities for goodness and eloquent also of human failings, to which both testaments of the Christian Bible bear witness. Over Pollan's glass abbatoir Barth would blazon the conviction of Romans 8:21 that humans' true freedom will be part of the healing of creation. Both these thinkers imply that keeping animals for meat may need to become a much less usual element in human life than it currently is. However, the forms of community that small-scale keeping of animals for meat can engender remain a positive value, and are not necessarily excluded by the imperatives either of justice or of freedom, or yet of ecological economics.

7.4 THE ETHICS OF EXTINCTION

Having investigated one possible proposal in eschatological ethics I now turn to consider another, more directly linked to my initial proposal about creation's "travail." I suggested that this could be read, in the light of evolutionary science, as being the travail of suffering and extinction out of which values of beauty, complexity, adaptiveness, and ultimately consciousness emerge in the biosphere (see chapter 1 and section 6.1). The driver that is natural selection has necessarily resulted in millions of extinctions—over 98 percent of all the species that have ever lived. For Rolston, this "groaning in travail is in the nature of things from time immemorial. Such travail is the Creator's will, productive as it is of glory."[41] As I noted in section 3.2, his view is that this system does not stand in need of redemption:[42] it contains within it its own processes of regeneration and therefore redemption. I made clear there, and at section 6.7, that I am not wholly in agreement with Rolston as to the character of redemption in the nonhuman creation. I do not follow his naturalistic inference that what *is* in a wild system is what *ought to be*. In the model I am developing here, based on a sense that the Cross is the hinge-point not merely of human but also of cosmic history, it is not enough to settle for the equation of what-the-nonhuman-world-is with what it should or will be. Eschatological hope should be a stronger influence on the Christian understanding than that. I do not consider that our interaction with wilderness should be confined to its protection from anthropogenic (human-induced) damage.

My proposal then is that we can not only take seriously Moltmann's understanding of Christ as evolution's redeemer (see section 5.4), but also the possibility of human partnership in this process. Not that humans could end or transform the process of predation; only God could do that. But I make the bold proposal that *a sign of our liberty as children of God starting to set free the whole creation would be that human beings, through a blend of prudential wisdom and scientific ingenuity, cut the rate of natural extinction.*

Extinction is an intrinsic part of the way that wild nature "works." For Rolston's cruciform naturalism there is no case for preventing it, if it is not human-induced. But extinction of a species means the loss of a whole way of being alive on the planet, a whole aspect of the goodness of creation, a whole way of praising God. Part of fulfilled human calling might be, by dint of our knowledge and ingenuity, to have a share in eliminating that phenomenon from the biosphere. That would mean a co-redeemerly "stewarding" (informed by our experience as priests and fellow-praisers) even of wilderness, but one that would take a great deal more wisdom as well as a great deal more knowledge than we currently possess. So one great human priority at present must be to gather (noninvasively) as much knowledge and wisdom as we can about the nonhuman world, and to reduce the very high rate of *human-induced* extinction to which the biosphere is currently subject.

But my proposal goes beyond that to suggest that humans could also make significant progress toward ending the process of biological extinction, and thereby take a very significant step toward the healing of creation.

Let me indicate the parameters of this claim. First, humans are at present rapidly accelerating the rate of extinction. As Michael Boulter indicates, this is not a new development. Ever since members of *H. Sapiens* emerged from Africa and acquired the skills of cooperative and systematic hunting we have been eliminating other species at a rapid rate. At first this was through hunting; an index of the efficiency of human hunting in this era is the rapid loss of species from North America after the arrival of human beings (chap. 6, note 38). Later anthropogenic extinction came through deforestation and agriculture. More recently it has also been through technological advance and the industrial pollution that it made possible. In the next phase of human life it may well be through the effects of human-accelerated climate change.[43] E. O. Wilson, in a chapter titled "The Planetary Killer,"[44] estimates that fifty thousand years ago the rate of extinction was low, perhaps one species per million per year, roughly equal to the rate of evolutionary replacement. Chiefly because of human activity, this rate now runs at over one thousand species per million per year. As John Cobb points out, if we take seriously the Prologue to the Fourth Gospel, and the immanence in creation of the divine Word, then to save a species must clearly be to enrich Christ's life.[45]

There is no question but that our calling under God must be to reduce that anthropogenic extinction, and indeed to endeavor to eliminate it. Since anthropogenic extinction often arises as a result of the extremity to which human populations are pushed by poverty and overpopulation, this will in turn mean radical changes in the way human goods are distributed. It will mean the ethical kenosis of aspiration, appetite, and acquisitiveness, especially on the part of the rich and powerful, that I have already noted as central for Christians to having that mind that was in Christ (see section 6.5). But can we go further and aim to end other types of extinction?

The ending of some not-wholly-anthropogenic extinctions is unproblematic. The giant panda is an animal that has captured human imagination. It is not, for whatever series of reasons, one of evolution's "successes." It has a low reproduction rate, and its population is easily threatened by any diminution in the quality of its environment. Even were its bamboo forests not under threat from human activity, the panda might struggle to survive. But there is no opposition, as far as I know, to strenuous attempts to preserve it both in the wild and in captivity.

Holmes Rolston is clear that anthropogenic extinctions differ from natural as profoundly as murder from death by natural causes. "Though harmful to a species, extinction in nature is no evil in the system; it is rather the key to tomorrow."[46] The crux of our disagreement is that Rolston is still looking to the natural unfolding of the creation, whereas I regard this as the eschatological phase of history, in which humans should be looking to their own liberation and to the relief of creation's groaning.

A test-case of the difference between my view and Rolston's comes from considering two of his own examples. He records the decision of the U.S. Fish and Wildlife Service and the California Department of Fish and Game to shoot two thousand feral goats to protect three endangered plant species indigenous to San Clemente Island.[47] I endorse that move. Rolston also notes the decision of the National Park Rangers at Yellowstone not to treat an outbreak of conjunctivitis in the bighorn sheep, an emblematic species of the park. Sixty percent of the bighorns died.[48] That is an instance in which, if the sheep had been threatened with extinction, I would have advocated intervention to save the species, although the disease threatening the sheep was entirely "natural."

As Neil Messer has pointed out, in work generally sympathetic to my approach to evolutionary theodicy, humans are unable "to protect the planet from the various kinds of natural catastrophe that are supposed to have precipitated previous mass extinctions."[49] I accept that as a limit on my proposal. But I do not regard it as a fundamental objection.[50] The Earth will not support life indefinitely—no conceivable action by any creature will prevent its eventual destruction by the expanding sun[51]—but that does not prevent humans from feeling a moral imperative, as well as a self-interested impulse, to protect the richness of our terrestrial environment as long as possible (see section 6.7). Likewise, we cannot by our own efforts protect every species indefinitely, but we can see the healing of extinction as a calling to participate in the saving work of God. In both cases, we are utterly dependent, finally, on God's transforming power. The present universe will "die" eventually; only God can preserve what is of value within it. But if the Cross and Resurrection of Christ is the hinge-point of its history, then that in itself is grounds for supposing that our partnership with God's healing efforts will not be in vain.

Sean McDonagh in his recent study of extinction is surely right when he says: "The reality of extinction disrupts [this] 'companioning' by the Spirit. It also forecloses countless possibilities, not just for the species involved, but for other species that depend on that species for their well-being and survival within the web of life."[52] McDonagh's own work in the Philippines has given him a particularly powerful ecological perspective, and he writes eloquently about the possibilities being lost as a result of the current "spasm" of extinction occasioned by human activity. But when McDonagh goes on, "It [extinction] also arrests the evolutionary journey of the biosphere in its tracks, leading to a more sterile planet,"[53] then it is clear that he is operating from a narrowly contemporary perspective. Previous spasms of extinction, notably that of the dinosaurs at the Cretaceous-Tertiary boundary, allowed the evolutionary journey of the biosphere to proceed in a different direction, ultimately allowing the evolution of hominids such as ourselves. So extinction, like the rest of the process of evolution, has been an ambiguous process over the long history of life on the planet. It has been part of the "labor pains" of producing the biosphere we now know.

But I warm to McDonagh's conviction (drawing on Col. 1:20) that the Resurrection of Christ inaugurates a new era of redemption, in which all creation is to be renewed. Extending this thought, I hold that the phase of evolution in which new possibilities are explored via competition and extinction is coming to an end, and it is to be superseded by the final phase in which new possibilities of reconciliation and self-transcendence among already existing species will be explored. The hymn in Colossians 1 stresses that this transformation is first and foremost the work of Christ. However, the enigmatic passage from Romans 8 that has informed this study implies that human beings have a key role in this phase; the labor pains of creation await our coming to live in freedom. And a sign of that freedom would be that we seek to prevent any species presently companioned by the Spirit from disappearing from the network of possibilities within creation.

This is how I would respond to the recent criticisms of my proposal published by Lisa Sideris in a volume in celebration of the work of Holmes Rolston. Sideris is concerned that by seeking to end extinction I would "put an end to the very system that creates and maintains value, beauty, sentience, and even, perhaps, intelligibility in the world we inhabit."[54] She continues:

Such proposals for reconciling evolution with religion, while holding tenaciously to human perspectives on suffering and justice, require so many additional theological postulates and refinements of biological data that they become unwieldy and unconvincing. Like the Ptole-maic model of astronomy requiring numerous epicycles, gears upon gears, in order to maintain the conviction that everything revolves around Earth, these solutions become cumbersome in their attempts to "save the phenomena." The simpler, and more elegant, solution would be to admit that humans, and their particular concerns and judgments and experiences, are not the center. This, as I see it, is the answer Rolston offers environmental ethicists. To my mind, no one has yet offered a better one—with the possible exception of God who said essentially the same thing to Job.[55]

This is a harsh criticism, but an interesting one. I considered in section 2.3 the theological option of a simpler account of God, a nonbenevolent God who answers, but does not answer, Job from the whirlwind, and is the author of weal and woe alike. For some (as for Wesley Wildman) this will be the "Coper-nican" model that resolves the complexities of holding to a personal God of love and redemption. We also saw, in sections 3.2–3.3, the complex and nuanced character of Rolston's own evolutionary theodicy. It is not yet, I would still claim, fully articulated *as* theodicy, but the combination of developmental and constitutive language generates a creative matrix for further development.

The whole argument of this book is that a combination of strategies is needed to understand the goodness of God in the context of the goodness and travail of creation. I would respond to Sideris in two ways. First, in regard to the doctrine of God. Whoever supposed that the story of God with God's crea-tures would be a simple one? Simple religion is, in fact, one of the greatest threats to the human project—and hence, necessarily, to the health of the planet—since the two are intimately coupled. (That is not to say that human interests are central, but human *activity* is.) Second, in relation to her theolog-ical ethics. There is no logical step from how-nature-is to how-it-should-be. As Rolston would be the first to insist, such a judgment rests on values; it can-not rest merely on science. My claim is merely the orthodox Christian confes-sion that this is the age of the Resurrection, the inauguration of God's consummation of all things, the age in which Paul described creation as await-ing the glorious freedom of the children of God, and that the ending of extinc-tion might be an expression of that freedom, of a desire to have a small part in ending nature's travail.[56]

This proposal of mine finds an interesting ally in an unexpected quarter. E. O. Wilson famously wrote in his *On Human Nature* (first published 1978), "Theology is not likely to survive as an independent intellectual discipline" (because scientific naturalism can explain the phenomenon of religion in sociobiological terms).[57] In *The Future of Life* (2002), Wilson is interestingly optimistic about the prospects for a program of dramatically reducing extinction.[58] He also thinks religion can have a significant role in developing such a program. In the evolution of ethics, "First into the new terrain venture saints and radical theologians."[59] This role for religion (of which Wilson sees hopeful signs in the pronouncements of Pope John Paul II and Patriarch Bartholomew I) will have to be combined with the unstoppable juggernaut of technology-based capitalism,[60] but he does not see this combination as impossible, or incompatible with a generally shared environmental ethic.

It is interesting to see Wilson's analysis, since as a biologist he might well have taken the view that extinction continues to be part of the driver of evolutionary adaptation, and so should not be prevented. Presumably his position is that, given the extent of the human impact on the planet, nonhuman biodiversity has reached its maximum possible richness, and this needs to be preserved if at all possible. The view set out here is rather different, namely that with the coming to freedom of human beings in Christ the travail of evolution has run its course. Humans can now take responsibility for honoring all current ways of being alive, and offering them to God. My proposal then is an essay in what Ted Peters has called "proleptic ethics,"[61] anticipation of the kingdom of God. Wilson's stems from his understanding of where conservation biology has brought us. But while the underlying understanding of the call to end biological extinction is very different from Wilson's, I agree wholeheartedly with his core proposal as to how to go forward.

Wilson believes that it is essential to salvage immediately the world's "hotspots" of biodiversity, and to keep intact the five remaining "frontier zones" of real wilderness forest (Amazon, Congo, New Guinea, Canada/Alaska, Russia/Finland/Scandinavia).[62] Among his other proposals are the completion of the mapping of the world's biodiversity (see below), increasing the capacity of zoos and botanical gardens, and making conservation profitable. I am not convinced that big capitalism as currently constructed will be an easy ally of a long-term environmental ethic. But I do embrace the notion that economics can be done differently, and in ways that make "good planetary medicine" (to use James Lovelock's phrase[63]), and also good financial sense. Even in today's systems the costs of Wilson's proposals look remarkably modest. For as little as 0.1 percent of the world's annual domestic product ($30 billion at 2002 values), Wilson thinks that "most of the task" could be accomplished. "The protection and management of the world's existing natural reserves . . . could be financed by a one-cent-per-cup tax on coffee."[64] But Wilson is clear that the initial creation of reserves is only the first step, and is not a lasting protection against extinctions. The reserves will need to be extended in a phase of "restoration," and connected by long corridors.[65]

I tease out here some of the implications of a great project to end extinction. This will mean a huge transfer of resources from the urban heartlands of human wealth to places of high biodiversity but relative human poverty.[66] It will mean a huge switching of research from weapons- and defense-related projects to the increased understanding of biological ecosystems. It will mean keeping some species in artificial environments, if competition would ordinarily mean their extinction. It may mean major (humane) culls of populous competing species (as in parts of the United Kingdom the alien import, the grey squirrel, is being removed to allow its smaller indigenous relative, the red squirrel, to survive). The cooperation of the human communities that live in the vicinity of endangered ecosystems will be essential. Their cultural understandings and sense of place will need to be treated with the utmost respect, and they will need to be compensated for changes in their lifestyle. So once again we are thrown back on the need for greater justice and equality of opportunity in human affairs, and for kenotic restraint on the part of the affluent. Ideally the flourishing of indigenous populations should be alongside that of the nonhuman biota, but there may be places and situations (as with the preservation of the tiger) where it is essential to have uninhabited areas in which endangered species can thrive.

This then is what might seem at first like a curious compound strategy. It calls for humans to use all their scientific ingenuity (depending as this does on the Western scientific and technological establishment, which in turn depends currently on a strongly capitalist economic basis) to find out what's there, even in the remotest areas of the world. Of a possible 55 million species currently in existence,[67] we have characterized only 1.7 million.[68] Both the fight to end extinction and the need to learn from nature's strategies (most obviously in combating disease, but also in understanding the "engineering" behind some extraordinary natural materials, such as spiders' webs) require this intensive inquiry into the natural world. It is a profoundly anthropocentric strategy (in the precise and narrow sense developed in section 6.1, of depending on a unique human calling). And yet the fruit of this inquiry will need to be a profound (and counter-capitalist) restraint as to our lives lived alongside these delicate ecosystems and their treasures.

A paradoxical strategy this may be, but I consider such a mixture of concentrated investigation and kenotic restraint to be deeply Christian—indeed, to be a variant of the saying recorded of Jesus in the Gospels that his disciples should be wise as serpents and gentle as doves (Matt. 10:16). The theme of wisdom has come to the fore in Christian writing recently, in a seminal essay by Dan Hardy and more recently in a number of works by Celia Deane-Drummond.[69] Wisdom involves concentrated attention to the creation, the sort of ruthlessly honest seeing to which John Berger and Annie Dillard[70]—in their very different ways—have called us (the same profound seeing-into as Gerard Manley Hopkins practiced in his search for the inscapes of things; see section 6.3). It involves a priestly celebration of that creation (see section 6.8), and by the same token, the sort of knowing, loving, skillful, and reverent sacramentalism to which Wendell Berry calls us. It must reject, as Berry so rightly points out, ignorant, greedy destructiveness.

It is fascinating to compare Wilson's "solution" with the deep-ecological view propounded by Arne Naess thirty years before.[71] The ecological crisis in general, and the problem of extinction in particular, have become much more intense in those thirty years; the hotspots of maximum biodiversity yet more depleted and endangered, and yet Wilson still believes that capitalism (allied to science and religion) can deliver conservation, through such ingenious measures as debt-for-nature swaps, land-lease purchases by NGOs, and carbon-credit trading. Naess, on the other hand, believed a "deep ecological" paradigm shift would require a transformation of "basic economic, technological and ideological structures."[72] For Wilson, religions (it seems) could help to provide the change of heart; capitalism will provide the mechanisms. (One may also contrast Wilson's view with that of Michael Boulter, for whom the scene is already set for a new mass extinction event.[73])

I side with Wilson at least insofar as I regard the suppression of extinction, of all kinds, as a contemporary priority, and that whatever social mechanisms are available should be used to achieve this. Also in that I consider that this will depend on humans taking responsibility for ecosystems, and using our distinctive gifts, especially those of scientific rationality, to achieve this. Naess was right that lasting and fundamental change requires deep-seated changes of attitude, but the particular way he framed this is not the one adopted here. Rather I see the attitude required as being one that recognizes the ambiguities of natural systems and seeks to participate in their eventual and divinely promised healing. This attitude, then, is resolutely anthropocentric, in recognizing the distinctive role of human beings in managing ecosystems. Management will often involve the creation of reserves from which unsustainable human activity is banned, but this will still be an active process, because of the need to police the reserves and to monitor the biotic systems they contain, which will necessarily be dynamic and ever-changing. Also because global influences, such as climate change and globally distributed pollutants, are becoming more and more important, such that systems are not secured simply by putting a fence around them. But the deeper change of attitude will involve not only claiming our role as created co-creators and co-redeemers (see section 6.7), but exercising a kenosis of self-assertion, of our own appetites and desires, truly coming to have "the mind of Christ Jesus," a profoundly kenotic mind in respect of our own attitudes and aspirations (see section 6.5).

We shall fulfill our co-redeeming role, becoming partners with God in the healing of our little corner of the cosmos, when we reveal our true Christ-likeness by having our minds set on servanthood. We shall transcend ourselves not by the consummation of all our desires but through reeducating them in wisdom, so as to liberate the nonhuman creation from this particular mark of its travail. It is my argument that this "renewing of [our] minds" (Rom. 12:2) stems most naturally from a contemplation of the self-giving creative love within the Trinity, and of the particular human opportunity and calling to become true selves, indwelling and indwelt by Father, Son, and Holy Spirit. As Denis Edwards helpfully reminds me, taking forward my own conviction about the human calling, it is the eucharist in which we, quintessentially, act out our eschatological role as contemplatives and priests, and draw near with all creation to the mystery of the triune life of God. The eucharist, he writes, is "a living, participatory memory of all God has done for us in creation and redemption. It is also an experience of the divine eschatological Communion. All creatures are embraced and loved in this divine Communion. To participate in God is to participate in God's feeling for individual creatures. It is to remember every sparrow that falls to the ground and to know that it has its place in God."[74]

7.5 CONCLUSION

So our journey into the deep problem of evolutionary theodicy ends—with proposals in environmental ethics, grounded in the most central Christian understandings of servanthood, contemplation, and worship. A consequence of the breadth of my approach, and my insistence that only a compound theodicy (such as I articulated in section 1.8) can do justice to this difficult area of exploration, may indeed be that my approach appears complex and "epicyclic" to some. But I hope that its very breadth may enable it to function as a guide to the debate, even for those with very different perceptions from my own.

I hope too that the reader comes away from the book with a sense of the importance of the problem it raises—a problem not to be dismissed either on the basis of a denial of the sufferings of nonhuman creatures, or on the basis of an unscientific denial of the ambiguity of the character of the creation, or by assigning that ambiguity to a spurious and equally unscientific appeal to a historical fall. Creation, then, has from the first emergence of life been "very good," in certain senses, and also "groaning in travail."

All theodicies that engage with real situations rather than philosophical abstractions, and endeavor to give an account of the God of the Christian Scriptures, arise out of protest and end in mystery. Theodicies never "work," in the sense of solving the problem of suffering in the world. But if a theodicy enables others to be challenged and fascinated by the questions they raise, and if it stirs those others to greater compassion for creaturely pain, to deeper prayer, and to partnering, in however small a way, the loving and merciful purposes of God, then it has done all that can be hoped of it.

Whether in the end this volume justifies the time and resources spent on it, and on my travels to Nara and the North-East Transvaal and the Juan de Fuca Strait, only the reader can decide.

Drewsteignton and Exeter, October 2007

Notes

Preface

1. Holmes Rolston III, "Naturalizing and Systematizing Evil," in *Is Nature Ever Evil? Religion, Science, and Value*, ed. Willem B. Drees, 67–86 (London: Routledge, 2003), esp. 67.
2. Douglas H. Chadwick, "Investigating a Killer," *National Geographic* 207, no. 4 (April 2005): 86–105, esp. 99.

Chapter 1

1. Alfred, Lord Tennyson, "In Memoriam A.H.H." LVI: 13–16, in *Tennyson: A Selected Edition*, ed. Christopher Ricks (1969; repr., Harlow: Longman, 1989), 399. It is often supposed that Tennyson was writing in response to Darwin's model of evolution by natural selection, but in fact these stanzas precede *The Origin of Species* by some years. Ricks believes they may have derived from Tennyson's reading of Lyell's *Principles of Geology* (which also greatly influenced Darwin); see *Tennyson: A Selected Edition*, first note to p. 398.
2. Charles Darwin, *On the Origin of Species by Means of Natural Selection, or the Preservation of Favored Races in the Struggle for Life* (London: John Murray, 1859).
3. Charles Darwin's letters are now being published in full on the World Wide Web. This excellent resource can be found through www.darwinproject.ac.uk. The letter to Hooker, dated July 13 1856, is cataloged as Letter No. 1924.
4. J. R. Illingworth, "The Problem of Pain: Its Bearing on Faith in God," in *Lux Mundi: A Series of Studies in the Religion of the Incarnation*, 3rd ed., ed. Charles Gore, 113–26 (1888; repr., London: John Murray, 1890). For a survey of theological responses to Darwin, see John Hedley Brooke, *Science and Religion: Some Historical Perspectives* (Cambridge: Cambridge University Press, 1991), esp. chap. 8.
5. For a more developed introduction, see Christopher Southgate, Michael Robert Negus, and Andrew Robinson, "Theology and Evolutionary Biology," in *God, Humanity and the Cosmos: Revised and Expanded as a Companion to the Science-Religion Debate*, 154–92 (London and New York: T&T Clark/Continuum, 2005). René van Woudenberg sums up the principle of natural selection as follows: "If many offspring must die (for not all can be accommodated in nature's limited *ecology*), and individuals in all species vary among themselves, then on average survivors will tend to be those individuals with variations that are best suited ('fitted') to their particular local environment. Since *genetic* heredity exists, the offspring of survivors will tend to resemble their successful parents. The accumulation of these favorable variants through time produces evolution-

ary change" ("Darwinian and Teleological Explanations: Are They Incompatible?" in *Evolution and Ethics: Human Morality in Biological and Religious Perspective*, ed. Philip Clayton and Jeffrey Schloss, 171–86 (Grand Rapids and Cambridge: Eerdmans, 2004], 178, emphases mine). Note that this is a modern version of Darwin's principle. The words in italics would not have been understood by Darwin in their modern sense, but the core principle is the same.

6. Predation is an excellent strategy for deriving energy from the environment, because in the bodies of organisms the energy comes in an already highly ordered form, together with the essential building blocks of life. So it is no surprise that whole pyramids of predation build up; these are what ecologists term "food chains."

7. Holmes Rolston III, *Science and Religion: A Critical Survey* (1987; repr., Philadelphia and London: Templeton Foundation Press, 2006), 134.

8. Darwin, *The Origin of Species*, 490. Fascinatingly in the second and subsequent editions Darwin inserted after "breathed" the words "by the Creator." For the complex textual history of *Origin*, see *The Origin of Species: A Variorum Text*, ed. Morse Peckham (1959; repr., Philadelphia: University of Pennsylvania Press, 2006), or the very helpful online versions of all Darwin's published work at www.darwin-online.org.uk. For insights into Darwin's own religious journey, see, for example, A. Desmond and J. Moore, *Darwin* (London: Michael Joseph, 1991).

9. Southgate, Negus, and Robinson, "Theology and Evolutionary Biology," 170–71. See also Eva Jablonka and Marion J. Lamb, *Evolution in Four Dimensions: Genetic, Epigenetic and Behavioral, and Symbolic Variation in the History of Life* (Cambridge, MA: MIT Press, 2005), and Marc W. Kirschner and John C. Gerhart, *The Plausibility of Life: Resolving Darwin's Dilemma* (New Haven, CT, and London: Yale University Press, 2005), for some radical new developments within the theory. I hasten to add that the continual evolution of the theory does not mean that its basic insights are under pressure. They still constitute one of the most robust theoretical frameworks on the whole of science, supported by evidence from a whole range of sciences from geology to molecular genetics.

As Niels Henrik Gregersen notes, the majority opinion among scientists is that natural selection is constrained by the character of self-organization ("The Complexification of Nature: Supplementing the Neo-Darwinian Paradigm?" *Theology and Science* 4, no. 1 [March 2006]: 5–31, especially 18). The options that can be explored within an evolutionary "fitness landscape" depend on physical and chemical constraints particular to that type of system. Certain options (such as having five digits on a hand, for instance) were set into the pattern of organismic development millions of years in the past. Some of these set patterns may be "frozen accidents," but others reflect the optimal solutions in terms of the symmetries of systems that organize themselves. Not every "hopeful monster" can be explored by evolution. For more on fitness landscapes, see section 4.4.

10. Holmes Rolston III, "Does Evolution Need to be Redeemed?" *Zygon* 29, no. 2 (June 1994): 205–29, quotation is on 213.

11. *The City of God*, 12, 4, quoted in A. Richard Kingston, "Theodicy and Animal Welfare," *Theology* 70 (November 1967): 482–88, 485. Of course, Augustine is right that we never see the picture whole, but merely to leave the subject there is to leave suffering as a matter of mystery. Theodicy is an effort at least to move as far as we rationally can into the enigma of God's ways with the world.

12. So I do not agree with Brian Hebblethwaite's judgment that "it is modern moral

sensibility rather than modern scientific knowledge that has accentuated the problem [of trying to find out why God allows so much evil in his creation]." See "The Problem of Evil" in *Keeping the Faith: Essays to Mark the Centenary of Lux Mundi*, ed. Geoffrey Wainwright, 54–77 (London: SPCK, 1989), 54–55. Rather I think that more attention to the implications of Darwinian science might have led theologians to a greater stress on the evolutionary as well as the moral component of theodicy.

13. I thank my wife Sandy for the gift of the suggestion that this is the sort of insight we might gain in heaven. That makes heaven, to me, a much more appealing place than some Christian descriptions suggest. See the opening sections of Yann Martel's novel *The Life of Pi* (2002; repr., Edinburgh: Canongate, 2003), for some counterintuitive assessments of the character of animal life in the wild. Also Thomas Nagel, "What Is It Like to Be a Bat?" *Philosophical Review* 83 (October 1974): 435–50, reprinted in T. Nagel, *Mortal Questions* (Cambridge: Cambridge University Press, 1979).

14. Patrick Bateson and Elizabeth L. Bradshaw, "Physiological Effects of Hunting Red Deer (Cervus elaphus)," *Proceedings of the Royal Society B* 264 (December 1997): 1707–14.

15. Wesley J. Wildman has made an important effort to clarify terminology in this field. He chooses the term "suffering" to cover everything from physical injury to a biological organism through "conscious pain" to "emotional distress" and "existential anxiety." Wildman is helpful in clarifying why we should not impute suffering either to a "dying" star, or yet to an ecosystem as a whole. He concludes rightly that suffering "can only exist in the context of intensely structured, biochemically regulated forms of being" (Wesley J. Wildman, "The Use and Meaning of the Term 'Suffering' in Relation to Nature," *Physics and Cosmology: Scientific Perspectives on the Problem of Evil in Nature*, ed. Nancey Murphy, Robert J. Russell, and William Stoeger, SJ, 53–66 [Berkeley, CA, and Vatican City: CTNS and Vatican Observatory, 2007]). However, I do not share his sense that the term "suffering" is a neutral word well suited to covering the range of meanings he asks of it. I think injury takes place in many organisms without pain being experienced; insects may well be an example (see David deGrazia, *Taking Animals Seriously: Mental Life and Moral Status* [Cambridge: Cambridge University Press, 1996], chap. 5), and pain where it is experienced may be momentary, succeeded either by relief (or by death). I would not regard such situations as necessarily involving *suffering*. Suffering seems to me to belong only to situations of intense pain, particularly where no relief is in sight, and prolonged distress, physical or psychic.

As deGrazia indicates in summarizing recent work on animal pain and suffering, there is ample evidence that animals feel pain. We see them avoiding noxious stimuli, and "saving" a hurt muscle or limb. We see social animals crying out for assistance. Importantly, we see behavior being modified in response to pain. (Contrast this with the opinion of Charles Raven in 1927 that "It may be doubted whether there is any real pain without a frontal cortex, a foreplan in mind, and a love which can put itself in the place of another, and these are the attributes of humanity" [*The Creator Spirit: A Survey of Christian Doctrine in the Light of Biology, Psychology and Mysticism* (London: Martin Hopkinson, 1927), 120.]).

DeGrazia defines suffering as "a highly unpleasant emotional state associated with more-than-minimal pain or distress." Clearly animals can suffer more-than-minimal pain, and they can suffer the distress that comes from difficulty in adapting to a new circumstance. DeGrazia also discusses the evidence for fear and anxiety in animals. Fear itself requires some sense of the future, however primitive. Tellingly, the neurophysiological responses we can measure in animals show very similar pathways of brain activity in response to stimuli giving rise to fear and anxiety. DeGrazia's conclusion is that "*the available evidence suggests that most or all vertebrates, and perhaps some invertebrates, can suffer*" (123, emphasis in original).

My own inclination is to see "suffering" not as a "neutral" word but as a word evoking a very negative experience, either acute or chronic, and hence to use the term more in deGrazia's sense than Wildman's.

16. Kenneth R. Miller, *Finding Darwin's God: A Scientist's Search for Common Ground between God and Evolution* (New York: HarperCollins, 1999), 246.

17. Robert J. Russell, "Natural Theodicy in an Evolutionary Context: The Need for an Eschatology of New Creation," in *Theodicy and Eschatology*, ed. Bruce Barber and David Neville, 121–52 (Hindmarsh, South Australia: Australian Theological Forum, 2005), see 128–29.

18. A religion such as Buddhism has very different strategies for confronting suffering.

19. Quentin Smith, "An Atheological Argument from Evil Natural Laws," *International Journal for Philosophy of Religion* 29, no. 3 (June 1991): 159–74, emphasis in original.

20. So also Thomas F. Torrance, *Divine and Contingent Order* (Oxford: Oxford University Press, 1981): "if we did not believe that God is good and that the temporal order of things he has conferred upon the universe serves his good will, we would have no problem with decay, decomposition, and death, or with entropy, nor would we find affliction and suffering intolerable for they would be treated merely as part of the natural process of things" (120).

21. See Michael Lloyd, "Are Animals Fallen?" in *Animals on the Agenda: Questions about Animals for Theology and Ethics*, ed. Andrew Linzey and Dorothy Yamamoto, 147–60 (London: SCM Press, 1997), esp. 147–48. For more on self-giving, see section 4.5.

22. A particularly telling example is the evolution (both in mammalian and marsupial lines) of saber-toothed cats. The dentition of the saber-toothed cat was excellently adapted to the ripping open of the throats of prey animals and to the slashing and puncturing of flesh. *Smilodon fatalis*, the saber-toothed tiger, flourished 2.5 million years ago, long before the advent of modern humans. (I thank Dr. Dennis Lamoureux for this example.)

23. See in particular Aldo Leopold, *A Sand County Almanac: With Essays on Conservation from Round River* (New York: Ballantine Books, 1966; *A Sand County Almanac* first published 1949), and Annie Dillard, *Pilgrim at Tinker Creek*, in *Three by Annie Dillard* (New York: HarperCollins, 2001).

24. Lisa H. Sideris, *Environmental Ethics, Ecological Theology, and Natural Selection* (New York: Columbia University Press, 2003), especially her critique of ecofeminist writers such as Sallie McFague and Rosemary Radford Ruether in chap. 2. See also a similar charge against ecofeminists in B. Jill Carroll, *The Savage Side: Reclaiming Violent Models of God* (Lanham, MD, and Oxford: Rowman and Littlefield, 2001).

25. Michael Pollan, *The Omnivore's Dilemma: A Natural History of Four Meals* (New York: Penguin, 2006), 322–23.

26. On seeing nature truly, see also Gary Snyder, "Blue Mountains Constantly

Walking," in *The Practice of the Wild* (1990; repr., New York: North Point Press, 1993), 97–115, esp. 110–11; Ruth Page, "God, Natural Evil and the Ecological Crisis," *Studies in World Christianity* 3, no. 1 (1997): 68–86.

27. And still continue to be an inspiration to those tracking evolution; see J. Weiner, *The Beak of the Finch* (London: Jonathan Cape, 1994).

28. David L. Hull, "God of the Galapagos," *Nature* 352 (August 1992): 485–86.

29. On the interplay of chance and law in scientifically informed Christian theologies of creation see in particular John Polkinghorne, *Science and Christian Belief: Reflections of a Bottom-up Thinker* (London: SPCK, 1994); Arthur Peacocke, *Theology for a Scientific Age: Being and Becoming—Natural, Divine and Human*, enlarged ed. (London: SCM Press, 1993); and Keith Ward, *God, Chance and Necessity* (Oxford: Oneworld, 1996).

30. So some of Dillard's horror at contemplating the activities of insects need not necessarily translate into a problem of suffering (see *Three by Annie Dillard*, 164–67, but note DeGrazia, *Taking Animals Seriously*, chap. 5, pointing out that the simplicity of insects' central nervous systems, and their lack of aversive behavior at noxious stimuli, suggests that they do not suffer as higher organisms do). To Dillard's more general response of wanting to "shake her fist" at creation, Holmes Rolston has responded that he would rather "raise both hands and cheer" ("Naturalizing and Systematizing Evil," in *Is Nature Ever Evil? Religion, Science and Value*, ed. Willem B. Drees, 67–86 [London: Routledge, 2003], 82). This underlines the subjectivity of our aesthetic responses.

31. A point particularly well made by Arthur Peacocke; see, for example, his "Biological Evolution—A Positive Theological Appraisal," in *Evolutionary and Molecular Biology: Scientific Perspectives on Divine Action*, ed. Robert J. Russell, William R. Stoeger, SJ, and Francisco J. Ayala, 357–76 (Vatican City: Vatican Observatory; Berkeley, CA: CTNS, 1998), esp. 366–67.

32. Cf. Holmes Rolston III, *Genes, Genesis and God: Values and Their Origins in Natural and Human History—The Gifford Lectures, University of Edinburgh 1997–1998* (Cambridge: Cambridge University Press, 1999), 304.

33. Rolston, "Naturalizing and Systematizing Evil," 83; Peacocke, "Biological Evolution," 369; also Denis Edwards, *The God of Evolution: A Trinitarian Theology* (Mahwah, NJ: Paulist Press, 1999), 38–39.

34. Cf. Patricia A. Williams, *Doing without Adam and Eve: Sociobiology and Original Sin* (Minneapolis: Fortress Press, 2001), 169–70; also Niels Henrik Gregersen, "The Cross of Christ in an Evolutionary World," *dialog: A Journal of Theology* 40, no. 3 (Fall 2001): 192–207, esp. 198.

35. Holmes Rolston III, *Environmental Ethics: Duties to and Values in the Natural World* (Philadelphia: Temple University Press, 1988), 95–106.

36. I owe this observation to Dr. Andrew Robinson.

37. And it is worth noting that a very high proportion of all the species that have ever lived, over 98 percent, are now extinct. As Richard W. Kropf notes, "The statistically usual outcome of evolution is not, then, the progressive appearance of higher forms but simply obliteration" (*Evil and Evolution: A Theodicy* [1984; repr., Eugene, OR: Wipf and Stock, 2004], 98, quoting the evolutionary biologist G. G. Simpson).

38. Daryl P. Domning and Monika K. Hellwig, *Original Selfishness: Original Sin in the Light of Evolution* (Aldershot and Burlington, VT: Ashgate, 2006), 75.

39. On Hume, see "Design arguments" in Brian Davies, ed., *Philosophy of Religion: A Guide and Anthology*, 245–303 (Oxford: Oxford University Press, 2000).

40. Darwin, Letter No. 2814 to Asa Gray, dated May 22, 1860, www.darwin project.ac.uk.

41. Quoted in John Hedley Brooke, "Darwin and Victorian Christianity," in *The Cambridge Companion to Darwin*, ed. Jonathan Hodge and Gregory Radick, 192–213 (Cambridge: Cambridge University Press, 2003), 206.

42. The phrase was first used by the Reverend Charles Kingsley (cited in Keith Ward, *Pascal's Fire: Scientific Faith and Religious Understanding* [Oxford: Oneworld, 2006], 40).

43. Quoted in Arthur Peacocke, *Paths from Science towards God: The End of All Our Exploring* (Oxford: Oneworld, 2001), 136. This motif of Darwinism as the disguised friend of Christianity has been a particular influence on Peacocke, and is also found in the writing of John F. Haught. See his *God after Darwin: A Theology of Evolution* (Oxford and Boulder, CO: Westview Press, 2000), esp. chap. 4.

44. Not that an "arm's-length," freedom-giving God is necessarily an answer to the problem of evolutionary suffering. Philip Kitcher writes, "Our conception of a providential Creator must suppose that He has constructed a shaggy-dog story, a history of life that consists of a three-billion-year curtain-raiser to the main event, in which millions of sentient beings suffer, often acutely, and that the suffering is not a by-product but constitutive of the script that the Creator has chosen to write. . . . The charge doesn't go away when the action of the Creator is made more remote. For a history of life dominated by natural selection is extremely hard to understand in providentialist terms" (*Living with Darwin: Evolution, Design and the Future of Faith* [Oxford: Oxford University Press, 2007], 123–24). For more on divine action in the world, see section 4.6.

45. C. C. J. Webb, *Problems in the Relations of God and Man* (London: James Nisbet & Co., 1911), 268; cf. John Hick, *Evil and the God of Love* (1966; repr., Basingstoke and London: Macmillan, 1985), 345.

46. So Hick can write: "The more fruitful question for theodicy is not why animals are liable to pain as well as pleasure—for this follows from their nature as living creatures—but rather why these lower forms of life should exist at all" (*Evil and the God of Love*, 350). Clearly he shows no sign here of engaging with an evolutionary narrative of the origin of humans and other creatures.

47. Southgate, Negus and Robinson, "Theology and Evolutionary Biology," 166.

48. C. S. Lewis, *The Problem of Pain* (1940; repr., New York: Macmillan, 1962), 138. For an overview of Lewis's approach, see Andrew Linzey, "C. S. Lewis's Theology of Animals," *Anglican Theological Review* 80, no. 1 (Winter 1998): 60–81.

49. Most famously by Lynn White Jr., "The Historical Roots of Our Ecologic Crisis," *Science* 155 (March 1967): 1203–7 (reprinted with anglicizations in *The Care of Creation: Focusing Concern and Action*, ed. R. J. Berry, 31–42 [Leicester: InterVarsity Press, 2000]).

50. Schweitzer was committed to an ethic of "Reverence for Life" and to the concept that humans had a responsibility to assist all life. For an introduction see Albert Schweitzer, *My Life and Thought: An Autobiography*, trans. C. T. Campion (1931; English ed., London: George Allen and Unwin, 1933), esp. chap. 21. Note also Karl Barth's sympathetic critique of Schweitzer in *Church Dogmatics*, III/4, trans. A. T. Mackay, T. H. L. Parker, H. Knight, H. A. Kennedy, and J. Marks (Edinburgh: T&T Clark, 1961), 349–50.

51. See Pierre Teilhard de Chardin, *The Phenomenon of Man, with an introduction by Sir Julian Huxley*, trans. Bernard Wall (1955; English ed., New York: Harper

and Row, 1975); *Christianity and Evolution*, trans. René Hague (1969; English ed., London: Collins, 1971).

52. See deGrazia, *Taking Animals Seriously*, chap. 5.

53. Andrew Elphinstone, *Freedom, Suffering and Love* (London: SCM Press, 1976); Arthur Peacocke, *Creation and the World of Science: The Bampton Lectures 1978* (Oxford: Clarendon Press, 1979); Kropf, *Evil and Evolution*; Rolston, *Science and Religion*; Paul S. Fiddes, *The Creative Suffering of God* (Oxford: Clarendon Press, 1988); Jürgen Moltmann, *God in Creation: An Ecological Doctrine of Creation (Gifford Lectures 1984–5)*, trans. M. Kohl (1985; English ed., London: SCM Press, 1985); Moltmann, *The Way of Jesus Christ: Christology in Messianic Dimensions*, trans. M. Kohl (1989; English ed., London: SCM Press, 1990).

54. For a dramatic example, see the article by the ecofeminist Val Plumwood about being severely injured in a crocodile attack. See her "Being Prey," *UTNE Reader*, July/August 2000, available at www.utne.com/issues/2000_100/features/1209-1.html.

55. Holmes Rolston III, "Disvalues in Nature," *The Monist* 75 (April 1992): 250–78, esp. 255–56.

56. Rolston, *Science and Religion*, "Disvalues in Nature," "Does Evolution Need to Be Redeemed?" and "Naturalizing and Systematizing Evil." See also section 3.3.

57. A phrase used by Gregersen in "The Cross of Christ," 201.

58. Robin Attfield, *Creation, Evolution and Meaning* (Aldershot and Burlington, VT: Ashgate, 2006), chaps. 6–7.

59. Cf. also Gregersen, "The Cross of Christ," 201: "The limitations of this theodicy [of the world as a 'package deal,' in which disvalues are necessary to experiences of value] should not go unnoticed. Only the presence of pain is explained, not the exuberance of pain in creation which is and should remain a challenge. . . . Moreover, an evolutionary theodicy assumes a global, systemic view of evil. It offers no comfort to the individual suffering person" [or nonhuman creature].

60. David Bentley Hart, *The Doors of the Sea: Where Was God in the Tsunami?* (Grand Rapids and Cambridge: Eerdmans, 2005).

61. Fyodor Dostoevsky, *The Karamazov Brothers, A New Translation by Ignat Avsey* (1880; English ed., 1994; repr., Oxford and New York: Oxford University Press, 1998).

62. Ibid., 306–8.

63. Hart, *The Doors of the Sea*, 70, emphasis in original.

64. Dostoevsky himself was clear as to the difference, as in this from earlier in Ivan's speech: "We often talk of man's 'bestial' cruelty, but this is terribly unjust and insulting to beasts: a wild animal could never be as cruel as man, as artistic, as refined in his cruelty. The tiger mauls and tears its prey because that is all it knows. It would never enter its head to leave people all night nailed by their ears, even if it could do it" *(Karamazov Brothers*, 299). And the human experience of suffering is rendered all the more extreme, compared with that of animals, by the human capacity for cruelty.

65. A famous example in the literature is William L. Rowe's in "The Problem of Evil and Varieties of Atheism," in *The Problem of Evil*, ed. Marilyn McCord Adams and Robert Merrihew Adams, 126–37 (Oxford: Oxford University Press, 1990). Rowe writes of a forest fire in which "a fawn is trapped, horribly burned, and lies in terrible agony for several days before death relieves its suf-

fering" (129–30), and claims that this is indeed truly pointless suffering.

66. These ideas were already in my mind in 1999; see Christopher Southgate, ed., *God, Humanity, and the Cosmos: A Textbook in Science and Religion* (Edinburgh: T&T Clark, 1999), 275. The only references I have since seen to the application of Dostoevsky's passage to evolutionary theodicy are in Kropf, *Evil and Evolution*, 124, and Jill Le Blanc, "A Mystical Response to Disvalues in Nature," *Philosophy Today* 45, no. 3/4 (Fall 2001): 254–65.

67. Richard Dawkins, *River out of Eden: A Darwinian View of Life* (London: Weidenfeld and Nicolson, 1995), 133.

68. P. Brown, T. Sunitka, M. J. Morwood, R. P. Soejono, Jatmiko, and E. W. Saptomo, "A New Small-Bodied Hominin from the Late Pleistocene in Flores, Indonesia," *Nature* 431 (October 2004): 1055–61. For a summary and comment, see Jared Diamond, "The Astonishing Micropygmies," *Science* 306 (December 2004): 2047–48.

69. Kropf, *Evil and Evolution*, 126. See also Ruth Page, "Panentheism and Pansyntheism: God in Relation," in *In Whom We Live and Move and Have Our Being: Panentheistic Reflections on God's Presence in a Scientific World*, ed. Philip Clayton and Arthur Peacocke, 222–32 (Grand Rapids and Cambridge: Eerdmans, 2004).

70. This link with the Romans passage is also made by (among others) Kropf, *Evil and Evolution*, 156; Rolston, *Science and Religion*, 146; and Haught, *God after Darwin*, 38. See section 6.1 for more detailed discussion of this passage.

71. Claus Westermann, *Genesis 1–11: A Commentary*, trans. J. J. Scullion, SJ (1974; English ed., London: SPCK, 1984), 166–67.

72. Cf. also John Polkinghorne, *Reason and Reality: The Relationship between Science and Theology* (London: SPCK, 1991), seeing the goodness of creation "in terms of fruitful potentiality . . . rather than original perfection" (99).

73. See Haught, *God after Darwin*, chap. 9, on nature as unfinished and as "promise" rather than fulfilled reality.

74. Wolfhart Pannenberg, *Systematic Theology*, Vol. 3, trans. G. W. Bromiley (1993; English ed., Edinburgh: T&T Clark, and Grand Rapids: Eerdmans, 1998), 645. See also Pannenberg's comment, "The goodness of all creation obviously depends on that of humans and their being in accord with the divine purpose in creation" (*Systematic Theology*, Vol. 2, trans. G. W. Bromiley [1991; English ed., Edinburgh: T&T Clark, 1994], 162). If a "fall" of humans from original perfection is ruled out (see section 2.6), this likewise suggests that the goodness of creation will not be fully realized until the consummation of the human "project" is complete. For a related approach, see Ted Peters and Martinez Hewlett, *Evolution from Creation to New Creation: Conflict, Conversation and Convergence* (Nashville: Abingdon Press, 2003), 172; also Karl Schmitz-Moormann, *Theology of Creation in an Evolutionary World*, in collaboration with James F. Salmon, SJ (Cleveland: Pilgrim Press, 1997), 116.

75. Colin E. Gunton, *The Triune Creator: A Historical and Systematic Study* (Edinburgh: Edinburgh University Press, 1998), 56. For more on Irenaeus's Trinitarian theology of creation, see section 4.4. An alternative is to take the line pursued by Neil Messer in his *Selfish Genes and Christian Ethics: Theological Reflections on Evolutionary Biology* (London: SCM Press, 2007) and draw a sharp distinction between God's creation, which is indeed, as we learn from scriptural revelation, "very good," and "nature," which has, at least as we discern it, a distinctly ambiguous character. (See, e.g., Messer, *Selfish Genes*, 84–88.) The

difficulty with this approach is that it makes it very hard for the theological picture of the world to be genuinely informed by scientific understandings.

76. See Jürgen Moltmann, *The Coming of God: Christian Eschatology*, trans. M. Kohl (1995; English ed., Minneapolis: Fortress Press, 2004), 265–67.

77. There is an interesting relation between this position, formulated as a theodicy, and Andrew Linzey's "confession," as he puts it, in relation to his "Animal Gospel." See *Animal Gospel: Christian Faith as though Animals Mattered* (London: Hodder and Stoughton, 1998), 8–9. I thank Professor Linzey for his response to a draft of my *Zygon* paper, and for directing my attention to his confession. For more on his work on the theology and ethics of our relation to animals, see section 7.2.

78. Quoted as one of the epigraphs to Gordon D. Kaufman's *In Face of Mystery: A Constructive Theology* (Cambridge, MA, and London: Harvard University Press, 1993). Interestingly, Kaufman begins his book from Ivan's diatribe in *The Brothers Karamazov* (see section 1.7).

Chapter 2

1. Ted Peters and Martinez Hewlett, *Evolution from Creation to New Creation: Conflict, Conversation, and Convergence* (Nashville: Abingdon Press, 2003).

2. For accessible summaries of that narrative, see Bill Bryson, *A Short History of Nearly Everything* (London: Random House, 2003); Richard Fortey, *Life: An Unauthorised Biography: A Natural History of the First 4,000,000,000 Years of Life on Earth* (London: HarperCollins, 1997).

3. For honest assessments of current problems, see Michael Ruse, *Darwinism and Its Discontents* (Cambridge: Cambridge University Press, 2006); Joan Roughgarden, *Evolution and Christian Faith: Reflections of an Evolutionary Biologist* (Washington, DC: Island Press, 2006).

4. So William A. Dembski, *The Design Revolution: Answering the Toughest Questions about Intelligent Design* (Downers Grove, IL, and Leicester: InterVarsity Press, 2004), chaps. 10–14.

5. On irreducible complexity, see Michael Behe, *Darwin's Black Box: The Biochemical Challenge to Evolution* (New York: Free Press, 1996). For evaluations of intelligent design, see, for example, Michael Ruse, *Darwin and Design: Does Evolution Have a Purpose?* (Cambridge: Cambridge University Press, 2003), chap. 15; John F. Haught, *Deeper Than Darwin: The Prospect for Religion in the Age of Evolution* (Oxford and Boulder, CO: Westview Press, 2003), chap. 7; Matt Young and Taner Edis, eds., *Why Intelligent Design Fails: A Scientific Critique of the New Creationism* (2004; repr., New Brunswick, NJ, and London: Rutgers University Press, 2006).

6. Robert J. Russell, "Special Providence and Genetic Mutation: A New Defense of Theistic Evolution," in *Evolutionary and Molecular Biology: Scientific Perspectives on Divine Action*, ed. Robert J. Russell, William R. Stoeger, SJ, and Francisco Ayala, 191–223 (Vatican City: Vatican Observatory; Berkeley, CA: Center for Theology and the Natural Sciences, 1998), esp. 221–23. At the same time Russell is clear that such divine action at the quantum level need not constitute an "intervention" in the flow of natural causes.

7. But if it is accepted that biological realities are mysteriously affected by a spiritual fall, it becomes yet harder to assert that some of them are the discrete result of insertions by an intelligent designer. See the work of John F. Haught, who writes: "One-sided appeals to the idea of God as an 'intelligent designer' ren-

der the issue of theodicy all the more intractable. Advocates of 'intelligent design' typically ignore the contingency, randomness and struggle in evolution" (*God After Darwin: A Theology of Evolution* [Oxford and Boulder, CO: Westview Press, 2000], 45).

8. A variant of this approach is that the preexistent material from which creation is fashioned is chaotic, or otherwise refractory to God's goodness. See Sjoerd L. Bonting, *Chaos Theology: A Revised Creation Theology* (Ottawa: Novalis, 2002). Many process thinkers also adopt a version of this position; see, for example, Ian Barbour, *Religion and Science: Historical and Contemporary Issues* (New York: SCM Press, 1998). For a recent reassertion of the importance of creation out of nothing in the light of contemporary cosmology, see Paul Copan and William Lane Craig, *Creation out of Nothing: A Biblical, Philosophical, and Scientific Exploration* (Grand Rapids: Baker Academic; Leicester: Inter-Varsity Press, 2004).

9. Alastair H. B. Logan, *Gnostic Truth and Christian Heresy: A Study in the History of Gnosticism* (Edinburgh: T&T Clark, 1996).

10. Malcolm Lambert, *The Cathars* (Oxford: Blackwell, 1998).

11. Wesley J. Wildman, "Incongruous Goodness, Perilous Beauty, Disconcerting Truth: Ultimate Reality and Suffering in Nature," in *Physics and Cosmology: Scientific Perspectives on the Problem of Evil in Nature*, ed. Nancey Murphy, Robert J. Russell, and William Stoeger, SJ (Berkeley, CA: CTNS; Vatican City: Vatican Observatory, 2007), 267–94.

12. B. Jill Carroll, *The Savage Side: Reclaiming Violent Models of God* (Lanham, MD, and Oxford: Rowman and Littlefield, 2001).

13. Charlene P. E. Burns, "Honesty about God: Theological Reflections on Violence in an Evolutionary Universe," *Theology and Science* 4, no. 3 (November 2006): 279–90.

14. Carroll, *Savage Side*, 116.

15. Walter Wink, *The Powers*, Vol. 2, *Unmasking the Powers: The Invisible Forces That Determine Human Existence* (Philadelphia: Fortress Press, 1986).

16. Burns, "Honesty about God," 283.

17. Ibid. The quotation from Kaufman is from his *In Face of Mystery: A Constructive Theology* (Cambridge, MA, and London: Harvard University Press, 1993), 275.

18. Burns, "Honesty about God," 285. See also Niels Henrik Gregersen, "The Cross of Christ in an Evolutionary World," *dialog: A Journal of Theology* 40, no. 3 (Fall 2001): 192–207, on the theology of Luther and his concept of the *opus alienum*.

19. Such a position links with the negative or apophatic tradition in theology—the conviction that positive statements about God are bound to be incomplete, if not just plain wrong.

20. Wildman, "Incongruous Goodness," 294. There is a fascinating section at the end of Jim Cheney's article on the work of Holmes Rolston and Frederick Ferré in relation to the problem of evil. Cheney writes: "Which do we want: a world governed by a God who either treats us like infants or is constrained to act with an inhuman ruthlessness toward our suffering, *or* a world well-suited, by and large, to human flourishing, a basically nurturing world that says, in effect, have at it, you are in a world that has brought your species into existence, a world to which the human species has been finely tuned by the forces of evolution? It is a world which will kill you one way or another; it is a world that, given your particular circumstances in life, may leave you one of the wretched of the Earth

through no fault of your own: you may not even get a start down the road. . . . The earth matrix doesn't care *about* you, but it cares *for* you in the most fundamental way: it is a nourishing matrix for you and your kind—with a little luck on your side that is, and if your human culture is favorable" (Jim Cheney, "Naturalizing the Problem of Evil," *Environmental Ethics* 19, no. 3 [Fall 1997]: 299–313, at 312, emphases in original). This poses the question sharply, albeit in the human-focused way I have already noted as a recurring problem in this area. Cheney's preferred understanding (which could be addressed just as well to any species as to humans) is one that would be very much in keeping with Wildman's ground-of-being theism. The world just is; it has in Wildman's terms "incongruous goodness" and "perilous beauty," but no benevolence, neither divine parenthood nor any promise of divine redemption. My answer is a simple one, though not simply arrived at or without feeling the profound force of the question. I prefer to understand myself as living by gift in a world "fathered-forth" by "him whose beauty is past change" (to quote from "Pied Beauty" by Gerard Manley Hopkins, on whose thought I draw in chaps. 4 and 6). And it is on the basis of that understanding that I then seek to understand the nonhuman world as also the recipient of divine love, both creative and redemptive. For another variant on the attempt to depersonalize God and do theology without reference to divine love, see James M. Gustafson, *Ethics from a Theocentric Perspective*, Vol. 1, *Theology and Ethics* (Chicago: University of Chicago Press, 1981). For a highly nuanced view of the "moral indifference" of God, see Brian Davies, *The Reality of God and the Problem of Evil* (London and New York: Continuum, 2006), 251–55.

21. This is a conviction simply but powerfully put by David E. Jenkins in his credo: "God is. He is as he is in Jesus. Therefore there is hope" (*God, Jesus, and Life in the Spirit* [London: SCM Press, 1988], 8).

22. Alfred North Whitehead, *Process and Reality: An Essay in Cosmology* (Cambridge: Cambridge University Press, 1929).

23. David Pailin, *God and the Processes of Reality: Foundations of a Credible Theism* (London: Routledge, 1989), 51.

24. Barbour, *Religion and Science*, 285.

25. For brief but clear expositions of process thought, see Paul S. Fiddes, *The Creative Suffering of God* (Oxford: Clarendon Press, 1988), 40–45, or Barbour, *Nature, Human Nature, and God* (Minneapolis: Fortress Press, 2002), 94–100, 111–18.

26. See Pailin, *God and the Processes of Reality*, chap. 4. Keith Ward wants to propose a different type of theism, but sees clearly the helpfulness of dipolarity. He writes: "The basic idea of divine dipolarity, with its associated place for temporality and possibility in God, may survive dissociation from general process metaphysics" (*Religion and Creation* [Oxford: Oxford University Press, 1996], 308).

27. Whitehead, *Process and Reality*, 532.

28. But interestingly David Pailin and Joseph Bracken (see next note) both restore this within their process schemes.

29. Joseph A. Bracken, SJ, *Christianity and Process Thought: Spirituality for a Changing World* (Philadelphia and London: Templeton Foundation Press, 2006).

30. Ibid., 31.

31. In his impressive *Theology and the Problem of Evil* (Oxford: Basil Blackwell, 1988), especially chaps. 4 and 5.

32. Hans Jonas, *Mortality and Morality: A Search for the Good after Auschwitz—A (Posthumous) Collection of Essays edited by Lawrence Vogel* (Evanston, IL: Northwestern University Press, 1996), 125.

33. Haught, *God after Darwin*, 184.

34. Pierre Teilhard de Chardin, *The Phenomenon of Man: With an Introduction by Sir Julian Huxley*, trans. B. Wall (1955; English ed., 1959; repr., New York: Harper and Row, 1975). For a brief, if critical, summary of Teilhard's work, see H. Paul Santmire, *The Travail of Nature: The Ambiguous Ecological Promise of Christian Theology* (Philadelphia: Fortress Press, 1985), 155–71; for new studies, see David Grumett, *Teilhard de Chardin: Theology, Humanity, and Cosmos* (Leuven: Peeters, 2005), and Arthur Fabel and Donald St. John, eds., *Teilhard in the 21st Century: The Emerging Spirit of Earth* (Maryknoll, NY: Orbis, 2003). See also a whole issue of *Ecotheology* devoted to Teilhard's thought: vol. 10, no. 2 (August 2005).

35. Peter Medawar, *The Strange Case of the Spotted Mice and Other Classic Essays in Science* (Oxford: Oxford University Press, 1996), 1–11, reprinting a review first published in *Mind* in 1961.

36. R. J. Berry, "The Lions Seek Their Prey from God: Response to the Boyle Lecture," *Science and Christian Belief* 17, no. 1 (April 2005): 41–56.

37. Holmes Rolston III, "Does Evolution Need to Be Redeemed?" *Zygon* 29, no. 2 (June 1994): 205–29, on 218.

38. John Polkinghorne, *Faith, Science, and Understanding* (London: SPCK, 2000), 95–99.

39. The end or ultimate purpose.

40. Teilhard de Chardin, *Phenomenon of Man*, 313, emphases in original.

41. Raymond J. Nogar, OP, writing in *The Lord of the Absurd* (1966; repr., Notre Dame, IN: University of Notre Dame Press, 1998), notes that "Father Teilhard saw unity wherever he looked" (119). But Nogar cannot see this; he sees rather "the disorder, the waste, the hectic disorganization of the fragments of the universe" (121). Likewise, Nogar is troubled by Teilhard's theology of the Cross. He quotes Teilhard as saying that "[this] is what the Cross means . . . the sublime aspect of a law common to *all* life" (122). Nogar finds this unacceptable; the cross must always be a "scandal to the Jews" and "folly to the Greeks" (124). F. W. Dillistone, however, in his classic study *The Christian Understanding of Atonement* (1968; repr., London: SCM Press, 1984), concludes: "However deficient Teilhard's system may be in its dealing with radical evil in nature and the proud rebellion of man to which I shall be referring later, it is an immensely impressive attempt to interpret the groaning and travailing of the natural order in the light of the experience of a life-time spent in first-hand scientific investigation" (see 59–62, quotation on 62).

42. As might be gathered from the title of a noted article on him by Ian G. Barbour, "Five Ways of Reading Teilhard," *Soundings* 51 (Spring 1968): 115–45.

43. For example, Jürgen Moltmann, *The Way of Jesus Christ: Christology in Messianic Dimensions*, trans. M. Kohl (1989; English ed., London: SCM Press, 1990), 292–97.

44. See John F. Haught, "The Boyle Lecture 2003: Darwin, Design and the Promise of Nature," *Science and Christian Belief* 17 (April 2005): 5–20 (note that this was actually the 2004 Lecture, given on February 4 of that year); Celia Deane-Drummond, "Sophia, Mary and the Eternal Feminine in Pierre Teilhard de Chardin and Sergei Bulgakov," *Ecotheology* 10, no. 2 (August 2005): 215–31.

45. Grumett, *Teilhard de Chardin*.

46. Cf. Brian Horne, *Imagining Evil* (London: Darton, Longman, and Todd, 1996): "Acceptance of a theory of evolution need not evacuate the [Edenic] myth of its potency, but it does require us to read it differently and see the relation between physical evil and moral evil (murder, cruelty, hatred, envy, etc.) in a different way. It will require us to view pain and death not as evil and outrageous, arising out of some act in the distant past, but as plain and inescapable facts of biological existence" (130).

47. See, for example, its intrusion into the otherwise very sophisticated treatment of the theodicy problem in David Bentley Hart's *The Doors of the Sea: Where Was God in the Tsunami?* (Grand Rapids and Cambridge: Eerdmans, 2005), 63.

48. Unless one takes the weird, and theologically extremely problematic, view espoused by William Dembski that God disordered creation in foreknowledge of human sin, in order to demonstrate to humans their insanity (see his "Christian Theodicy in Light of Genesis and Modern Science," available at www.designinference.com, accessed on August 14, 2007). As A. Richard Kingston noted forty years ago, any theory that blames God's response to human sin for the violence in nature, or concedes that God allowed human sin to pervert the goodness of creation resulting in wholesale animal suffering, also "fails the moral test" of behavior consistent with a good God ("Theodicy and Animal Welfare," *Theology* 70 [November 1967]: 482–88, at 483).

49. Polkinghorne, *Reason and Reality* (London: SPCK, 1991), 99.

50. Arthur Peacocke, *Theology for a Scientific Age: Being and Becoming—Natural, Divine and Human*, enlarged ed. (Oxford: Blackwell, 1993), 222–23, italics in original. Cf. also Paul Tillich, *Systematic Theology*, Vol. 2 (1957; repr., London: James Nisbet & Co., 1964): "Theology must clearly and unambiguously represent 'the Fall' as a symbol for the human situation universally, not as the story of an event that happened 'once upon a time'" (33).

51. Patricia A. Williams, *Doing without Adam and Eve: Sociobiology and Original Sin* (Minneapolis: Fortress Press, 2001), chaps. 3–6. See also Claus Westermann, *Genesis 1–11: A Commentary*, trans. John J. Scullion, SJ (1974, 1976 (2nd ed.); London: SPCK; Minneapolis: Augsburg Publishing House, 1984), 275–77. I do not myself altogether concede this criticism of Paul. It seems to me a perfectly appropriate strategy for the community of interpreters prayerfully to decide that a certain text is a "hermeneutical lens" that allows a particular theme in Scripture to be understood in a particular way. So I make use in chaps. 4 and 6 of the concept of kenosis, self-emptying, as a way of understanding the character of God, and of human action after the example of Christ. That concept rests on a single word in Phil. 2:7 acting as a lens through which something profound about the nature of God can be inferred within the broad sweep of the New Testament. So also it would be perfectly valid to regard Paul's understanding of fall and redemption in Rom. 5 as such a lens. That this is not the only way Paul understands the human predicament is something I seek to show in section 6.1.

52. For other authors deploying versions of the "only way" argument, see sections 3.2–3.3. Williams herself adopts it in her treatment of the problem of evil (see *Doing without Adam and Eve*, chap. 10). She writes: "The source of evil is not some divine opponent of God. The source of evil is not even human sin. Rather the sources of evil lie in attributes so valuable that we would not even consider eliminating them in order to eradicate evil" (179).

53. Michael Lloyd, "Are Animals Fallen?" in *Animals on the Agenda: Questions about Animals for Theology and Ethics*, ed. Andrew Linzey and Dorothy Yamamoto (London: SCM Press, 1998), 147–60. So Lloyd cannot accept formulations such as that of Austin Farrer who praised the enormous vitality of force in creatures seeking to absolutize themselves and could not imagine a world where every system makes space for the other (Austin Farrer, *Love Almighty and Ills Unlimited: An Essay on Providence and Evil Containing the Nathaniel Taylor Lectures for 1961* [London: Collins, 1962], 53. This language of Farrer's finds an echo in my account of "selving" in section 4.4). The sort of world Lloyd wants to imagine is one that would reflect "the vitality and love of our triune, servant-minded self-sacrificial God. Why," he asks, "should a Christian theodicy adopt a definition of vitality which includes the will to power . . . ?" (149).

54. Lloyd, "Are Animals Fallen?" 151.

55. Michael Lloyd, "The Humanity of Fallenness," in *Grace and Truth in a Secular Age*, ed. Timothy Bradshaw, 66–82 (Grand Rapids: Eerdmans, 1998).

56. See, for example, Ernst M. Conradie, "On Responding to Human Suffering: A Critical Survey of Theological Contributions in Conversations with the Sciences," in *Can Nature Be Evil or Evil Natural?* ed. Cornel W. du Toit, 165–87 (Unisa, South Africa: Research Institute for Theology and Religion, 2006).

57. Lloyd, "The Humanity of Fallenness," 76.

58. To say this is not to minimize the complexities of the debate on homosexuality. For an introduction to its puzzles, see *Some Issues in Human Sexuality: A Guide to the Debate* (London: Church House Publishing, 2003), where a whole range of positions is explored and plausibly defended.

59. Lloyd, "Are Animals Fallen?" 156.

60. Implicitly this is the position of Hart in *Doors of the Sea*.

61. Lloyd, "Are Animals Fallen?" 159.

62. T. F. Torrance, *Divine and Contingent Order* (Oxford: Oxford University Press, 1981), 112.

63. Ibid., 113.

64. Ibid., 116.

65. Ibid., 122.

66. Ibid., 125.

67. Ibid., 130. For more on human priesthood of creation, see sections 6.7–6.8.

68. The language of Barth himself is very careful, but his talk of the shadow side of creation is, as Fiddes notes, still a "good example of the tendency to smooth away the offensive shock of natural evil." See Fiddes, *Creative Suffering of God*, 223–24, working from Karl Barth, *Church Dogmatics*, III/3, ed. G. W. Bromiley and T. F. Torrance, trans. G. W. Bromiley and R. J. Ehrlich (Edinburgh: T&T Clark, 1961), 297–301. Fiddes also refers in the same passage to John Macquarrie's assessment of dysteleological elements of natural evil—such as parasitism—as "loose ends that are not integrated into the main creative process or into God's providential act" (*Principles of Christian Theology*, rev. ed. [London: SCM Press, 1977], 257–59, at 258). This is to fail to face the teleological aspect of evolutionary theodicy. It *is* the main creative process that gives rise to suffering in the nonhuman creation.

69. Torrance, *Divine and Contingent Order*, 139.

70. Clark H. Pinnock, *Most Moved Mover: A Theology of God's Openness* (Carlisle, UK: Paternoster, 2001), 133–34.

71. Ibid., 134.

72. Interestingly, such a classic liberal theological thinker as Keith Ward still finds a logical place for the reality of spiritual evil (cf. *Rational Theology and the Creativity of God* [Oxford, Blackwell, 1982], 205).

73. On the doctrine of creation out of nothing, see Keith Ward, *Religion and Creation* (Oxford: Oxford University Press, 1996), 288–93.

74. R. J. Berry, *God's Book of Works: The Nature and Theology of Nature*, Glasgow Gifford Lectures (London and New York: T&T Clark/Continuum, 2003), 231. Berry is pointing to the tendency to advance what might be called a "fall of the gaps" argument, by analogy with the "God of the gaps" arguments notorious in the history of theology's engagement with the sciences.

75. R. J. Berry, "This Cursed Earth: Is 'the Fall' Credible?" *Science and Christian Belief* 11, no. 1 (1999): 29–49.

76. Berry, *God's Book of Works*, 231.

77. Peter D. Ward and Donald Brownlee, *Rare Earth: Why Complex Life is Uncommon in the Universe* (New York: Copernicus Books, 2004), 110, 144.

78. Ward, *Rational Theology*, 203.

79. Paul S. Fiddes, *Freedom and Limit: A Dialogue between Literature and Christian Doctrine* (Macon, GA: Mercer University Press, 1999), chap. 3, quotations at 47.

80. Williams, *Doing without Adam and Eve*, 179.

81. Daryl P. Domning and Monika K. Hellwig, *Original Selfishness: Original Sin and Evil in the Light of Evolution* (Aldershot and Burlington, VT: Ashgate, 2006). But see Philip Hefner, "Theological Perspectives on Fall and Original Sin," *Zygon* 28, no. 1 (March 1993): 77–101, warning against a simplistic nature-culture dualism. Both are the product of evolutionary processes, and they cannot be simply disentangled. Hefner sees the Fall as "articulat[ing] symbolically our awareness that our human identity is constructed very significantly on foundations bequeathed to us from a prehuman evolutionary history in ways that are not available to us as humans" (89). There may be dissonances in the directions in which our nature and our culture would take human behavior.

But it is not to be supposed that culture is always more "enlightened" and "co-operative" than the inheritance of our genes. An example that occurs to me is that of the decision of some societies to constitute themselves around free-market capitalism. That cultural decision may actually be less co-operative than strategies that are part of our genetic inheritance. See also John Bowker, *Is God a Virus? Genes, Culture, and Religion: The Gresham Lectures 1992–3* (London: SPCK, 1995), on the ambiguity of our evolutionary inheritance.

82. London: SCM Press, 1976.

83. A distinguished exception is Fiddes's *Creative Suffering of God*, e.g., 218ff. Elphinstone's work is also taken up by John V. Taylor in *The Christlike God* (London: SCM Press, 1992), e.g., 201–5 (see section 4.7).

84. Elphinstone, *Freedom, Suffering, and Love*, 1.

85. Ibid., 24.

86. Ibid., 46.

87. Ibid., 48.

88. Cf. Colin Gunton, *The Triune Creator: A Historical and Systematic Study* (Edinburgh: Edinburgh University Press, 1998), 201–2.

89. Elphinstone, *Freedom, Suffering and Love*, 131.

90. Ibid., 34.

91. Ibid.

92. This is an important motif in the work of Arthur Peacocke; see, e.g., his *Theology for a Scientific Age*, 77.
93. Elphinstone, *Freedom, Suffering and Love*, 64.
94. Ibid., 65.
95. At the same time the image of scaffolding is an interesting one. There is a sense in which I hold that the evolving physical substrate of the universe was a way—the only way as far as we know—in which the values associated with myriad ways of being alive could be realized. But as Elphinstone insists, "Evolution was not *intended* to lead to perfection" (ibid., 132, emphasis in original).
96. See Robert John Russell, "Natural Theodicy in an Evolutionary Context: The Need for an Eschatology of New Creation," in *Theodicy and Eschatology*, ed. Bruce Barber and David Neville, 121–52 (Hindmarsh, South Australia: Australian Theological Forum, 2005).
97. One thinks not only of the behavior of civil servants in totalitarian states such as Nazi Germany, but of those psychological experiments where volunteers have been persuaded to inflict great pain on innocent subjects.
98. Elphinstone, *Freedom, Suffering and Love*, 73.
99. Ibid. This begs a question related to one which "bedevils" the divine action debate: how can the human psyche and spirit be influenced except through the medium of human neurophysiology, and if the devil interacts with human neurons, can that being not also interact with other matter? For a discussion of whether divine action can be understood purely in terms of communication at the level of the mental, see Philip Clayton and Steven Knapp, "Divine Action and the 'Argument from Neglect,'" in *Physics and Cosmology: Scientific Perspectives on the Problem of Evil in Nature*, ed. Nancey Murphy, Robert J. Russell, and William Stoeger, SJ, 179–94 (Berkeley, CA: CTNS; Vatican City: Vatican Observatory, 2007).
100. E.g., in his mention of "strange natural disasters and incomprehensible diseases," Elphinstone, *Freedom, Suffering and Love*, 105.

Chapter 3

1. I am aware that to make any guess as to what constitutes a fulfilled life depends on assumptions about the experience of nonhuman creatures. As I indicated in section 1.3, these are risky assumptions at best. I explore this concept further in section 4.4.
2. Thomas Aquinas, *Summa theologica*, trans. by the Fathers of the English Dominican Province (New York: Benziger Brothers, 1947); the quotation is from 1, q.42, a.2.
3. I pointed out in section 1.3 that the harms in evolution pose no problem if no creator God is postulated, and in section 2.3 that there is an important variant of theism (what Wesley Wildman calls "ground-of-being theism") that does not claim goodness or benevolence as a constant feature of the character of God. It is the "determinate-entity theism" of the mainstream of the Christian tradition, in which the creation is the good outcome of the loving work of a personal God who also is the ultimate ground of hope for redemption, that makes this type of analysis of goods and harms particularly challenging and necessary.
4. Christopher Southgate and Andrew Robinson, "Varieties of Theodicy: An Exploration of Responses to the Problem of Evil Based on a Typology of Good-Harm Analyses," in *Physics and Cosmology: Scientific Perspectives on the Problem of Evil in Nature*, ed. Nancey Murphy, Robert J. Russell, and William R. Stoeger,

SJ, 67–90 (Vatican City: Vatican Observatory; Berkeley, CA: Center for Theology and the Natural Sciences, 2007). Much of sections 3.2–3.3 follows the analysis of this article.

5. See John Hick, *Evil and the God of Love* (1966; repr., Basingstoke and London: Macmillan, 1979), parts 3 and 4.

6. As Southgate and Robinson show, a good-harm analysis is only one element in a "thick defense" of God (the term is Thomas F. Tracy's). "Thin defenses" try and show the logical possibility of the coexistence of harms with goods in a world created and loved by God (see Tracy, "The Lawfulness of Nature and the Problem of Evil," in *Physics and Cosmology: Scientific Perspectives on the Problem of Evil in Nature*, ed. Nancey Murphy, Robert J. Russell, and William R. Stoeger, SJ, 153–78 (Vatican City: Vatican Observatory; Berkeley, CA: Center for Theology and the Natural Sciences, 2007). Thick defenses try and frame that good-harm analysis within an overall account of the creative and redemptive purposes of God.

7. Christopher Southgate, "God and Evolutionary Evil: Theodicy in the Light of Darwinism," *Zygon* 37, no. 4 (December 2002): 803–24. An alternative term is "biophysical evil," which indicates the larger context of "cosmic theodicy" within which evolutionary considerations are set (see section 3.3). Both of these terms are an effort to distinguish, within the traditional category "natural" or "physical" evil, the harms that come to nonhuman creatures. So many discussions of natural evil focus only on earthquakes, volcanoes, etc., and their propensity to cause seemingly arbitrary suffering to human beings. Moral evil—that intentionally caused by moral agents—can include suffering inflicted on either humans or nonhuman creatures. Natural evil includes the suffering of humans, and evolutionary (or biophysical) evil.

8. C. S. Lewis, *The Problem of Pain* (1940; repr., New York: Macmillan, 1962), 129.

9. Thomas F. Tracy, "Evolution, Divine Action, and the Problem of Evil," in *Evolutionary and Molecular Biology: Scientific Perspectives on Divine Action*, ed. Robert J. Russell, William R. Stoeger, SJ, and Francisco J. Ayala, 511–30 (Vatican City: Vatican Observatory; Berkeley, CA: Center for Theology and the Natural Sciences, 1998).

10. Ibid., 523. Cf. also Robin Attfield, "Evolution, Theodicy, and Value," *Heythrop Journal* 41 (July 2000): 281–96: "what must be added to the balance of the argument [effectively the good-harm analysis] is the intrinsic value of the flourishing of each flourishing creature that has ever lived" (292–93).

11. Tracy, "Evolution, Divine Action, and the Problem of Evil," 522–23, emphasis in original.

12. Ibid., 523.

13. Patricia A. Williams, *Doing without Adam and Eve: Sociobiology and Original Sin* (Minneapolis: Fortress Press, 2001), 176.

14. Nancey Murphy and George F. R. Ellis, *On the Moral Nature of the Universe: Theology, Cosmology and Ethics* (Minneapolis: Fortress Press, 1996), 246. For an update of this, see Nancey Murphy, "Science and the Problem of Evil: Suffering as a By-product of a Finely Tuned Cosmos," in *Physics and Cosmology: Scientific Perspectives on the Problem of Evil in Nature*, ed. Nancey Murphy, Robert J. Russell, and William Stoeger, SJ, 131–51 (Vatican City: Vatican Observatory; Berkeley, CA: Center for Theology and the Natural Sciences, 2007). See Stephen R. L. Clark, "Progress and the Argument from Evil," *Religious Studies* 40 (2004): 181–92, for another variant of the by-product argument.

15. See John Polkinghorne, *Science and Providence: God's Interaction with the World* (London: SPCK, 1989), 66–68. In outlining the "free-process" defense he writes: "In his great act of creation I believe God allows the physical world to be itself . . . in that independence which is Love's gift to the one beloved. That world is endowed in its fundamental constitution with an anthropic potentiality which makes it capable of fruitful evolution. The exploration and realization of that potentiality is achieved by the universe through the continual interplay of chance and necessity within its unfolding process" (66). "God no more expressly wills the growth of a cancer than he expressly wills the act of a murderer, but he allows both to happen. He is not the puppetmaster of either men or matter" (67).

16. Richard W. Kropf, *Evil and Evolution: A Theodicy* (1984; repr., Eugene, OR: Wipf and Stock, 2004).

17. Ibid., 125.

18. Ibid., 116.

19. Ibid., 123.

20. Ibid., 124. Kropf thus substitutes "chance" for "vanity" or "futility" (Greek: *mataiotēs*). See section 6.1 for further discussion of a reading of the word "futility" in Rom. 8:20 in evolutionary terms.

21. For further exploration of the analogy of music, see section 4.4, and the work of Arthur Peacocke cited there.

22. Kropf, *Evil and Evolution*, 126.

23. Ibid., 127.

24. Ibid., quoting Pierre Teilhard de Chardin, *The Phenomenon of Man: With an Introduction by Sir Julian Huxley*, trans. B. Wall (1955; first English ed., 1959; repr., New York: Harper and Row, 1975), 313.

25. Kropf, *Evil and Evolution*, 158.

26. Ibid., 164.

27. Ibid., 165.

28. See especially Holmes Rolston III, *Science and Religion: A Critical Survey* (1987; repr., Philadelphia and London: Templeton Foundation Press, 2006); "Naturalizing and Systematizing Evil," in *Is Nature Ever Evil? Religion, Science, and Value*, ed. Willem B. Drees, 67–86 (London: Routledge, 2003); also Lisa Sideris, "Writing Straight with Crooked Lines: Holmes Rolston's Ecological Theology and Theodicy," in *Nature, Value, Duty: Life on Earth with Holmes Rolston III*, ed. Christopher J. Preston and Wayne Ouderkirk, 77–101 (Dordrecht: Springer, 2007); and Mark Wynn, *God and Goodness: A Natural Theological Perspective* (London and New York: Routledge, 1999), esp. 102–15.

29. Holmes Rolston III, "Does Nature Need to Be Redeemed?" *Zygon* 29, no. 2 (June 1994): 205–29, at 218.

30. Holmes Rolston III, "Disvalues in Nature," *The Monist* 75 (April 1992): 250–78, at 254.

31. For a collection of Rolston's examples see Lisa H. Sideris, *Environmental Ethics, Ecological Theology, and Natural Selection* (New York: Columbia University Press, 1983), and references to Rolston therein. A similar developmental instrumental position is adopted by Daryl P. Domning and Monika K. Hellwig, *Original Selfishness: Original Sin in the Light of Evolution* (Aldershot and Burlington, VT: Ashgate, 2006), chap. 12.

32. E.g., Wayne Ouderkirk, "Can Nature Be Evil? Rolston, Disvalues and Theodicy," *Environmental Ethics* 21 (1999): 135–50; Jill Le Blanc, "A Mystical

Response to Disvalue in Nature," *Philosophy Today* 45, nos. 3/4 (Fall 2001): 254–65; but see Mark Wynn, *God and Goodness: A Natural Theological Perspective* (London and New York: Routledge, 1999), 102–15, and Attfield, "Evolution, Theodicy, and Value," for more positive responses to Rolston.

33. Rolston, "Naturalizing and Systematizing Evil," 84.

34. Rolston, "Does Nature Need to Be Redeemed?" 218.

35. Sideris, "Writing Straight with Crooked Lines," esp. 82–83.

36. Helpful here is Jay B. McDaniel's categorization of senses of the term "redemption." He writes: "The word 'redemption' has different meanings. It can mean 1) freedom from the consequences of sin, in which case it applies almost exclusively to humans. But it can also mean 2) freedom from what distresses or harms, 3) contribution to lives beyond one's own, and 4) transformation into an improved state of existence" (*Of God and Pelicans: A Theology of Reverence for Life* [Louisville, KY: Westminster/John Knox Press, 1989], 42). Rolston also seeks to "take the moral component out of redemption" or rather to "restrict the moral component to the redemption of humans" ("Does Nature Need to Be Redeemed?" 218). So he eliminates McDaniel's (1) from the question of the redemption of the nonhuman creation. His theology of redemption by regeneration satisfies meaning (3), but leaves hanging the question of meanings (2) and (4)—what for the individual sufferer constitutes freedom from what distresses or harms, and transformation into an improved state of existence?

37. Rolston, *Science and Religion*, 144. Though Kropf does not use this term his thought clearly runs along the same lines; see *Evil and Evolution*, 126–27. Cf. also Teilhard: "Physical and moral evil originate from a process of becoming; everything which evolves experiences suffering and moral failure. . . . The Cross is the symbol of the pain and toil of evolution, rather than the symbol of expiation" (quoted in Ralph G. Wilburn, "Reflections on the Problem of Evil," *Lexington Theological Quarterly* 16, no. 4 [October 1981]: 126–41, at 136).

That Rolston developed his concept of creation as "cruciform" independently of Teilhard and Kropf is strongly suggested by the fact that in *Science and Religion: A Critical Survey*, in which the idea first appears, he does not cite Kropf and makes only minimal mention of Teilhard as "[a] sort of Roman Catholic representative [of process theism]" (346). Fascinatingly Wynn thinks "Rolston's work could be viewed as a contemporary reworking of Teilhardian themes" (*God and Goodness*, 55), a conclusion that might come as a surprise to some of Teilhard's critics (see R. J. Berry, "The Lions Seek Their Prey from God: A Response to the Boyle Lecture," *Science and Christian Belief* 17, no. 1 [April 2005]: 41–56).

The earliest use of this idea of "cruciformity" in creation that I have found is in Charles E. Raven. He quotes Jean Henri Fabre (1823–1915), "If each creature is what it is only because it is a necessary part of the plan of the supreme Artificer who has constructed the universe, why have some the right of life and death, and others the terrible duty of self-immolation? Do not both obey, not the gloomy law of carnage, but a kind of sovereign and exquisite sacrifice, some sort of unconscious idea of submission to a superior and collective interest?" Raven goes on, "That is the testimony of one who would not have called himself a Christian; and it amounts to this—that woven into the very woof and warp of the universe is the pattern of the Cross, that Nature is baptized in the Spirit of Jesus, that man's creation was accomplished by the same means as his redemption" (*The Creator Spirit: A Survey of Christian Doctrine in the Light of Biology, Psychology and Mysticism* [London: Martin Hopkinson, 1927], 124).

It is possible, however, that this thought goes back yet further to the thought of the Anabaptist Hans Hut (c. 1490–1527) and his followers; see Murphy and Ellis, *On the Moral Nature*, 248. The Anabaptist view that redemption comes only through suffering is expressed in such sayings as this: "By the Gospel of all creatures nothing is said or preached but Christ crucified—not Christ the head alone, but the whole Christ with all His members, the Christ which all creatures preach and teach" (quoted in Rollin Stely Armour, *Studies in Anabaptist and Mennonite History: No 11, Anabaptist Baptism: A Representative Study* [Scottdale, PA: Herald Press, 1966], 82).

38. Rolston, *Science and Religion*, 144–46.
39. Rolston, "Naturalizing and Systematizing Evil," 67. The analysis of different foci of theodicy that follows is adapted from Southgate and Robinson, "Varieties of Theodicy."
40. Douglas H. Chadwick, "Investigating a Killer," *National Geographic* 207, no. 4 (April 2005): 86–105.
41. Rolston, *Science and Religion*, 144, italics in original. Humans' sense of the beauty and importance of these interdependent systems is shown in many films of wildlife. The camera operator does not intervene to rescue the limping impala calf from the hyenas, any more than U.S. National Park officials intervene in cases of nonanthropogenic suffering in animals under their care. Though it operates by way of suffering that on occasion seems tragic, the system tends to be depicted by the filmmakers as good and necessary, the suffering being intimately and inseparably bound up with values, indeed with beauty. If a theodicy were being mounted, it would be a constitutive-based one.
42. Ibid., 137–9.
43. Ibid., 144.
44. Ibid., 145.
45. Holmes Rolston III, "Kenosis and Nature," in *The Work of Love: Creation as Kenosis*, ed. J. Polkinghorne, 43–65 (London: SPCK; Grand Rapids and Cambridge: Eerdmans, 2001), 60.
46. It would be easy to give too anthropocentric an account here, and say that it is human freedom that requires this morally ambiguous universe as a stage to work on (as in the free-will defense to moral evil), or as a school in which to learn virtue (as in the "Irenaean" approach of John Hick). But that would be to suppose that human experience is the principal focus of value, and that the experience of other creatures, however full of struggle and suffering, is of little account. This would pose even more considerable problems of theodicy than the evolutionary process poses in itself. See section 5.6 for further discussion of why God did not simply create heaven.
47. Robin Attfield, *Creation, Evolution, and Meaning* (Aldershot and Burlington, VT: Ashgate, 2006), 109–50. This only-way argument is essentially the approach defended by Michael Ruse, in his *Can a Darwinian Be a Christian? The Relationship between Science and Religion* (Cambridge: Cambridge University Press, 2001), 130–38, and Richard L. Fern, *Nature, God, and Humanity: Envisioning an Ethics of Nature* (Cambridge: Cambridge University Press, 2002), 152–53, 222. See also Domning, *Original Selfishness*: "I would say that theodicy has done enough by explaining the data actually before us—by demonstrating

that *up to now* the Creator has had no alternative, and hence needs no defense" (166, emphasis in original).

For a helpful statement of the argument (and a look beyond it) see Neil Messer, *Selfish Genes and Christian Ethics: Theological and Ethical Reflection on Evolutionary Biology* (London: SCM Press, 2007), 197–99. And see sections 3.5 and 5.1 for the need for an eschatological dimension to a complete evolutionary theodicy; also the work of Robert J. Russell, n50–51, this chapter.

48. Richard Dawkins, *River out of Eden: A Darwinian View of Life* (London: Weidenfeld and Nicolson, 1995), 133.

49. Michael Ruse, *Darwinism and Its Discontents* (Cambridge: Cambridge University Press, 2006), 288–89, quoting from Richard Dawkins, "Universal Darwinism," in *Evolution from Molecules to Men*, ed. D. S. Bendall, 403–25 (Cambridge: Cambridge University Press, 1983), 423.

50. Robert J. Russell, "Natural Theodicy in an Evolutionary Context: The Need for an Eschatology of New Creation," in *Theodicy and Eschatology*, ed. Bruce Barber and David Neville, 121–52 (Hindmarsh, South Australia: Australian Theological Forum, 2005), 131, emphases in original.

51. Ibid., 132.

52. Ruth Page, *God and the Web of Creation* (London: SCM Press, 1996).

53. Quoted in Nancey Murphy, "Theological Reflections on the Moral Nature of Nature," in *Creative Creatures: Values and Ethical Issues in Theology, Science, and Technology*, ed. Ulf Görman, Willem B. Drees, and Hubert Meisinger, 92–106 (London and New York: T&T Clark/Continuum, 2005), 101.

54. Sideris, "Writing Straight with Crooked Lines," 89–90.

55. Denis Edwards, *The God of Evolution: A Trinitarian Theology* (New York and Mahwah, NJ: Paulist Press, 1999), 36–39.

56. Denis Edwards, "Every Sparrow that Falls to the Ground: The Cost of Evolution and the Christ-Event," *Ecotheology* 11, no. 1 (March 2006): 103–23. The point Edwards makes in criticism of Rolston's theology of the cross is the same point Nogar makes against Teilhard's (see section 2.5).

57. Ibid., 108.

58. We see the misanalogy between nonhuman suffering and human suffering of and in Christ also when Rolston writes, "Every life is chastened and christened, straitened and baptized in struggle" (*Science and Religion*, 291). It is Christians, not nonhuman creatures, who are baptized through their free self-giving choice into Christ's self-giving sacrificial death (Rom. 6:3). That is not at all the same as other creatures' self-interested struggle. Rolston goes on to make a further misanalogy when he adds: "Everywhere there is vicarious suffering" (ibid.). Admittedly, there are many cases of creatures entering into situations of pain to protect the interests of (notably) their young. Ironically it used to be thought that the pelican tore out her own breast to sustain her young—hence the bird being used as a symbol for Christ. But we see in Rolston's very helpful example of the insurance pelican chick precisely the opposite point: the nesting white pelican will not feed the insurance chick, and if it falls out of the nest will not allow it back in. The suffering the insurance chick does on behalf of others is not freely chosen suffering for others, on the analogy of Christ and by extension the Christian (cf. Col. 1:24), but suffering forced upon it by the evolutionary strategy pelicans have evolved.

59. Rolston, "Does Evolution Need to Be Redeemed?" 218. For a critique of this approach as ignoring the suffering of the individual, and as embedding an

anthropocentric assumption that aesthetic perceptions are better than mere sensory experience, see Le Blanc, "A Mystical Response to Disvalues in Nature," in turn analyzed by Sideris, "Writing Straight with Crooked Lines," 93–94.

60. Rolston, *Science and Religion*, 146.
61. Arthur Peacocke, *Paths from Science towards God: The End of All Our Exploring* (Oxford: Oneworld, 2001), 86. A similar approach is found in Keith Ward, *God, Chance, and Necessity* (Oxford: Oneworld, 1996), 191.
62. Arthur Peacocke, "Biological Evolution—A Positive Theological Appraisal," in *Evolutionary and Molecular Biology: Scientific Perspectives on Divine Action*, ed. Robert J. Russell, William R. Stoeger, SJ, and Francisco J. Ayala, 357–76 (Vatican City: Vatican Observatory; Berkeley, CA: Center for Theology and the Natural Sciences, 1998), 372.
63. Arthur Peacocke, "The Cost of New Life," in *The Work of Love: Kenosis as Creation*, ed. J. Polkinghorne, 21–42 (London: SPCK; Grand Rapids and Cambridge: Eerdmans, 2001), 42.
64. Arthur Peacocke died in October 2006, much mourned by the science-religion community. For tributes to his work see *Reviews in Science and Religion* 49 (May 2007): 7–18, and *Theology and Science* 5, no. 1 (March 2007): 1–19.
65. Peacocke, "Cost of New Life," 36–37.
66. Haught, *God after Darwin*, 41. See also Ruth Page's use of the concept of divine "letting-be," discussed in section 4.4.
67. Haught, *God after Darwin*, 43.
68. Ibid., 50.
69. Properly framed, this is a telling theological combination. However, it is not necessary to go all the way to a panexperientialist metaphysic as in process thought (see section 2.4), or to an optimistic arrow of evolution as in Teilhard (see section 2.5), in order to hold in tension these same motifs of God's persuasive love and ultimately sovereign, redemptive will. There are other ways to combine a model of God who respects the autonomy of creatures with a belief that God's costly redeeming love will not in the end be denied. Such a model is what I attempt in chaps. 4 and 5.
70. Cf. McDaniel, *Of God and Pelicans*, chap. 1.
71. Kenneth Surin, *Theology and the Problem of Evil* (Oxford: Basil Blackwell, 1988), 91. Surin goes on to point out, "What the process theodicy lacks is an eschatology, a resurrection-perspective, in which the almighty God on the cross of the powerless Nazarene is affirmed in faith to have inaugurated a radically new world by this very deed on the cross" (91–92). I take up the significance of the cross at section 4.7, and the question of eschatology in chap. 5.
72. McDaniel, *Of God and Pelicans*, 48–49.
73. For more on creaturely selves, see section 4.4.
74. There is a link here with Tracy's conviction that "To *be* is to be in relation to God, and in this lies the good of every creature of every kind" (see section 3.2). The relationship persists and represents value to the creature, even in its suffering.
75. Rolston, *Science and Religion*, 140, quoted in McDaniel, *Of God and Pelicans*, 19.
76. Cf. also Edwards, "Every Sparrow That Falls to the Ground."
77. McDaniel, *Of God and Pelicans*, 45.
78. Jay B. McDaniel, "Can Animal Suffering Be Reconciled with Belief?" in *Animals on the Agenda: Questions about Animals for Theology and Ethics*, ed. Andrew Linzey and Dorothy Yamamoto, 161–70 (London: SCM Press, 1998), 168.

79. Ibid.
80. Ted Peters and Martinez Hewlett, *Evolution from Creation to New Creation: Conflict, Conversation, and Convergence* (Nashville: Abingdon Press, 2003), chap. 6.
81. Ibid., 158.
82. Philip Hefner, "Biocultural Evolution: A Clue to the Meaning of Nature," in *Evolutionary and Molecular Biology: Scientific Perspectives on Divine Action*, ed. Robert J. Russell, William R. Stoeger, SJ, and Francisco J. Ayala, 329–56 (Vatican City: Vatican Observatory; Berkeley, CA: CTNS, 1998), 351, cited in Peters and Hewlett, *Evolution from Creation*, 148.
83. Peters and Hewlett, *Evolution from Creation*, 172.
84. Ibid., 173. Cf. also Hefner, ending the sentence cited in n83, [evil] "is a phenomenon that will be transmuted into goodness eternally" ("Biocultural Evolution," 351).

Chapter 4

1. Cf. Thomas Weinandy, OFM, Cap., *Does God Suffer?* (Edinburgh: T&T Clark, 2000), 19. Moreover, the assertion that Christ is of the very being of God, and that a distinction arises between the life of that intradivine being and the economy of salvation, was an important ingredient in the church's rejection of Arianism, and hence in the way Trinitarian thought came to its full flowering. See Catherine M. LaCugna, *God for Us: The Trinity and Christian Life* (London: HarperCollins, 1991), 8, 35.
2. Keith Ward, *Religion and Creation* (Oxford: Clarendon Press, 1996), 19–24; Paul S. Fiddes, *The Creative Suffering of God* (Oxford: Clarendon Press, 1988), 18–25.
3. Jürgen Moltmann, *The Crucified God: The Cross of Christ as the Foundation and Criticism of Christian Theology*, trans. R. A. Wilson and J. Bowden (1973; English ed., London: SCM Press, 1974), e.g., 235–49.
4. Kenneth Surin, *Theology and the Problem of Evil* (Oxford: Blackwell, 1986), chap. 4.
5. Sarah Coakley, "Kenosis: Theological Meanings and Gender Connotations," in *The Work of Love: Creation as Kenosis*, ed. John Polkinghorne, 192–210 (London: SPCK; Grand Rapids and Cambridge: Eerdmans, 2001), esp. 203–4; cf. also Herbert McCabe, *God Matters* (London: Geoffrey Chapman, 1987), chap. 4.
6. McCabe, *God Matters*, 41.
7. Weinandy, *Does God Suffer?*
8. McCabe, *God Matters*, 48.
9. Weinandy, *Does God Suffer?* esp. 168–70.
10. Fiddes, *Creative Suffering of God*, chap. 3.
11. An important emphasis in the work of Keith Ward; see his "Cosmos and Kenosis," in Polkinghorne, ed., *Work of Love*, 152–66, esp. 157–58. This is an interesting view of divine omniscience—that it must include the capacity for the uttermost empathy with all creaturely experience. Divine omnipotence can also be seen in terms as the power to give love without limit. See Denis Edwards, *Breath of Life: A Theology of the Creator Spirit* (Maryknoll, NY: Orbis Books, 2004), chap. 7.
12. LaCugna, *God for Us*, e.g., 300–301.
13. Fascinatingly, when the important Catholic theologian Hans Urs von Balthasar asks himself whether there is suffering in God, he responds, "There is something in God that can develop into suffering. This suffering occurs when the

recklessness with which the Father gives away himself (and all that is his) encounters a freedom that, instead of responding in kind to this magnanimity, changes it into a calculating, cautious self-preservation. This contrasts with the essentially divine recklessness of the Son, who allows himself to be squandered, and of the Spirit who accompanies him" (*Theodrama: Theological Dramatic Theory*, Vol. 4, *The Action*, trans. G. Harrison (1980; English ed., San Francisco: Ignatius Press, 1994), 328. This links with the necessary self-assertion of biological selves to which I point later in the chapter. Where I seek to expand the thought of von Balthasar is in seeing this move to self-preservation, as opposed to self-giving, as not confined to humans who might employ calculation, but being a characteristic of all living things. See also David N. Power, *Love without Calculation: A Reflection on Divine Kenosis* (New York: Crossroad Publishing, 2005), 45.

14. Paul S. Fiddes, *Participating in God: A Pastoral Doctrine of the Trinity* (London: Darton, Longman, and Todd, 2000), 176.

15. See sections 3.2–3.5. Note in particular John F. Haught, citing Holmes Rolston's phrase about "cruciform creation" (3.2), and commenting, "The cruciform visage of nature reflected in Darwinian science invites us to depart, perhaps more decisively than ever before, from all notion of a deity untouched by the world's suffering" (*God after Darwin: A Theology of Evolution* [Oxford and Boulder, CO: Westview Press, 2000], 46).

16. See Polkinghorne, ed., *Work of Love*. Particularly relevant to the current study are the papers in that collection by Moltmann on the explorations of kenosis in Lutheran theology and the Trinitarianism of von Balthasar, and Polkinghorne's own article, in which he lists four types of kenosis:

  1. Kenosis of omnipotence—the divine allowing of the creation to be and to act.
  2. Kenosis of eternity—God allows God's self a temporal pole which is responsive, in a way appropriate to the character of creation at that time.
  3. Kenosis of omniscience—even God does not know a future that has not yet become.
  4. Kenosis of causal status—God allowing divine special providence to "become as a cause among causes" to allow providential and creaturely causalities to become interwoven. This, for Polkinghorne, happens most dramatically at the Incarnation ("Kenotic Creation and Divine Action," in *Work of Love*, 90–106, 104).

17. A shift in my position from my "God and Evolutionary Evil: Theodicy in the Light of Darwinism," *Zygon* 37, no. 4 (December 2002): 803–24.

18. Most notably in Jürgen Moltmann's work—see, e.g., *God in Creation: An Ecological Doctrine of Creation, The Gifford Lectures 1984–85*, trans. M. Kohl (1985; English ed., London: SCM Press, 1985), 87–89.

19. For a critique see Coakley, "Kenosis," 200–205.

20. Arthur Peacocke, "The Cost of New Life," in *Work of Love*, 21–42, 38, emphases in original.

21. In a critique of the invocation of kenosis as a way of mitigating God's direct responsibility for pain and suffering within evolution, Ted Peters and Martinez Hewlett have attacked the concept of self-limitation of divine power. They allege that this is to misunderstand the nature of God's relation to the world. Power, for example, is not a zero-sum game, a "fixed amount of pie" (Ted Peters and Martinez Hewlett, *Evolution from Creation to New Creation: Conflict, Conversation and Convergence* [Nashville: Abingdon Press, 2003], 143), and neither is

freedom. Created entities acquire their power and their freedom not because God has *limited* God's power and freedom, but because the divine power and freedom makes the creation what it is. Colin Gunton has also criticized the use of the concept of kenosis in creation, especially with respect to Moltmann's image of God withdrawing Godself to make space for what is not-God. Gunton asks, "If God as creator is the one who gives reality to the other, must he do it by making space within rather than without himself? . . . [Kenosis] is a concept designed to deal with God's bearing in relation to a fallen world, not to be applied promiscuously to any of God's relations to the world. . . . There is no suggestion in the Bible that the act of creation is anything but the joyful giving of reality to the other" (Colin Gunton, *The Triune Creator: A Historical and Systematic Study* [Edinburgh: Edinburgh University Press, 1998], 141). As Niels Henrik Gregersen has written, "Kenosis has to be seen, not as a divine withdrawal, but as the self-realization of the power of love, which God is" ("The Complexification of Nature: Supplementing the Neo-Darwinian Paradigm?" in *Theology and Science* 4, no. 1 [March 2006]: 5–31, 25).

Keeping in mind Peters and Hewlett's criticism of kenosis as implying a zero-sum game, a "fixed amount of pie," it may be asked what is necessarily and intrinsically kenotic, in the sense of divine self-limitation, about the movements that Polkinghorne lists (see n17). Each of the first two could be redescribed as a movement of God's creative initiative and accepting love. Whether the concept of kenosis of causal status is operative depends on whether any account can be accepted of divine causation lying behind the pattern of causation that science describes. Polkinghorne has always dismissed an account of providence such as Austin Farrer's, based on "double agency" (see, e.g., John Polkinghorne, *Belief in God in an Age of Science* [New Haven, CT, and London: Yale University Press, 1998], 58–59). But it is not necessary to subscribe wholly to a neo-Thomist account of double agency to consider that God's general action in sustaining the world always lies behind the events we characterize as caused. On any model, except pure occasionalism, God's activity is one cause that stands in relation to others. So, again, it is not clear that divine creation of causal systems must mean divine self-limitation in the way Polkinghorne implies. Of Polkinghorne's four categories of proposed kenosis, only knowledge may qualify as a "fixed amount of pie." To the extent that human choices are free, there are human choices, which divine forbearance permits, that may well be taken to limit God's knowledge of the future. Such forbearance would then properly qualify as kenosis of omniscience.

22. See in particular von Balthasar, *Theological Dramatic Theory*, Vol. 4. As Coakley explains, "For Balthasar . . . the idea of kenotic self-surrender is too pervasive and important a characteristic of divine love to circumscribe its significance in Christology alone; it is eternally true of the perichoretic and reciprocal interrelations of the persons of the Trinity, not something newly impressed on the divine by the events of the incarnation" ("Kenosis," 199).

23. So William C. Placher, *The Triune God: An Essay in Postliberal Theology* (Louisville, KY: Westminster John Knox Press, 2007): "The Word's distance from the one he calls Father is so great that no one falls outside it, and the Spirit fills all that space with love" (155).

24. Cf. Gunton, *Triune Creator*, 141.

25. Cf. von Balthasar, *Theological Dramatic Theory*, 4:327: "Any world only has its

place within that distinction between Father and Son that is maintained and bridged by the Holy Spirit."

26. Moltmann himself has called this move of von Balthasar's going beyond "the interpretations of the nineteenth-century kenotics," "the next logical step" in exploring a theology of kenosis (*Science and Wisdom*, trans. M. Kohl [2002; English ed., London: SCM Press, 2003], 58).

27. And it is otherness, as John Zizioulas has emphasized, *held in communion*, so the ontological distinctness between God and creation, on which Christian theology has insisted, does not constitute separation. See John D. Zizioulas, *Communion and Otherness: Further Studies in Personhood and the Church*, ed. Paul McPartlan (London and New York: T&T Clark/Continuum, 2006), 19ff.

28. Holmes Rolston III, *Environmental Ethics: Duties to and Values in the Natural World* (Philadelphia: Temple University Press, 1988), chap. 3; also Stuart Kauffman, *Investigations* (Oxford: Oxford University Press, 2000), chap. 3.

29. Southgate, "God and Evolutionary Evil," 806.

30. Holmes Rolston III, "Naturalizing and Systematizing Evil," in *Is Nature Ever Evil? Religion, Science and Value*, ed. Willem B. Drees, 67–86 (London: Routledge, 2003), 67.

31. Except on a process metaphysic that sees all entities of any complexity as having experience and in some measure agency (see section 2.4). This is not, of course, to say that there are not great values in aspects of the nonliving world, even that God may delight hugely in those aspects, whether they be the Antarctic ice sheet or the rings of Saturn. But the values are there by dint of others valuing them, not—as I am arguing here for living organisms—because there are evaluating selves that are themselves centers of value. Living organisms also, of course, make artifacts that may themselves be centers of value—the Parthenon, for example.

32. On the importance of this and of Irenaeus's thought in general, see Gunton, *Triune Creator*, esp. 52–56.

33. Neil Messer, *Selfish Genes and Christian Ethics: Theological and Ethical Reflections on Evolutionary Biology* (London: SCM Press, 2007), 78.

34. My main sources on Maximus and "logoi" are Andrew Louth, "The Cosmic Vision of Saint Maximus the Confessor," in *In Whom We Live and Move and Have Our Being: Panentheistic Reflections on God's Presence in a Scientific World*, ed. Philip Clayton and Arthur Peacocke, 184–96 (Grand Rapids and Cambridge: Eerdmans, 2004); Kallistos Ware, "God Immanent yet Transcendent: The Divine Energies according to Saint Gregory Palamas," in *In Whom We Live and Move and Have Our Being*, Clayton and Peacocke, eds., 157–68; Hans Urs von Balthasar, *Cosmic Liturgy: The Universe according to Maximus the Confessor*, trans. Brian E. Daley, SJ (1988; English ed., San Francisco: Ignatius Press, 2003).

35. Edwards, *Breath of Life*.

36. Ware, "God Immanent yet Transcendent," 159.

37. Louth, "Cosmic Vision," 188.

38. Ware, "God Immanent yet Transcendent," 160.

39. Colin Gunton, *The One, the Three, and the Many: God, Creation, and the Culture of Modernity—The Bampton Lectures 1992* (Cambridge: Cambridge University Press, 1993), 56n21; cf. also Louth, "Cosmic Vision," 188.

40. A fitness landscape is a multidimensional graph that plots how a range of different parameters affect the evolutionary fitness of organisms at a particular time and place. The peaks in the landscape represent particular evolutionary

strategies which are successful in that time and place. However individuals in any given species will not all be in the same location in the landscape, and the landscape itself will continually shift depending on both the physical environment and the activities of other species.

For a brief introduction to this type of thinking see Per Bak, *How Nature Works: The Science of Self-Organized Criticality* (Oxford: Oxford University Press, 1997), 118–23. Organisms and species, then, exist in a phase space of possibilities, which the theologian will necessarily regard as ultimately deriving from God. That this is not wholly out of keeping with the thought of Maximus is shown by his comment: "All created things are defined in their essence and in their way of developing, by their own ideas (logoi) and by the ideas of the beings that provide their external context; through these ideas they find their defining limits" (quoted in von Balthasar, *Cosmic Liturgy*, 117). Beings do not receive their form, or develop, in a merely idealized way, without reference to (as we would say) their environment.

41. Arthur Peacocke, *Paths from Science towards God: The End of All Our Exploring* (Oxford: Oneworld, 2001), 77–78, 136–37; also Arthur Peacocke and Ann Pederson, *The Music of Creation* (Minneapolis: Fortress Press, 2006).

42. Edwards, *Breath of Life*, esp. chaps. 8–9. The importance of this work is particularly clear when it is compared with Paul Fiddes's compelling *Participating in God*, which offers an eloquent and dynamic way of understanding the Trinity, but has, in the last analysis, little place for the role of the Spirit.

43. Cf. also Niels Henrik Gregersen, "Complexity: What Is at Stake for Religious Reflection?" in *The Significance of Complexity: Approaching a Complex World through Science, Theology, and the Humanities*, ed. Kees van Kooten Niekerk and Hans Buhl, 135–66 (Aldershot and Burlington, VT: Ashgate, 2004), regarding the Holy Spirit as "the eternal energizer of divine life, who is present in all vital functions of all living beings, and who continues to release the ambience of mutuality in the world." I thank Professor Gregersen for the opportunity to view this text before its publication.

44. Edwards, *Breath of Life*, 134–35.

45. See Haught, *God after Darwin*.

46. Edwards, *Breath of Life*, 135. I noted this invocation of the book of Job in section 3.4.

47. Ibid.

48. Translating Duns Scotus's term *haecceitas*, a key term in the metaphysics of Hopkins. Fascinatingly, *haecceitas* was also of interest to another great idiosyncratic thinker, working slightly later than Hopkins, the American pragmatist philosopher C. S. Peirce (see T. L. Short, *Peirce's Theory of Signs* [Cambridge: Cambridge University Press, 2007], 50, 78). For a theory of Trinitarian creation based on Peirce, see my colleague Andrew Robinson's "Continuity, Naturalism and Contingency: A Theology of Evolution drawing on the Semiotics of C. S. Peirce and Trinitarian Thought," *Zygon* 39, no. 1 [March 2004]: 111–136).

49. There is a fine section in John V. Taylor's *The Christlike God* (London: SCM Press, 1992) on self-transcendence, drawing on the work of Karl Rahner. First Taylor shows that in the human being "the capacity to surpass or step forth beyond one's own being" is an important way of understanding humans as being in the image of God (113; see section 4.5). Then he asks if the term is meaningful in the nonhuman creation, and sees its application in terms of the sys-

tems of creation being open to the future, "open towards a higher level and order" (116, quoting Rahner). I note that the possibility of an organism exploring a higher level of complexity is most often through cooperation with another entity. Examples would be the symbiosis among bacteria that led to the first eukaryotic cells with interior organelles, and the cooperation that makes possible structure in plants, sexual behavior, social structures in insect communities, and cooperative hunting in animals.

Following my observations on kenosis in creation (n21 for this chapter), I have to reject the conclusion of, for example, Haught, that such self-transcendence is only possible if the divine infinity "contracts itself" (*God after Darwin*, 112). The very *presence* of God's Spirit, in longing and self-giving love, not that Spirit's withdrawal, makes possible creaturely self-transcendence.

50. The Nicene-Constantinopolitan Creed confesses the Holy Spirit as "the Lord, the Giver of Life."

51. *Poems and Prose of Gerard Manley Hopkins: Selected with an Introduction and Notes by W. H. Gardner* (Harmondsworth: Penguin, 1953), 51.

52. Von Balthasar himself writes on Hopkins; see his *The Glory of the Lord*, Vol. 3, *Studies in Theological Style: Lay Styles*, trans. A. Louth, J. Saward, M. Simon, and R. Williams, ed. J. Riches, 353–99 (1962; English ed., Edinburgh: T&T Clark, 1986, in association with Ignatius Press, San Francisco). To my knowledge the only theologians who have invoked Hopkins's insights in relation to a scientifically informed theology are Sallie McFague in *Super, Natural Christians: How We Should Love Nature* (London: SCM Press, 1997), 26, 58, and Paul S. Fiddes, *Freedom and Limit: A Dialogue between Literature and Christian Doctrine* (Macon, GA: Mercer University Press, 1999), chap. 6. McFague points to the vital importance of paying attention to the creation in a way of which, one feels, Hopkins would thoroughly have approved. I take up this theme of contemplation in section 6.3. Fiddes, writing of the sonnet that has concerned us in this chapter, notes, "There is contact and communion between the selves of all creatures, including human personalities" (117). Again, I take up humans' "instressing" of creaturely selves in section 6.3.

53. See Ian Bradley, *God Is Green: Christianity and the Environment* (London: Darton, Longman, and Todd, 1990), 39–45; also see sections 6.7–6.8.

54. Rolston, *Science and Religion: A Critical Survey* (1987; repr., Philadelphia and London: Templeton Foundation Press, 2006), 137–39.

55. I acknowledge that not all creatures have reproductive opportunities, and also that in some sexually reproducing species there may be social roles that constitute "fulfillment" for an organism without the need to be reproductively active.

56. Note that theology of creation is a different sort of discourse from scientific explanation (so Messer, *Selfish Genes*, 77), so the two can coexist without there necessarily being conflict between them.

57. *How much* of such flourishing constitutes the consummation of a creaturely life is something that can be known only to God.

58. An example given by John F. Haught, "The Boyle Lecture 2003: Darwin, Design and the Promise of Nature," *Science and Christian Belief* 17 (April 2005): 5–20, 8. Note that this was actually the 2004 Lecture, given on February 4 of that year.

59. On the grieving of God's "Shekinah" over the self-seeking of creatures, see Jürgen Moltmann, *The Spirit of Life: A Universal Affirmation*, trans. M. Kohl (1991; English ed., London: SCM Press, 1992), 50. I explore in the next chapter the

suggestion that the creature is given fulfillment (in a form appropriate to itself) at the eschaton.

60. Cf. Jared Diamond, "The Evolution of Human Inventiveness," in *What Is Life? The Next Fifty Years: Speculations on the Future of Biology*, ed. M.P. Murphy and L. A. J. O'Neill, 41–55 (Cambridge: Cambridge University Press, 1995), 45–46.

61. Cf. Ian Tattersall, *Becoming Human: Evolution and Human Uniqueness* (New York: Harcourt and Brace, 1998); J. Wentzel van Huyssteen, *Alone in the World: Human Uniqueness in Science and Theology: The Gifford Lectures, University of Edinburgh Spring 2004* (Grand Rapids and Cambridge: Eerdmans, 2006).

62. See Holmes Rolston III, *Genes, Genesis, and God: Values and Their Origins in Natural and Human History* (Cambridge: Cambridge University Press, 1999), for a listing of such evolutionary strategies, and for cautions about extending this analysis to human behavior. See also Frans de Waal, *Good Natured: The Origins of Right and Wrong in Humans and Other Animals* (Cambridge, MA, and London: Harvard University Press, 1996), and "The Perennial Debate about Human Goodness: The Primate Evidence," in *Creative Creatures: Values and Ethical Issues in Theology, Science and Technology*, ed. U. Görman, W. B. Drees, and H. Meisinger, 75–91 (London and New York: T&T Clark/Continuum, 2005).

63. Fiddes, *Creative Suffering of God*, 228.

64. As Rev. 13:8 hints.

65. Von Balthasar, *Theological Dramatic Theory*, 4:329.

66. Patricia A. Williams, "The Fifth R: Jesus as Evolutionary Psychologist," *Theology and Science* 3, no. 2 (July 2005): 133–43.

67. For a discussion of these concepts and an evaluation of their application to theology, see Rolston, *Genes, Genesis and God*, chap. 5.

68. See www.lewa.org/oryx-lioness-facts.php, accessed August 15, 2007.

69. This is the very problematic imaginative stretch of the vision of Isa. 11:6–9. There, animals that seem defined by, and indeed beautiful in, their hurting and destroying, are pictured as not hurting or destroying on the holy mountain, but rather lying down with their prey. I take up this problem in 5.5.

70. De Waal, *Good Natured*. These conclusions in primatology are hotly debated, and the whole field is very controversial. This is bound to be the case, because in studying another species we are always imposing our own thought modes upon it. In considering, for example, the intelligence or language learning of chimpanzees, we are always, necessarily, asking human questions and performing human tests. We cannot get beyond these. It is always the case to some extent, but especially evident in this field that our own presuppositions strongly condition our conclusions. For example, a sociobiologist who did not believe in the possibility of altruism would find it impossible to observe same, because he or she would always and only search for nonaltruistic explanations of apparently selfless behavior. See George C. Williams for a similar conclusion, quoted in Messer, *Selfish Genes and Christian Ethics*, 138.

71. Only with the evolution of the human do we see the full extent of the possibilities inherent in a yes which is the yes beyond the self, the yes of the self-given self (see section 4.5).

72. Fiddes, *Participating in God*, 186.

73. Ibid., 185.

74. Cf. Wolfhart Pannenberg: "Like pain and suffering, evil is possible because of the finitude of existence, and especially of living creatures that seek to maintain themselves autonomously and thus incline to aim at a radical independence. . . .

Asserting themselves against one another, creatures do so also against the Creator. . . . For the autonomous creature self-independence conceals dependence on God, just as for the scientific observer the autonomy of natural processes hides their origin in God. At the same time, the results of creaturely autonomy seem to refute belief in a good Creator of this world. We have here two aspects of one and the same fact" (*Systematic Theology*, Vol. 2, trans. G. W. Bromiley [1991; English ed., Edinburgh: T&T Clark, 1994], 172–73).

In putting the dynamics of creaturely response in these terms I would not want to be misunderstood. No *blame* attaches to nonhuman creatures for being themselves. Nor is this an effort to introduce fallenness-language by the back door. It is a way of saying that self-interest both characterizes and limits creation, and postulating in all tentativeness that God both delights in creaturely selves and also longs for fuller realization of relationships of love and cooperation. Pierre Teilhard de Chardin hints at the same insight when he writes: "Wherever being *in fieri* [in process of becoming] is produced, suffering and wrong immediately appear as its shadow: not only as a result of the tendency towards inaction and selfishness found in creatures, but also (which is more disturbing) as an inevitable consequence of their effort and progress. Original sin is the essential reaction of the finite to the creative act. It is the *reverse side* of creation. We must retain an original sin as vast as the world" (*Christianity and Evolution*, trans. R. Hague [1969; English ed., London: Collins, 1971], 40). The language of original sin is dubiously helpful in considering creatures who are not moral agents, and Teilhard seems to miss the point that this is *God's way* of eliciting "progress"—both selving and self-transcendence—in creatures, but he has understood how closely coupled the "yes" and the "no" of the creature must be. Kropf too hints at the sort of formulation I develop here. He writes, "We might speak of a certain 'recalcitrance' in the structure of things that resists transformation and in so doing occasions further 'pain' or 'suffering'— at the same time we might also speak of a kind of unbounded 'exuberance' of nature" (Richard W. Kropf, *Evil and Evolution: A Theodicy* [1984; repr., Eugene, OR: Wipf and Stock, 2004], 165).

75. It may be objected that I am positing that God both delights in and grieves at the same event, if it be for instance an eagle's quartering of a Scottish hillside that exhausts and hunts down a mountain hare. I would only point out that such events evoke profound ambiguities even in human observers, thin though our resources are for experiencing either beauty or compassion.

76. The yes contains the no and vice versa. Compare Karl Barth: creation "praises its Creator and Lord even in its shadowy side" (*Church Dogmatics*, III/3, *The Doctrine of Creation*, trans. G. W. Bromiley and R. J. Ehrlich [Edinburgh: T&T Clark, 1961], 297–301, 297). "The diversities and frontiers of the creaturely world contain many 'nots'" (349).

It may be asked what type of theodicy my model leads to. Are we dealing here with a free-will defense, of the sort traced back to Augustine, in which freedom is a good which is worth the disvalues (such as the abuse of freedom) that go with it? Are we dealing with a "free-process defense" in Polkinghorne's terms (see *Science and Providence: God's Interaction with the World* [London: SPCK, 1989], 66–67), in which freedom is a good that requires certain physical and biological processes to exist? Or are we dealing with a "vale of soul-making" defense, of the sort traced back to Irenaeus, in which an ambiguous environment is necessary to teach creatures maturity? At first sight the argument is none of these. Nonhuman creatures are not generally deemed to possess moral freedom in the way human agents are typically regarded as possessing it, although the way we have described creatures is as expressing a "yes" and a "no," which might be taken to be the equivalent of freedom. Nor do these creatures learn moral maturity, though they do "learn," under the Darwinian pressures of their environments, to be the adaptive creatures they are.

This is where I consider that the traditional demarcations of theodicy fall down, because they have been framed in respect of freely choosing moral creatures, or creatures who are presumed to be able to grow in moral maturity. Even the nuanced and expanded versions of Augustinian and Irenaean approaches offered by R. J. Russell ("Natural Theodicy in an Evolutionary Context: The Need for an Eschatology of New Creation," in *Theodicy and Eschatology*, ed. Bruce Barber and David Neville, 121–52 [Adelaide: Australian Theological Forum, 2005]), do not describe this argument exactly. I therefore refer the reader to Southgate and Robinson's classification of theodicies in section 3.2, and identify this aspect of my approach as the constitutive element in a good-harm analysis which also includes developmental instrumental and developmental by-product elements.

77. Arthur Peacocke, *Creation and the World of Science: The Bampton Lectures 1978* (Oxford: Clarendon Press, 1979), 105–6; Peacocke and Pederson, *Music of Creation*.

78. It should be noted that this model presumes whole cosmos shot through with the love and *energaiai* of God, but does not presuppose any particular "causal joint" at which divine action is mediated. It does presume that God would not have allowed the possibility of complex life on earth to be altogether obliterated, either in its early phases, or during the great extinction events that have punctuated the evolutionary narrative (see section 4.6 on God's providential action).

79. See Ruth Page, *God and the Web of Creation* (London: SCM Press, 1996), esp. part 3, and "God, Natural Evil, and the Ecological Crisis," *Studies in World Christianity* 3, no. 1 (1997): 68–86.

80. Page, *God and the Web of Creation*, 104.

81. Ibid., 43–44.

82. Moreover, Page is quite content to invoke resurrection in a fairly traditional fashion even though she is at such pains to remove any talk of the providential action of God (ibid., 61).

83. Page, "God, Natural Evil, and the Ecological Crisis," 84; see also "Panentheism and Pansyntheism: God in Creation," in *In Whom We Live and Move and Have Our Being: Panentheistic Reflections on God's Presence in a Scientific World*, ed. Philip Clayton and Arthur Peacocke, 222–32 (Grand Rapids and Cambridge: Eerdmans, 2004), 228; also Christopher Southgate, "A Test Case—Divine Action," in *God, Humanity and the Cosmos*, 2nd ed., *Revised and Expanded as a Companion to the Science-Religion Debate* (London and New York: T&T Clark/Continuum, 2005), 284–85. Haught takes a similar line: "God acts powerfully in the world by offering to it a virtually limitless range of new possibilities within which it can become something relatively autonomous and distinct from its creator" (*God after Darwin*, 56).

84. Austin Farrer, *A Science of God?* (London: Bles, 1966), 76, cited (incorrectly) in Page, "God, Natural Evil, and the Ecological Crisis," 78.

85. Cf. Peter D. Ward and Donald Brownlee, *The Life and Death of Planet Earth:*

How the New Science of Astrobiology Charts the Ultimate Fate of Our World (2003; repr., New York: Owl Books, 2004).

86. Page, "God, Natural Evil, and the Ecological Crisis," 69.

87. This is not to say that the Creator does not delight in and appreciate the sharkness of sharks, rather to say that additional delight comes when a symbiotic relationship forms with pilot fish.

88. Peacocke, *The Palace of Glory: God's World and Science* (Adelaide: Australian Theological Forum, 2005), 66.

89. As with process-theological schemes, moreover, the strength of Page's proposal is also its weakness: the world has been distanced a vast way from being in any direct sense God's creation. Nor is it clear why such a merely companioning God should be the object of worship, or yet the recipient of prayer. Page's is a God neither of power nor of (long-term) purpose (here we can see the resemblance to Jonas's God [see section 2.4] who has consciously emptied Godself of these). For all its attractions, such a model gives purchase, in the end, neither on the realities of living in a world of natural disasters nor on the problem of loving the God who created them.

90. In this model the crucifying of Jesus stands as the ultimate "no" to God from creatures who were not only in God's image but were given a living, breathing example of God's love, and how that love offers possibilities of going beyond power expressed through violence, community expressed through exclusion.

91. See Brian Horne, *Imagining Evil* (London: Darton, Longman, and Todd, 1996): "The transcendence of our determination as purely natural beings, subject to the laws that govern all natural processes, will be accomplished not by regarding those laws as evil but by using those processes as occasions for love" (131).

92. Reg Morrison, *The Spirit in the Gene: Humanity's Proud Illusion and the Laws of Nature* (Ithaca, NY: Cornell University Press, 1999), 96–98.

93. J. Wentzel van Huyssteen, "Human Origins and Religious Awareness: In Search of Human Uniqueness," *Studia Theologica* 59, no. 2 (December 2005): 1–25, 22.

94. Paulos mar Gregorios, *The Human Presence: Ecological Spirituality and the Age of the Spirit* (Amity, NY: Amity House, 1987), 68.

95. See Kevin Mongrain, *The Systematic Thought of Hans Urs von Balthasar: An Irenaean Retrieval* (New York: Crossroad Publishing, 2002): "Believers are prepared by the Spirit to make 'an attempt at total self-renunciation, at dying to all self-will' so that they will be able to bear divine fruit in love for one another through concrete deeds" (126, quoting von Balthasar's *Theodrama IV*).

96. The sestet of the Hopkins sonnet I quoted above reads:

> I say more, the just man justices;
> Keeps grace: that keeps all his goings graces;
> Acts in God's eye what in God's eye he is—
> Christ—for Christ plays in ten thousand places,
> Lovely in limbs, and lovely in eyes not his
> To the Father through the features of men's faces.

The just human being can do *more* than the kingfisher or the hung bell. She or he can "keep grace," keep to self-givingness, and thereby return exactly—in that moment—the "yes" that is the "yes" of the Son, undiluted by the "no" of self-preservation. That—to return for a moment to Irenaeus—is the glory of God, a human being fully alive. In the "justicing" human, as in the perfectly hung bell and the flashing kingfisher of the first stanza, the perfectly tuned *logoi*, to use Maximus's expression, correspond in that moment exactly to the Logos. They return exactly to the Father—in that moment, in the power of the life-giving Spirit—that "yes" that is the "yes" of the Son. And this "yes" is from all eternity, not merely as a function of Incarnation. Hopkins has a fine simile to convey when a human being is most himself and is in all things conformed to Christ: "as the lettering on a sail or device upon a flag are best seen when it fills" (*The Sermons and Devotional Writings of Gerard Manley Hopkins*, ed. Christopher Devlin, SJ [London: Oxford University Press, 1959], 195), a most felicitous image since it conveys that always hard-to-picture role of the Holy Spirit, as the breath of God that fills the sail of a human being and enables that being to tell out truly what deep down (s)he is.

97. To grasp at it would be to fall precisely into von Balthasar's "no."

98. Gould advances this view particularly in his study of the organisms of the "Burgess Shale," an extraordinary geological site in the Canadian Rockies. The Burgess Shale contains fossils of a great diversity of creatures which evolved during the so-called "Cambrian explosion" of multicellular organisms. See Stephen Jay Gould, *Wonderful Life: The Burgess Shale and the Nature of History* (1989; repr., London: Penguin, 1991).

99. Simon Conway Morris, *Life's Solution: Inevitable Humans in a Lonely Universe* (Cambridge: Cambridge University Press, 2003).

100. But reflection on the long history of life on the Earth does lead to conundra in the divine action debate. For example, the extinction event at the boundary between the Cretaceous and the Tertiary periods, some 65 million years ago, that ended the era of the dinosaurs, although it must have caused huge quantities of distress in the dominant creatures of the biosphere, might be regarded as a "good" event in terms of the evolution of freely choosing self-conscious life forms. Indeed, the extinction event could even be seen as an instrument of God's purpose, whereas an ecological catastrophe destroying the hominids of East Africa 2 million years ago would presumably have been a "bad" event in not only causing great suffering but also ending a particular set of possibilities for conscious life. How are we to construe divine action, and theodicy, in respect of these cases? Might we not think of God permitting the first event, but preventing—if the possibility arose—the second? See Southgate, "A Test-Case: Divine Action," esp. 284–93.

101. Robert John Russell, "Divine Action and Quantum Mechanics: A Fresh Assessment," in *Quantum Mechanics: Scientific Perspectives on Divine Action*, ed. Robert John Russell, Philip Clayton, Kirk Wegter-McNelly, and John Polkinghorne, 293–328 (Vatican City: Vatican Observatory; Berkeley, CA: Center for Theology and the Natural Sciences, 2001).

102. For a general survey of God's possible action in relation to evolution, see Keith Ward, *Pascal's Fire: Scientific Faith and Religious Understanding* (Oxford: Oneworld, 2006), chap. 5.

103. Austin Farrer, *Love Almighty and Ills Unlimited: An Essay on Providence and Evil Containing the Nathaniel Taylor Lectures for 1961* (London: Collins, 1962), 51.

104. Keith Ward, *Rational Theology and the Creativity of God* (Oxford: Blackwell, 1982), 208.

105. Quoted in Philip Clayton and Steven Knapp, "Divine Action and the 'Argument from Neglect'" in *Physics and Cosmology: Scientific Perspectives on the Problem of Evil in Nature*, ed. Nancey Murphy, Robert J. Russell, and William

Stoeger, SJ, 179–94 (Vatican City: Vatican Observatory; Berkeley, CA: Center for Theology and the Natural Sciences, 2007).

106. Clayton and Knapp, "Divine Action and the 'Argument from Neglect.'"

107. Farrer, *Love Almighty*, 51.

108. Three books that have particularly helped my own thinking—none of them new, but all of them important—are Colin E. Gunton, *The Actuality of Atonement: A Study of Metaphor, Rationality, and the Christian Tradition* (Edinburgh: T&T Clark, 1988); Paul S. Fiddes, *Past Event and Present Salvation: The Christian Idea of Atonement* (London: Darton, Longman, and Todd, 1989); and Vernon White, *Atonement and Incarnation: An Essay in Universalism and Particularity* (Cambridge: Cambridge University Press, 1991).

109. Niels Henrik Gregersen, "The Cross of Christ in an Evolutionary World," *dialog: A Journal of Theology* 40, no. 3 (Fall 2001): 192–207. Key insights in his article include: the concept of "deep incarnation"—Christ is incarnate in putting on not only human nature but "also a scorned social being and a human-animal body, at once vibrant and vital and yet vulnerable to disease and decay" (193)—and the perception that Christ is in solidarity with victims of the evolutionary arms race, as one put to death without genetic offspring.

110. A major difference in emphasis between my position and Teilhard de Chardin's (see section 2.5).

111. Moltmann, *Crucified God*, e.g., 242–43—"Because God 'does not spare' his Son, all the godless are spared. . . . The delivering up of the Son to godforsakenness is the ground for the justification of the godless."

112. Jürgen Moltmann, *The Way of Jesus Christ: Christology in Messianic Dimensions*, trans. M. Kohl (1989; English ed., London: SCM Press, 1990), 291–305.

113. Fiddes, *Creative Suffering of God*, 7–12.

114. Arthur Peacocke, "Biological Evolution—A Positive Theological Appraisal," in *Evolutionary and Molecular Biology: Scientific Perspectives on Divine Action*, ed. Robert J. Russell, William R. Stoeger, SJ, and Francisco J. Ayala, 357–76 (Vatican City: Vatican Observatory; Berkeley, CA: CTNS, 1998), 372.

115. This is a view foreshadowed by the last paragraph of Andrew Elphinstone's *Freedom, Suffering and Love* (London: SCM Press, 1976), when he writes: "Dare we discern anything so outrageous as the idea that here [in Gethsemane and on the cross] God is making an atonement towards man for all that his desired creation costs man in the making: that he was making love's amends to all those who feel, and have felt, that they cannot forgive God for all the pains which life has foisted, unwanted, upon them?" (147). See also Taylor, *Christlike God*, 201–5. The concept of God experiencing suffering as a human individual, and thereby gaining the moral authority to overcome suffering and death, is explored further in White, *Atonement and Incarnation*, e.g., 39–41.

116. Karl Schmitz-Moormann, *Theology of Creation in an Evolutionary World*, in collaboration with James F. Salmon, SJ (Cleveland: Pilgrim Press, 1997), 116.

117. Helpful here is Gregersen's formulation in an earlier article, "God has taken the costs of evolution into the very being of Godself: the Son of God dies the death that is required by nature, and in doing so, he dies the death of pain (as a biological organism) and the death of social scorn (as a social being). And with Jesus' resurrection from the dead death, weakness and pain are brought into God's experience so that they will never be forgotten" ("Theology in a Neo-Darwinian World," *Studia Theologica* 48 [1994]: 125–49, 147). Cf. also "The Cross of Christ," 204: "*God, the giver of life, who produced the package deal*

of natural order and disorder, is also the co-carrier of the costs of creation" (emphasis in original).

118. See n109, this chapter.

Chapter 5

1. Keith Ward, *The Concept of God* (Oxford: Basil Blackwell, 1974), 223.

2. Keith Ward, *Rational Theology and the Creativity of God* (Oxford: Basil Blackwell, 1982), 202. Cf. also Ward, *Pascal's Fire: Scientific Faith and Religious Understanding* (Oxford: Oneworld, 2006), 255–56.

3. John Wesley, "The General Deliverance," in *Sermons on Several Occasions*, Vol. 2 (London: J. Kershaw, 1825), 121–32, 131.

4. See Andrew Linzey and Tom Regan, eds., *Animals and Christianity* (London: SPCK, 1989), 93–105.

5. David H. Kelsey, *Imagining Redemption* (Louisville, KY: Westminster John Knox Press, 2005); Marguerite Shuster, "The Redemption of the Created Order: Sermons on Romans 8.18–25," in *The Redemption: An Interdisciplinary Symposium on Christ as Redeemer*, ed. Stephen T. Davis, Daniel Kendall, SJ, and Gerald O'Collins, SJ, 321–42 (Oxford: Oxford University Press, 2004), 330.

6. At the time of writing the latest calculations suggest that heat death is the more likely.

7. See Peter D. Ward and Donald Brownlee, *The Life and Death of Planet Earth: How the New Science of Astrobiology Charts the Ultimate Fate of Our World* (2003; repr., New York: Owl Books, 2004).

8. Ted Peters, *God as Trinity: Relationality and Temporality in the Divine Life* (Louisville, KY: Westminster/John Knox Press, 1993), 175–76.

9. For an introduction to their views see John Polkinghorne, *Science and the Trinity: The Christian Encounter with Reality* (London: SPCK, 2004), chap. 6; Robert J. Russell, "Eschatology and Physical Cosmology: A Preliminary Reflection," in *The Far-Future Universe: Eschatology from a Cosmic Perspective*, ed. George F. R. Ellis, 266–315 (Radnor, PA: Templeton Foundation Press, 2002).

10. Robert J. Russell, "Divine Action and Quantum Mechanics: A Fresh Assessment," in *Quantum Mechanics: Scientific Perspectives on Divine Action*, ed. R. J. Russell, P. Clayton, K. Wegter-McNelly, and J. Polkinghorne, 293–328 (Vatican City: Vatican Observatory; Berkeley, CA: Center for Theology and the Natural Sciences, 2001).

11. See the recent work of Denis Edwards for an attempt to see even the resurrection of Christ as a "non-interventionist" action of God (Edwards, "Resurrection and the Costs of Evolution: A Dialogue with Rahner on Noninterventionist Theology," in *Theological Studies*, forthcoming). I thank Professor Edwards for allowing me access to this article before its publication. However, I am not sure how well Edwards's Rahnerian theology of divine action, based on double agency, really fits with the categories of interventionism and noninterventionism as usually used in the divine action debate (for instance, by Russell).

12. Robert J. Russell, "Special Providence and Genetic Mutation: A New Defense of Theistic Evolution," in *Evolutionary and Molecular Biology: Scientific Perspectives on Divine Action*, ed. R. J. Russell, W. R. Stoeger, and F. J. Ayala, 191–223 (Vatican City: Vatican Observatory; Berkeley, CA: Center for Theology and the Natural Sciences, 1998), 223.

13. John Polkinghorne, *Scientists as Theologians: A Comparison of the Writings of Ian Barbour, Arthur Peacocke, and John Polkinghorne* (London: SPCK, 1996), 54–55.

14. Process theologians (see section 2.4) are divided as to whether to regard all existence after death as "objective immortality"—the holding of the experience of that creature in the memory of God—or to postulate any "subjective immortality," in which entities continue to experience themselves in this new state. McDaniel, as we saw in section 3.5, postulates a "pelican heaven"; others follow Charles Hartshorne in not seeing any need for this. See section 5.5.

15. Colin Gunton, *Christ and Creation: The Didsbury Lectures* (Carlisle, UK: Paternoster Press; Grand Rapids: Eerdmans, 1992), 33–34.

16. Polkinghorne, *Science and the Trinity*, 154–63.

17. Robert J. Russell, "Entropy and Evil," *Zygon* 19, no. 4 (December 1984): 449–68; see also his *Cosmology, Evolution, and Resurrection Hope: Theology and Science in Creative Mutual Interaction*, ed. Carl S. Helrich (Kitchener, Ontario: Pandora Press; Hindmarsh, South Australia: ATF Press, 2006), chap. 3; and Mark William Worthing, *God, Creation, and Contemporary Physics* (Minneapolis: Fortress Press, 1996), chap. 4.

18. So John F. Haught: "In the same act of gathering the separate moments of each human life into the divine depths, and endowing them with the coherence of 'new creation,' a trustworthy God concerned with our own bodily resurrection would also assimiliate and redeem the whole cosmic drama. . . . Any theology that deliberately shuts its eyes to the intimate connection of our own existence to that of the larger evolutionary and cosmic totality would be insufferably trifling" (*Deeper than Darwin: The Prospect for Religion in an Age of Evolution* [Oxford and Boulder, CO: Westview Press, 2003], 155).

19. Holmes Rolston III, "Does Nature Need to Be Redeemed?" *Zygon* 29 (June 1994): 205–29.

20. Jürgen Moltmann, *The Way of Jesus Christ: Christology in Messianic Dimensions*, trans. M. Kohl (1989; English ed., London: SCM Press, 1990), 296–97.

21. Denis Edwards, "Every Sparrow That Falls to the Ground: The Cost of Evolution and the Christ-event," *Ecotheology* 11, no. 1 (March 2006): 103–23.

22. Jay B. McDaniel, *Of God and Pelicans: A Theology of Reverence for Life* (Louisville, KY: Westminster/John Knox Press, 1989), 45.

23. Polkinghorne, *Science and the Trinity*, 147.

24. Ibid., 152. C. S. Lewis made the same exception. For Lewis, "A tame animal acquires a 'self' or 'personality' in relation to its human owner and therefore as the human subject is resurrected so will its animal companion" (Andrew Linzey, "C. S. Lewis' Theology of Animals," *Anglican Theological Review* 80, no. 1 (Winter 1998): 60–81.

25. Russell, *Cosmology, Evolution, and Resurrection Hope*, 52, emphasis mine. C. S. Lewis also thought that the immortality of wild animals will be, at most, as types. He writes with characteristic eloquence that maybe God will give "this rudimentary self" [of lionhood] "a body no longer living by the destruction of the lamb, yet richly leonine in the sense that it also expresses whatever energy and splendor and exulting power dwelled within the visible lion on earth" (*The Problem of Pain* [1940; repr., New York: Macmillan, 1962], 143).

26. In drawing a distinction between creatures whose individual experiences merit an individual redeemed life, and those whose lives may be represented by a type, I acknowledge both that there is a spectrum of creaturely experience with few sharp discontinuities within it, and also that we cannot formulate with any accuracy how that distinction might actually work itself out at the eschaton.

27. Polkinghorne, *Science and the Trinity*, 150.

28. See n16, this chapter.

29. Jürgen Moltmann, *The Coming of God: Christian Eschatology*, trans. M. Kohl (1995; English ed., Minneapolis: Fortress Press, 2004), 132.

30. McDaniel, *Of God and Pelicans*, 47.

31. Thomas Sieger Derr, "The Challenge of Biocentrism," in *Creation at Risk? Religion, Science, and Environmentalism*, ed. Michael Cromartie, 85–104 (Cambridge: The Ethics and Public Policy Center; Grand Rapids: Eerdmans, 1995), 97.

32. Lisa H. Sideris, *Environmental Ethics, Ecological Theology, and Natural Selection* (New York: Columbia University Press, 2003), 119.

33. I am not a biblical specialist, but colleagues working in the area have been unable to convince me that the biblical vision is of the restoration of creation to its original state. There may be hints of this—for instance, in the reappearance of the Tree of Life in the book of Revelation—but it is not clearly demonstrated and should not be taken for granted in the formulation of an ethic. Note also my discussion earlier in section 2.6. Interestingly Jay McDaniel edges toward the same conclusion when he writes: "The second dream [God's vision for creation] is not exactly a duplication of the first; it is not exactly a return to the primal integrity of creation. Too much has happened in the interim" (Jay B. McDaniel, "A God Who Loves Animals and a Church That Does the Same," in *Good News for Animals? Christian Approaches to Animal Well-Being*, ed. Charles Pinches and Jay B. McDaniel, 75–102 (Maryknoll, NY: Orbis, 1993), 90. See Carolyn Merchant, *Reinventing Eden: The Fate of Nature in Western Culture* (New York and London: Routledge, 2003), for the evolution of a myth of "recovery." The difficulty in picturing the final state of the new creation is not helped by trying to picture the also unpicturable, and scientifically unsupported, character of an original garden of harmony.

34. The phrase was coined by Whitehead in his *Process and Reality*; see Haught, *Deeper Than Darwin*, 154, and n14, this chapter.

35. Haught, "The Boyle Lecture 2003: Darwin, Design and the Promise of Nature," *Science and Christian Belief* 17 (April 2005): 5–20, 17.

36. Thomas E. Hosinski, "How Does God's Providential Care Extend to Animals?" in *Animals on the Agenda: Questions about Animals for Theology and Ethics*, ed. Andrew Linzey and Dorothy Yamamoto, 137–43 (London: SCM Press, 1998), 143.

37. Jay B. McDaniel, "Can Animal Suffering Be Reconciled with Belief?" in *Animals on the Agenda: Questions about Animals for Theology and Ethics*, ed. Andrew Linzey and Dorothy Yamamoto, 161–70 (London: SCM Press, 1998), 169.

38. Ibid., 170.

39. Alfred Lord Tennyson, "In Memoriam," LIV:9, 12, in *Tennyson: A Selected Edition*, ed. Christopher Ricks (1969; repr., London: Longman, 1989), 396.

40. Haught, *Deeper Than Darwin*, 154.

41. Ibid.

42. Ibid., 157–58. The reason for this preference may very well lie in Haught's interest in Whiteheadian metaphysics, with its emphasis on event, rather than entity.

43. McDaniel, *Of God and Pelicans*, 45.

44. Edwards, "Every Sparrow That Falls to the Ground."

45. Moltmann, *Way of Jesus Christ*: "There is therefore no meaningful hope for the future of creation unless 'the tears are wiped from every eye'. But they can only

be wiped away when the dead are raised, and when the victims of evolution experience justice through the resurrection of nature" (297). "What is eschatological is the new creation of all things which were and are and will be. What is eschatological is the bringing back of all things out of their past, and the gathering of them into the kingdom of glory. What is eschatological is the raising of the body and the whole of nature" (303).

46. Edwards, "Every Sparrow That Falls to the Ground," 116, citing Ernst Conradie, "Resurrection, Finitude, and Ecology," in *Resurrection: Theological and Scientific Assessments*, ed. Ted Peters, Robert J. Russell, and Michael Welker, 277–96 (Grand Rapids: Eerdmans, 2002).

47. Conradie, "Resurrection," 292.

48. Ibid., 295.

49. Here he is in accord with C. S. Lewis's point that if creatures have no developed sentient self, with no sense at all of the integration of successive experiences, then there is little point in attributing to them a subjective immortality (*Problem of Pain*, chap. 9).

50. Edwards, "Every Sparrow That Falls to the Ground," 118–21; see also sections 6.2, 6.8.

51. In *Staying Alive: Real Poems for Unreal Times*, ed. Neil Astley (Tarset, Northumberland, UK: Bloodaxe, 2002), 221–22, and reproduced here from Dickey's collection "The Whole Motion" by permission of The Wesleyan Press.

52. Note that this is a dynamic vision, one of continuing consummation (cf. John Macquarrie, *Principles of Christian Theology*, rev. ed. [1966; repr., London: SCM Press, 1977], 356).

53. An important attempt to delineate what can and cannot helpfully be said is Robert J. Russell's "Natural Theodicy in an Evolutionary Context: The Need for an Eschatology of New Creation," in *Theodicy and Eschatology*, ed. Bruce Barber and David Neville, 121–52 (Adelaide: Australian Theological Forum, 2005).

54. Haught, *Deeper Than Darwin*, 158.

55. Wesley J. Wildman, "Incongruous Goodness, Perilous Beauty, Disconcerting Truth: Ultimate Reality, and Suffering in Nature," in *Physics and Cosmology: Scientific Perspectives on the Problem of Evil in Nature*, ed. Nancey Murphy, Robert J. Russell, and William Stoeger, SJ, 267–94 (Vatican City: Vatican Observatory; Berkeley, CA: Center for Theology and the Natural Sciences, 2007), emphasis in original, 292.

Chapter 6

1. Some of section 6.1 was presented by Cherryl Hunt, David G. Horrell, and myself as "An Environmental Mantra? Ecological Interest in Romans 8:18–23 and a Modest Proposal for Its Narrative Interpretation," at the British New Testament Conference, Exeter, September 2007. I thank my colleagues for permission to make use of their insights here. All quotations from Hunt et al. in the text are from this still unpublished paper. See also David G. Horrell, Cherryl Hunt, and Christopher Southgate, "Appeals to the Bible in Ecotheology and Environmental Ethics: A Typology of Hermeneutical Stances," *Studies in Christian Ethics*, 21, no. 2 (2008, forthcoming).

2. Robert Jewett, *Romans: A Commentary*, Hermeneia Series (Minneapolis: Fortress Press, 2007), 504.

3. See Ron Elsdon, "Eschatology and Hope," in *The Care of Creation: Focusing Concern and Action*, ed. R. J. Berry, 161–66 (Leicester: InterVarsity Press, 2000);

Michael S. Northcott, *The Environment and Christian Ethics* (Cambridge: Cambridge University Press, 1996), 204; H. Paul Santmire, *Nature Reborn: The Ecological and Cosmic Promise of Christian Theology* (Minneapolis: Fortress Press, 2000), 42.

4. E.g., Steven Bouma-Prediger, *For the Beauty of the Earth: A Christian Vision for Creation Care* (Grand Rapids: Baker Book House, 2001), 40.

5. Reprinted in R. J. Berry, ed., *The Care of Creation: Focusing Concern and Action* (Leicester: InterVarsity Press, 2000), 17–22, 19.

6. R. J. Berry, *God's Book of Works: The Nature and Theology of Nature* (London and New York: T&T Clark/Continuum, 2003), 230–32.

7. Neil Messer, *Selfish Genes and Christian Ethics: Theological and Ethical Reflections on Evolutionary Biology* (London: SCM Press, 2007), 214.

8. Charles Raven writes of this passage, "St Paul is far too good a theist, far too close a student of the Old Testament, to believe that the imperfection of creation is due to any act of devil or man: only God is in control of the world" (*Natural Religion and Christian Theology: The Gifford Lectures 1952*, Vol. 1, *First Series: Science and Religion* [Cambridge: Cambridge University Press, 1953], 36).

9. Lukas Vischer, "Listening to Creation Groaning: A Survey of Main Themes in Christian Theology," in *Listening to Creation Groaning: Report and Papers from a Consultation on Creation Theology Organized by the European Christian Environmental Network at the John Knox International Reformed Center from March 28 to April 1, 2004*, ed. Lukas Vischer, 11–31 (Geneva: Centre International Réformé John Knox, 2004), see 21–22.

10. The Earth Bible Team, "Guiding Ecojustice Principles," in *Readings from the Perspective of Earth, The Earth Bible, Volume One*, ed. Norman C. Habel, 38–53 (Sheffield: Sheffield Academic Press; Cleveland: Pilgrim Press, 2000).

11. Brendan Byrne, SJ, "Creation Groaning: An Earth Bible Reading of Romans 8.19–22," in *Readings from the Perspective of Earth, The Earth Bible, Volume One*, ed. Norman C. Habel, 193–203 (Sheffield: Sheffield Academic Press; Cleveland: Pilgrim Press, 2000), 198.

12. Richard Bauckham, *God and the Crisis of Freedom: Biblical and Contemporary Perspectives* (Louisville: Westminster John Knox Press, 2002), 173.

13. Christian believers are significant here, not because they represent the few who alone will be redeemed—an anthropomonist and exclusivist doctrine of salvation—but because for Paul they are the ones in whom the promise of renewal and transformation is already coming to fruition: just as they have the firstfruits of the Spirit, so, in a sense, they are the firstfruits of a redeemed creation, the "deposit" that guarantees the remainder (cf. 2 Cor. 1:22; 5:5).

14. In terms of the narrative types outlined by Northrop Frye and developed theologically by James Hopewell, in his study of the different kinds of stories congregations tell, I suggest that in this aspect of the Pauline vision there is more than a hint of a romantic (for Hopewell a "charismatic") genre (James Hopewell, *Congregation: Stories and Structure* [1987; repr., London: SCM Press, 1988], 58–62). As Hunt et al. put it, "The 'heroes' of this sub-drama in God's great drama of salvation are 'the children of God' as they undertake their 'quest,' longing to be transformed from one degree of glory to another, to come into that full liberty for which the creation as a whole also longs. In this they follow *the* central hero-figure, Christ himself, who, having faithfully accepted the path of suffering and death, has become the firstborn among many siblings (8:29), the firstfruits from the dead (1 Cor. 15:20)."

Jewett has argued that this Pauline narrative may represent a countercultural contrast to a received narrative of the Augustan Age (which would be in Frye's terms "comic"), in which the crisis of the break-up of the Roman Republic is replaced by an (ultimately illusory) harmonious union of *urbs et orbs* in the person of the emperor (Jewett, *Romans*, 516–17). The focus of the Pauline communities is the Jerusalem collection, the relief of the suffering of the poor; the believers thus set up a countercultural relation with that world (about relief of suffering rather than the imposition of grain quotas to run a great imperial infrastructure). In stressing the character of this passage as a narrative of struggle and quest, rather than of the once-for-all reversal of the sin of Adam, I am associating the key to the passage very much with Rom. 1 (and behind that the book of Ecclesiastes) and the "futility" to which God has subjected the creation, rather than with Rom. 5:12–21 and behind that the sin of Adam, as in Byrne's reading ("Creation Groaning," 195–99).

15. N. T. Wright also sees the futility of creation in the natural rhythms of the seasons and of birth and death (*Evil and the Justice of God* [Downers Grove, IL: InterVarsity Press, 2007], 117). Richard W. Kropf in *Evil and Evolution: A Theodicy* (1984; repr., Eugene, OR: Wipf and Stock, 2004) sees the futility as residing in the operation of chance in the evolutionary process (124). Cf. also Holmes Rolston: "'Groaning in travail' is in the nature of things from time immemorial. Such travail is the Creator's will, productive as it is of glory" ("Naturalizing and Systematizing Evil," in *Is Nature Ever Evil?* ed. Willem B. Drees, 67–86 (London and New York: Routledge, 2003), 85.

16. See Dietrich Bonhoeffer, *Ethics*, ed. Eberhard Bethge, trans. N. Horton Smith (1949; English ed., London: Collins, 1964), 125–43.

17. Cf. Luzia Sutter Rehmann, "To Turn the Groaning into Labor: Romans 8.22–23," in *A Feminist Companion to Paul*, ed. A.-J. Levine and M. Bickenstaff, 74–83 (Cleveland: Pilgrim, 2004).

18. Norman C. Habel, unpublished paper on Gen. 1 given to the Society for Biblical Literature Conference, Washington, DC, November 2006.

19. For Denis Edwards it is the Spirit who is the true midwife; see his *Breath of Life: A Theology of the Creator Spirit* (Maryknoll, NY: Orbis Books, 2004), 110–12.

20. Indeed the interior logic of the passage suggests that creation's "futility" is part of God's (profoundly mysterious) solution to the problem of "bondage to decay," rather than being a concept with a parallel meaning to "bondage to decay," as many commentators assume (cf. J. D. G. Dunn, *Romans 1–8* [Dallas: Word Books, 1988], 470; Jewett, *Romans*, 513–15; Brendan Byrne, *Romans* [Collegeville, MN: The Liturgical Press, 1996], 260).

21. This then is a heuristic hermeneutic, interpreting the biblical text in terms of its consonance with scientific narrative, what Sallie McFague calls "the common creation story," and in terms of the capacity of the text to generate constructive proposals in ethics. At the same time I endeavor to remain as faithful as possible to the mainstream of the Christian tradition. This then is not *merely* a remythologization with "ethical or pragmatic concern" (Sallie McFague, *The Body of God: An Ecological Theology* [London: SCM Press, 1993], 81), and it allows the tradition more of a controlling influence than is the case with McFague's own theology (cf. the critique of McFague's general approach by Daphne Hampson in her *Theology and Feminism* [Oxford: Basil Blackwell, 1990], 161).

22. A related reading is that of Richard Kropf, who describes the "subjection" in

Rom 8:20 as "simply part of an even broader movement of co-creative love and unitive fulfilment" (*Evil and Evolution*, 156). Kropf transates v. 22 as "the entire creation . . . has been groaning and is in one great act of giving birth" (156). The positive, generative aspects of the word *sunōdinō*, "to suffer together the agony of giving birth," have been neglected by many commentators, but see Rehmann, "To Turn the Groaning into Labor."

23. Metropolitan John Zizioulas of Pergamon, "Creation Theology: An Orthodox Perspective," in *Listening to Creation Groaning*, ed. Lukas Vischer, 90–104 (Geneva: Centre International Réformé John Knox, 2004), 93.

24. Ibid., 94.

25. Ibid., emphases in original.

26. See in particular the work of Alexander Schmemann, such as *The World as Sacrament* (1965; repr., London: Darton, Longman, and Todd, 1966).

27. Cf. Andrew Elphinstone, *Freedom, Suffering, and Love* (London: SCM Press, 1976), chap. 12.

28. What follows draws on my "From the Bison at Niaux to the Kyoto Protocol," in *The Evolution of Rationality: Interdisciplinary Essays in Honor of J. Wentzel van Huyssteen*, ed. LeRon Shults, 183–96 (Grand Rapids and Cambridge: Eerdmans, 2006).

29. For two very different construals of inscape, see Walter Ong, SJ, *Hopkins, the Self, and God* (Toronto: University of Toronto Press, 1986), and Bernadette Ward, *World as Word: Philosophical Theology in Gerard Manley Hopkins* (Washington, DC: Catholic University of America Press, 2001).

30. The scholastic precursor is *haecceitas*, coined by Duns Scotus, who greatly influenced Hopkins.

31. See Paul S. Fiddes, *Freedom and Limit: A Dialogue between Literature and Christian Doctrine* (Macon, GA: Mercer University Press, 1999), 120, reflecting on Hopkins's "The Wreck of the *Deutschland*," stanza 5.

32. This phrase is John V. Taylor's in his *The Go-Between God: The Holy Spirit and the Christian Mission* (1972; repr., London: SCM Press, 1984).

33. It is important to admit that my use of "inscape" and "instress" in what follows is an inference from Hopkins's thought, rather than an effort to follow his not-always-clear system exactly.

34. In *Nature*, 27, no. 681 (November 1882), 53; 29, no. 733 (November 1883), 55; 29, no. 740 (January 1884), 222–23; 30, no. 783 (October 1884), 633.

35. W. H. Gardner, *Gerard Manley Hopkins: A Study of Poetic Idiosyncrasy in Relation to Poetic Tradition*, Vol. 2 (1949; repr., London: Oxford University Press, 1958), 350.

36. J. Wentzel van Huyssteen, "Human Origins and Religious Awareness: In Search of Human Uniqueness," *Studia Theologica* 59, no. 2 (December 2005): 1–25, 22. See also his *Alone in the World? Human Uniqueness in Science and Theology—The Gifford Lectures, University of Edinburgh, Spring 2004* (Cambridge and Grand Rapids: Eerdmans, 2006), esp. 276–300, "Interdisciplinary Perspectives."

37. Reg Morrison, *The Spirit in the Gene: Humanity's Proud Illusion and the Laws of Nature* (Ithaca, NY: Cornell University Press, 1999), 99.

38. Indeed, the extinction record shows precisely the reverse. Within a few thousand years of humans' arrival in North America, 70 percent of the species of large mammals were extinct. See Michael Boulter, *Extinction: Evolution and the End of Man* (2002; repr., London: HarperCollins, 2003), 9. For more on extinction, human-induced and other, see section 7.4.

39. Morrison, *Spirit in the Gene*, 139–41. Morrison's own thesis seems to be that humans' spiritual bent acts as the biosphere's insurance policy, ensuring that we do *not* look wisely to our own ecological self-interest, and therefore are certain to die back at the end of each plague cycle. That is the reverse of the case van Huyssteen and I would want to make, which is that spirituality is intrinsic to the growth of human rationality. But the events of Easter Island, where the building of vast statues continued although the means to move them, and the means to ensure food supplies and continue to communicate with the outside world, had been destroyed by deforestation, surely constitute Morrison's most telling example. On the unsustainability of human societies, see also Jared Diamond, *Collapse: How Societies Choose to Fail or Survive* (London: Penguin, 2005).

40. The vast prairie lands, now grain lands, of the American Midwest are in the middle of this process. Their extraordinary fecundity derived from the last Ice Age; they are still incredibly productive, but suffering appreciable and continuing erosion. They will not recover until the next glaciation. See William F. Ruddiman, *Plows, Plagues, and Petroleum: How Humans Took Control of Climate* (Princeton, NJ, and Oxford: Princeton University Press, 2005).

41. Morrison, *Spirit in the Genes*, 96–98.

42. Thomas Berry goes as far as to describe the situation of modern scientific and mechanistic humanity as "autistic": "Emotionally," he writes, "we cannot get out of our confinement, nor can we let the outer world flow into our own beings. We cannot hear the voice [of the universe] or speak in response" (*The Dream of the Earth* [San Francisco: Sierra Club, 1988], 16–17).

43. Hopkins's own translation of *harpagmon* in Phil. 2:6. See Christopher Devlin's introduction to *The Sermons and Devotional Writings of Gerard Manley Hopkins*, ed. Christopher Devlin, 107–21 (London: Oxford University Press, 1959), 108.

44. Ibid., 115.

45. This has been an important motif in the work of Arthur Peacocke, who summarizes his approach in his *Paths from Science towards God: The End of All Our Exploring* (Oxford: Oneworld Press, 2001). The implications of the text from Acts are explored in a variety of ways in *In Whom We Live and Move and Have Our Being: Panentheistic Reflections on God's Place in a Scientific World*, ed. Philip Clayton and Arthur Peacocke (Grand Rapids and Cambridge: Eerdmans, 2004).

46. This point is trenchantly made by Lisa H. Sideris in her *Environmental Ethics, Ecological Theology, and Natural Selection* (New York: Columbia University Press, 2003).

47. In elaborating an ethics of kenosis I am well aware of the critique of the term from a feminist perspective. See Sarah Coakley, "Theological Meanings and Gender Connotations," in *The Work of Love: Creation as Kenosis*, ed. John Polkinghorne, 192–210 (London: SPCK; Grand Rapids and Cambridge: Eerdmans, 2001), for a judicious analysis. As Coakley so wisely says, although we may deploy the hermeneutics of suspicion in relation to the language of self-sacrifice, "It does not follow that *all* attempts to rethink the value of moral kenosis, or of 'sacrificial' love, founder on the shoals of gender essentialism" (208, italics in original).

48. Simone Weil, *Waiting for God*, trans. E. Craufurd (New York: Harper and Row, 1951), 159–60.

49. Cf. James D. G. Dunn, *The Theology of Paul the Apostle* (Grand Rapids: Eerdmans, 1998), 112. Also Byrne, "Creation Groaning," on "the sin story."

50. I avoid the term "resources" here as that carries the implication that the good things of the world are defined by their availability for use by human beings.

51. This, and much of what follows, is taken from my chapter "Stewardship and Its Competitors: A Spectrum of Relationships between Humans and the Non-Human Creation," in *Environmental Stewardship*, ed. R. J. Berry, 185–95 (London and New York: T&T Clark/Continuum, 2006).

52. John Habgood, *The Concept of Nature* (London: Darton, Longman, and Todd, 2002), 70.

53. Southgate, "Stewardship and Its Competitors."

54. Philip Hefner, *The Human Factor: Evolution, Culture and Religion* (Minneapolis: Fortress Press, 1993).

55. E.g., Ted Peters, *Playing God? Genetic Determinism and Human Freedom* (London and New York: Routledge, 1997), and *Science, Theology, and Ethics* (Aldershot and Burlington, VT: Ashgate, 2003).

56. Hefner, *Human Factor*, 264.

57. Peters, *Science, Theology, and Ethics*, 215.

58. Józef Życiński, *God and Evolution: Fundamental Questions of Christian Evolutionism*, trans. K. W. Kemp and Z. Maslanka (Washington, DC: Catholic University of America Press, 2006), 192.

59. Ronald Cole-Turner, *The New Genesis: Theology and the Genetic Revolution* (Louisville, KY: Westminster/John Knox Press, 1993), 96–97.

60. Cole-Turner, *New Genesis*, 102, emphasis in original.

61. Arthur Peacocke, *Creation and the World of Science: The Bampton Lectures 1978* (Oxford: Clarendon Press, 1979), 295–97.

62. T. F. Torrance, *Divine and Contingent Order* (Oxford: Oxford University Press, 1981), 128–30; Ruth Page, *God and the Web of Creation* (London: SCM Press, 1996), 161–64.

63. Wendell Berry, *The Gift of Good Land: Further Essays Cultural and Agricultural* (San Francisco: North Point Press, 1981), 281.

64. Vladimir Lossky, *The Mystical Theology of the Eastern Church*, trans. Members of the Fellowship of St. Alban and St. Sergius (London: J. Clarke, 1957), 111.

65. John Zizioulas, "Priest of Creation," in *Environmental Stewardship*, ed. R. Berry, 273–90 (London and New York: T&T Clark/Continuum, 2006), 274.

66. Elizabeth Theokritoff, "Creation and Priesthood in Modern Orthodox Thinking," *Ecotheology* 10, no. 3 (December 2005): 344–63.

67. Theokritoff, commenting on the work of Metropolitan Anthony Bloom, looks for a middle position which is neither a "self-interested tinkering" nor "simply . . . leaving the world alone even where that is a possible option" ("Creation and Priesthood," 349).

68. Paulos mar Gregorios, *The Human Presence: Ecological Spirituality and the Age of the Spirit* (Amity, NY: Amity House, 1987), 90.

69. Theokritoff, "Creation and Priesthood," 351.

70. See Michael Northcott, *The Environment and Christian Ethics* (Cambridge: Cambridge University Press, 1996): "The metaphor [of priesthood] elides or misses the extraordinary difference and otherness of life which is not human and not God, and the potential for nonhuman life, albeit partially obscured by the Fall, and for nature, like humanity, to render praise to God in its beauty and order" (134). Also Richard Bauckham, "Joining Creation's Praise of God," *Ecotheology* 7, no. 1 (July 2002): 45–59, esp. 49–51. For a response to the critiques of Northcott and Bauckham, see Theokritoff, "Creation and Priesthood," 354–56.

71. Though Zizioulas, interestingly, argues the reverse, that "because man, unlike the angels..., forms an organic part of the material world ... he is able to carry with him the whole of creation to its transcendence. The fact that the human is also an *animal*, far from being an insult to the human race, constitutes the *sine qua non* for his glorious mission in creation" ("Priest of Creation," 286).

72. Arne Naess, "The Shallow and the Deep, Long-range Ecology Movement. A Summary," *Inquiry* 16 (1973): 95–100.

73. Aldo Leopold, *A Sand County Almanac: With Essays on Conservation from Round River* (Oxford: Oxford University Press, 1966), 262. (The original *Sand County Almanac* was published in 1949.)

74. Thomas Sieger Derr, "The Challenge of Biocentrism," in *Creation at Risk? Religion, Science, and Environmentalism*, ed. Michael Cromartie, 85–104 (Cambridge: Ethics and Public Policy Center; Grand Rapids: Eerdmans, 1995).

75. Cf. Berry, *God's Book of Works*, 249–50.

76. Derr, "Challenge of Biocentrism," 100.

77. Such as Clare Palmer's denunciation of stewardship as being (in the sense in which it is popularly used) unbiblical. See her "Stewardship: A Case Study in Environmental Ethics," in *The Earth Beneath: A Critical Guide to Green Theology*, ed. Ian Ball, Margaret Goodall, Clare Palmer, and John Reader, 67–86 (London: SPCK, 1992). Bauckham confirms that the explicit understanding within the Christian tradition that humans are stewards of nature dates only to the seventeenth century; see his "Stewardship and Relationship" in *The Care of Creation: Focusing Concern and Action*, ed. R. J. Berry, 99–106 (Leicester: InterVarsity Press, 2000). Anne Primavesi condemns the concept of stewardship as exploitative and unecological; see her *From Apocalypse to Genesis: Ecology, Feminism, and Christianity* (Tunbridge Wells: Burns and Oates, 1991), 106–7. Sean McDonagh is concerned that "within the context of this analogy the earth is reified and becomes either inert property to be cared for or financial resources to be managed in a way that gives a good return on the investment." See his *Passion for the Earth: The Christian Vocation to Promote Justice, Peace, and the Integrity of Creation* (London: Geoffrey Chapman, 1994), 130. Edward Echlin claims that stewardship "easily lends itself to a detached, manipulative view of creation" and that it "has not moved hearts" (*The Cosmic Circle: Jesus and Ecology* [Blackrock, Co. Dublin: Columba Press, 2004], 16). Bill McKibben regards stewardship as "so lacking in content as to give us very little guidance about how to behave in any given situation" (*The Comforting Whirlwind: God, Job and the Scale of Creation* [Grand Rapids: Eerdmans, 1994], 51).

78. Cf. Herman E. Daly and John B. Cobb Jr., *For the Common Good: Redirecting the Economy towards Community, the Environment and a Sustainable Future* (1989; repr., London: Green Print, 1990).

79. Lawrence Osborn, *Guardians of Creation: Nature in Theology and Human Life* (Leicester: Apollos, 1993), pp 143–44.

80. See J. Gleick, *Chaos: Making a New Science* (London: Cardinal, 1988), for an introduction.

81. Sideris, *Environmental Ethics*, chap. 2.

82. Holmes Rolston III, *Environmental Ethics: Duties to and Values in the Natural World* (Philadelphia: Temple University Press, 1988); Rolston, *Conserving Natural Value* (New York: Columbia University Press, 1994).

83. Holmes Rolston III, "Naturalizing and Systematizing Evil," in *Is Nature Ever Evil? Religion, Science and Value*, ed. Willem B. Drees, 67–86 (London and New York: Routledge, 2003), 84.

84. A major nuclear event would be much more disastrous even than the sort of asteroid impact that seems to have precipitated the last great extinction event, the disappearance of the dinosaurs, because the resulting radiation would effectively sterilize the surface of the planet for a long period.

85. James Lovelock, *The Revenge of Gaia: Why the Earth Is Fighting Back—and How We Can Still Save Humanity* (London: Penguin, 2006), 43–44.

86. First made in Southgate, "Stewardship and Its Competitors."

87. See James Lovelock, *The Ages of Gaia: A Biography of Our Living Earth* (1988; repr., Oxford: Oxford University Press, 1989), and for a chilling update, *Revenge of Gaia*.

88. See McKibben, *The Comforting Whirlwind;* for a conspectus of deep ecologists, see George Sessions, ed., *Deep Ecology for the Twenty-first Century* (Boston: Shambhala, 1995).

89. For a passionate account of this type of attention to the natural world, see Annie Dillard, *Pilgrim at Tinker Creek*, in *Three by Annie Dillard* (New York: HarperCollins, 2001).

90. In Berry, *God's Book of Works*, 232.

91. I am grateful to the Right Reverend Bill Ind, former bishop of Truro, for a sermon including this motif of seeing creation whole.

92. In Hopkins, *Sermons and Devotional Writings*, 239, emphasis in original.

93. David Bentley Hart, *The Doors of the Sea: Where Was God in the Tsunami?* (Grand Rapids and Cambridge: Eerdmans, 2005), 63.

94. Ware, "The Value of the Material Creation," *Sobornost* 6, no. 3 (Summer 1971): 154–65, 155–56.

95. Theokritoff, "Creation and Priesthood," 346.

96. Cf. Zizioulas, "Priest of Creation," 289.

97. Theokritoff, "Creation and Priesthood," quoting John Chryssavgis.

98. Ware, "Value of the Material Creation," 157. See also Andrew Louth, "The Cosmic Vision of Saint Maximos the Confessor," in *In Whom We Live and Move and Have Our Being*, ed. Philip Clayton and Arthur Peacocke, 184–96 (Grand Rapids and Cambridge: Eerdmans, 2004), 189.

99. Theokritoff, "Creation and Priesthood," 347, quoting Schmemann.

100. Ibid., 348, quoting Ware.

101. Ibid., 357, quoting Sherrard.

102. Ibid., 345, quoting Zizioulas.

103. Cf. Olivier Clément, *On Human Being: A Spiritual Anthropology*, trans. J. Hummerstone (1986; English ed., London: New City, 2000), 118.

104. Theokritoff, "Creation and Priesthood," 349, quoting Basil Osborne.

105. Bishop Kallistos of Diokleia (Kallistos Ware), *Through the Creation to the Creator* (London: Friends of the Centre, 1997), 9. Interestingly Ware in turn is drawing here on Elizabeth Barrett Browning's verse in *Aurora Leigh*.

106. I exclude Thomas Gold's proposed "deep hot biosphere," and perhaps the remotest parts of the deep ocean, as being effectively beyond the ambit of our care (see Gold, *The Deep Hot Biosphere* [New York: Springer-Verlag, 1999]). An example of the care that needs to be taken in our investigations of the nonhuman world is Lake Vostok, under the East Antarctic Ice Sheet, an ecosystem effectively isolated from any other. E. O. Wilson notes that to drill through to the liquid water to analyze this fascinating location "would contaminate one of the last remaining pristine habitats on Earth" (*The Future of Life* [London: Little, Brown, 2002], 9).

Chapter 7

1. Andrew Linzey, *Animal Theology* (London: SCM Press, 1994), 84–85, 98–99. This ignoring of the scientific evidence clouds unnecessarily Linzey's appeal to vegetarianism as an eschatological sign of our hope and response to the Gospel. There is no reason to believe that just because God used a long evolutionary process to give rise to the biosphere we know, God may not have inaugurated a redemptive movement that will heal that process. Indeed Moltmann is convinced this must be so; see section 5.4.

2. Ibid., 55. On human priesthood of creation, see section 6.2, 6.7–6.8.

3. Ibid., 72.

4. Richard Bauckham, "Jesus and Animals II: What Did He Practise?" in *Animals on the Agenda: Questions about Animals for Theology and Ethics*, ed. Andrew Linzey and Dorothy Yamamoto, 49–60 (London: SCM Press, 1998), 57–58.

5. Andrew Linzey, "The Vampire's Dilemma: Animal Rights and Parasitical Nature," in *Good News for Animals? Christian Approaches to Animal Well-Being*, ed. Charles Pinches and Jay B. McDaniel, 128–41 (Maryknoll, NY: Orbis, 1993), 139.

6. Ibid., 140. Again note the reference to creation's longing (Rom. 8:19).

7. N. T. Wright, *The Resurrection of the Son of God* (London: SPCK, 2003), 258.

8. Karl Barth, *Church Dogmatics*, III/4, *The Doctrine of Creation*, ed. G. W. Bromiley and T. F. Torrance, trans. A.T. Mackay, T. H. L. Parker, H. Knight, H. A. Kennedy, and J. Marks (Edinburgh: T&T Clark, 1961), 355.

9. Ibid.

10. Ibid. I note in passing that most commentators agree that it was God, not humans, who "subjected" creation to bondage; so section 6.1 and, for example, John Ziesler, *Paul's Letter to the Romans* (London: SCM Press; Philadelphia: Trinity Press International, 1989), 220. This is also Barth's position in *The Epistle to the Romans*, trans. from the 6th ed. by E. C. Hoskyns (London: Oxford University Press, 1933), 309.

11. Barth, *Church Dogmatics*, III/4, 355.

12. Those coming to this account from outside the Christian tradition may well note with surprise the strongly anthropocentric implication of these invocations of Rom. 8. It is at least possible to argue that the movements for animal rights and animal liberation are just as anthropocentric—that their claims project human valuation of individuals onto the natural world, at the expense of recognizing the value of systems (cf. Pollan, *The Omnivore's Dilemma: A Natural History of Four Meals* [New York: Penguin, 2006], 323–24). I would hold that the passage from Romans does indeed imply a very high doctrine of humanity and its influence. I recall here Vischer's distinction, noted in section 6.1, between anthropocentrism and anthropomonism, and call for a resolute anthropocentrism, a conviction that humans are called to a specific role in the world. See also Charles Pinches on not being afraid of an anthropocentrism which recognizes that to care for other creatures and ecosystems is to be a good human and hence to serve a sort of human interest ("Each According to Its Kind: A Defense of Theological Speciesism," in *Good News for Animals? Christian Approaches to Animal Well-Being*, ed. Charles Pinches and Jay B. McDaniel, 187–205 [Maryknoll, NY: Orbis Books, 1993]).

13. Barth, *Church Dogmatics* III/4, 355.

14. I am aware that the argument from community can run both ways. Walter Houston quotes Porphyry's position that "we do not slaughter . . . any of those

animals that share our labor but do not enjoy its fruits" ("What Was the Meaning of Classifying Animals as Clean or Unclean?" in *Animals on the Agenda: Questions about Animals for Theology and Ethics*, ed. Andrew Linzey and Dorothy Yamamoto, 18–24 [London: SCM Press, 1998], 22). If farm animals are in some measure members of the human community, it could be argued that they gain the rights of community members—not only the right not to be used merely as means to an end, but the right to life as well. The problem with this view is that if animals were not to be killed, then very few animals would be kept (particularly given the resource cost of keeping animals into old age).

15. A point that seems to be missed by Gary L. Comstock in his efforts to press the analogy between meat eating and slavery; see his "Pigs and Piety: A Theocentric Perspective on Food Animals," in *Good News for Animals? Christian Approaches to Animal Well-Being*, ed. Charles Pinches and Jay B. McDaniel, 105–27 (Maryknoll, NY: Orbis Books, 1993).

16. I accept, then, McDaniel's point that habitat depletion and the violent manipulation of animals through science, hunting, or commercial livestock production both reduce our bonding with animals, and yet I believe that animal husbandry *can* be part of our fulfilling of our "need to be bonded with animals for fullness of life." It can be an example of communion with animals exhibiting, in McDaniel's terms, both empathy, sharing of one another's life situations, and eros, desiring the well-being of the other. See his "A God Who Loves Animals and a Church That Does the Same," in *Good News for Animals? Christian Approaches to Animal Well-Being*, ed. Charles Pinches and Jay B. McDaniel, 75–102 (Maryknoll, NY: Orbis Books, 1993), 81.

17. Martin Buber, *I and Thou*, trans. Ronald Gregor Smith (1923; first English ed., 1937; repr., London: Continuum, 1958). Buber extended I-Thou relationships very widely, even to encounters with trees, but realized that they are always in danger of slipping into I-It relations, in which the "It" may be traded as a commodity.

18. As in the telling example of Nathan's illustration to David of the loved lamb in 2 Sam. 12, see George L. Frear Jr., "Caring for Animals: Biblical Stimulus for Ethical Reflection," in *Good News for Animals? Christian Approaches to Animal Well-Being*, ed. Charles Pinches and Jay B. McDaniel, 3–11 (Maryknoll, NY: Orbis Books, 1993), esp. 6.

19. Rosemary Radford Ruether, "Men, Women, and Beasts: Relations to Animals in Western Culture," in *Good News for Animals? Christian Approaches to Animal Well-Being*, ed. Charles Pinches and Jay B. McDaniel, 12–23 (Maryknoll, NY: Orbis Books, 1993), 20. L. Shannon Jung, in the same volume, notes that we tend to regard pets as friends, but all other animals as strangers ("Animals in Christian Perspective: Strangers, Friends, or Kin?" in *Good News for Animals?* 47–61). He prefers to explore the possibility of regarding all animals as kin and potential friends. I suggest rather that the concept of the animal as stranger accords with our ignorance of what it is really like to be another creature, and would enable Christian ethicists to draw on the strong vein in the Hebrew Bible of care for the stranger who is found within the community. The same concept of the animal as stranger invited into the human community, to whom hospitality is then owed, is found in Charles Pinches's "Each According to Its Kind," esp. 203.

20. H. Paul Santmire, *Nature Reborn: The Ecological and Cosmic Promise of Christian Theology* (Minneapolis: Fortress Press, 2000).

21. Richard Alan Young, *Is God a Vegetarian? Christianity, Vegetarianism, and Animal Rights* (Chicago and La Salle, IL: Open Court, 1999), 124.

22. Ibid., 145.

23. So Michael Pollan: "The industrial animal factory offers a nightmarish glimpse of what capitalism is capable of in the absence of any moral or regulatory constraint whatsoever" (*Omnivore's Dilemma*, 318).

24. Young cites in this connection that fine saying of F. F. Bruce's, "A truly emancipated spirit such as Paul's is not in bondage to its own emancipation," *Commentary on Acts* (Grand Rapids: Eerdmans, 1954), quoted in Young, *Is God a Vegetarian?* 124.

25. Barth, *Church Dogmatics* III/4, 356.

26. Ibid.

27. Wendell Berry, *The Gift of Good Land: Further Essays Cultural and Agricultural* (San Francisco: North Point Press, 1981), 281.

28. After drafting this section I was encouraged to pick up my colleague Timothy Gorringe's *Harvest: Food, Farming, and the Churches* (London: SPCK, 2006) and to note that he reaches a similar conclusion (64–66).

29. David Grumett, "Hebrew Food Rules in Christian Dietary Practice," in *Eating and Believing: Interdisciplinary Perspectives on Vegetarianism and Theology*, ed. R. E. Muers and D. J. Grumett (London and New York: T&T Clark/Continuum, 2008, forthcoming).

30. Rachel Muers, "Women and Other Animals, Gender, Diet and Theology," in *Eating and Believing: Interdisciplinary Perspectives on Vegetarianism and Theology*, ed. R. E. Muers and D. J. Grumett (London and New York: T&T Clark/Continuum, 2008, forthcoming). See Dietrich Bonhoeffer, *Ethics*, ed. Eberhard Bethge, trans. N. Horton Smith, 125–43 (1949; English ed., London: Collins, 1964), and Neil Messer, *Selfish Genes and Christian Ethics: Theological and Ethical Reflections on Evolutionary Biology* (London: SCM Press, 2007), 207–9, for a recent appropriation of this concept.

31. Muers, "Women and Other Animals."

32. On the importance of prudential wisdom in ethics, see Celia Deane-Drummond, *The Ethics of Nature* (Edinburgh: T&T Clark, 2004), esp. chap. 9.

33. As pointed out by Ruether, "Men, Women and Beasts," 21, among many others. Mary Midgley points out that, paradoxically, the most telling argument for vegetarianism is not derived from animal care but from appeal to human welfare. See her *Animals and Why They Matter* (Athens: University of Georgia Press, 1984), 26–27.

34. A quarter-pound hamburger requires around eleven cubic meters of water to produce (Reg Morrison, *The Spirit in the Gene: Humanity's Proud Illusion and the Laws of Nature* [Ithaca, NY: Cornell University Press, 1999], 46).

35. Methane, produced in the stomachs of ruminants, is around twenty times as potent a greenhouse gas as carbon dioxide (ibid., 23). It is estimated that the global greenhouse effect of domestic cattle now exceeds that of all human modes of transport combined.

36. Pollan, *Omnivore's Dilemma*, 326–27.

37. See also Gorringe, *Harvest*, 65; also Colin Tudge, *So Shall We Reap* (London: Penguin, 2003).

38. Cf. my chapters on environmental ethics in *Bioethics for Scientists*, ed. John Bryant, Linda Baggott LaVelle, and John Searle (Chichester, UK: Wiley, 2002), chaps. 3–5 [chap. 5 written with Alex Aylward]; also H. E. Daly and J. B. Cobb

Jr., *For the Common Good: Redirecting the Economy toward Community, the Environment and a Sustainable Future* (1989; repr., London: Greenprint, 1990).

39. Published in John Berger, *About Looking* (New York: Vintage International, 1991).

40. Pollan, *Omnivore's Dilemma*, 333.

41. Holmes Rolston III, "Naturalizing and Systematizing Evil," in *Is Nature Ever Evil? Religion, Science, and Value*, ed. Willem B. Drees, 67–86 (London: Routledge, 2003), 85.

42. Holmes Rolston III, "Does Nature Need to Be Redeemed?" *Zygon* 29, no. 2 (June 1994): 205–29.

43. See Mark Lynas, *Six Degrees: Our Future on a Hotter Planet* (London: Fourth Estate, 2007), and Elizabeth Kolbert, *Field Notes from a Catastrophe* (New York: Bloomsbury, 2006). Even if the nations of the world act vigorously to mitigate the increase in greenhouse gases, a significant human-induced warming of the global mean surface temperature now seems unavoidable. Significant extinctions in various areas in which change will be rapid currently seem inevitable; this only points to the urgency of the proposals outlined here.

44. In Edward O. Wilson's *The Future of Life* (London: Little, Brown, 2002), chap. 4.

45. John B. Cobb Jr., "All Things in Christ?" in *Animals on the Agenda: Questions about Animals for Theology and Ethics*, ed. Andrew Linzey and Dorothy Yamamoto, 173–80 (London: SCM Press, 1998), esp. 177–80.

46. Holmes Rolston III, *Environmental Ethics: Duties to and Values in the Natural World* (Philadelphia: Temple University Press, 1988), 154.

47. Holmes Rolston III, *Philosophy Gone Wild: Essays in Environmental Ethics* (Buffalo, NY: Prometheus Books, 1986), 211.

48. Rolston, *Environmental Ethics*, 53.

49. Messer, *Selfish Genes and Christian Ethics*, 232.

50. Though, of course, humans will do everything in their power to avoid, for example, a major asteroid impact, for their own self-interest if for no other reason.

51. Peter D. Ward and Donald Brownlee, *The Life and Death of Planet Earth: How the New Science of Astrobiology Charts the Ultimate Fate of Our World* (New York: Henry Holt and Co., 2002), chap. 9.

52. Sean McDonagh, *The Death of Life: The Horror of Extinction* (Blackrock, C. Dublin: Columba Press, 2004), 97.

53. Ibid.

54. Lisa Sideris, "Writing Straight with Crooked Lines: Holmes Rolston's Ecological Theology and Theodicy," in *Nature, Value, Duty: Life on Earth with Holmes Rolston III*, ed. Christopher J. Preston and Wayne Ouderkirk, 77–101 (Dordrecht: Springer, 2007), 96.

55. Ibid.

56. This thinking is in line with Messer's appropriation of the concept of the penultimate (see n30, this chapter). He writes: "We cannot and need not perfect or save the world by our own efforts; this ultimate work is God's, not ours. But it leaves us the 'penultimate' responsibility of acting in the world so as to 'shape the future,' or to improve the world and the conditions of human life within it. Not to do so would be a refusal of our vocation and a betrayal of our responsibility that would perpetuate the distortion of our relations with God, one another and the world. . . . Truly responsible action . . . will also, within this penultimate sphere, be characterized by its conformity to the shape of God's saving activity" (*Selfish Genes and Christian Ethics*, 211).

57. E. O. Wilson, *On Human Nature* (1978; repr., London: Penguin, 1995), 192.

58. Wilson, *Future of Life*, chap. 7. Compare this with the pessimistic tone of Michael Boulter's *Extinction: Evolution and the End of Man* (2002; repr., London: HarperCollins, 2003), chap. 7.

59. Wilson, *Future of Life*, 157.

60. Ibid., 156.

61. Ted Peters, *God—The World's Future: Systematic Theology for a New Era* (Minneapolis: Fortress Press, 2000), chap. 12.

62. The need to preserve the world's forest, especially the great tropical moist forest of Amazonia, is also stressed by James Lovelock in *The Revenge of Gaia: Why the Earth Is Fighting Back—And How We Can Still Save Humanity* (London: Penguin, 2006), and received additional support from recent findings that deforestation is a major contributor to global warming (cited in *The Independent*, May 14, 2007). Logging should be practiced only with the greatest restraint, and Wilson believes the logging of all old-growth forests should cease forthwith. (There is a fascinating echo in Wilson's *Future of Life*, 158–59, of the passage from Barth about the "honourable butcher" [see section 7.2]. Wilson quotes a young poet, Janisse Ray, who writes: "If you clear a forest, you'd better pray continuously. While you're pushing a road through and rigging the cables and moving between trees on the dozer, you'd better be talking to God." There is the same implication that what is so often done for human profit and without thought needs to be done only reverently and humbly.)

63. James Lovelock, *The Ages of Gaia: A Biography of Our Living Earth* (1988; repr., Oxford: Oxford University Press, 1989), chap. 7.

64. Wilson, *Future of Life*, 164.

65. Plans for some such corridors are already in place. See Wilson, *Future of Life*, 178–79.

66. Wilson too acknowledges this. He writes: "The poor, some 800 million of whom live without sanitation, clean water and adequate food, have little chance to advance in a devastated environment. Conversely, the natural environments where most biodiversity hangs on cannot survive the press of land-hungry people with nowhere else to go" (*Future of Life*, 189).

67. Boulter, *Extinction*, 138.

68. McDonagh, *Death of Life*, 18.

69. Daniel W. Hardy, "The God Who Is with the World," in *Science Meets Faith: Theology and Science in Conversation*, ed. Fraser Watts, 136–53 (London: SPCK, 1998); Deane-Drummond, *The Ethics of Nature*.

70. Berger, *About Looking*; Annie Dillard, *Pilgrim at Tinker Creek* in *Three by Annie Dillard* (New York: HarperCollins, 2001).

71. In 1972 Arne Naess wrote a significant article calling for a "deep, long-range ecology movement": "The Shallow and the Deep, Long-range Ecology Movement: A Summary," *Inquiry* 16 (1973): 95–100. For his summary of his ideas, see Naess, "The Deep Ecological Movement: Some Philosophical Aspects," in *Environmental Ethics: An Anthology*, ed. Andrew Light and Holmes Rolston III, 262–74 (Oxford: Blackwell, 2003).

72. Naess, "Deep Ecological Movement," 264.

73. Boulter, *Extinction*, 189.

74. Denis Edwards, "Every Sparrow That Falls to the Ground: The Cost of Evolution and the Christ-Event," *Ecotheology* 11, no. 1 (March 2006): 103–23, 121.

Index